GROUNDED INNOVATION

GROUNDED INNOVATION
STRATEGIES FOR CREATING
DIGITAL PRODUCTS

LARS ERIK HOLMQUIST

AMSTERDAM • BOSTON • HEIDELBERG • LONDON
NEW YORK • OXFORD • PARIS • SAN DIEGO
SAN FRANCISCO • SINGAPORE • SYDNEY • TOKYO

Morgan Kaufmann is an imprint of Elsevier

ELSEVIER

Acquiring Editor: Steve Elliot
Development Editor: David Bevans
Project Manager: Danielle S. Miller
Designer: Joanne Blank

Morgan Kaufmann is an imprint of Elsevier
225 Wyman Street, Waltham, MA 02451, USA

Notices
Knowledge and best practice in this field are constantly changing. As new research and experience broaden our understanding, changes in research methods or professional practices, may become necessary. Practitioners and researchers must always rely on their own experience and knowledge in evaluating and using any information or methods described herein. In using such information or methods they should be mindful of their own safety and the safety of others, including parties for whom they have a professional responsibility.

To the fullest extent of the law, neither the Publisher nor the authors, contributors, or editors, assume any liability for any injury and/or damage to persons or property as a matter of products liability, negligence or otherwise, or from any use or operation of any methods, products, instructions, or ideas contained in the material herein.

Library of Congress Cataloging-in-Publication Data
Holmquist, Lars Erik, 1966-
 Grounded innovation : strategies for inventing smart products/Lars Erik Holmquist.
   p. cm.
 ISBN 978-0-12-385946-4
 1. Microprocessors–Technological innovations. 2. Microcomputers–Technological innovations. 3. Digital electronics–Technological innovations. 4. Creative ability in technology. I. Title.
 QA76.5.H6356 2012
 004.16–dc23

                                                                                    2011044872

British Library Cataloguing-in-Publication Data
A catalogue record for this book is available from the British Library

ISBN: 978-0-12-385946-4

Printed and bound by CPI Group (UK) Ltd, Croydon, CR0 4YY

Transferred to digital print 2012

Working together to grow
libraries in developing countries

www.elsevier.com | www.bookaid.org | www.sabre.org

ELSEVIER   BOOK AID International   Sabre Foundation

For information on all MK publications visit our website at www.mkp.com

CONTENTS

ABOUT THE AUTHOR

Lars Erik Holmquist leads the Mobile Innovations group at Yahoo! Labs in Santa Clara, California. Previously, he was Professor in Media Technology at Södertörn University and manager of the Interaction Design and Innovation lab at the Swedish Institute of Computer Science. He was a co-founder and research leader at the Mobile Life Centre, a joint research venture between academia and industry hosted at Stockholm University, with major partners including Ericsson, Microsoft, Nokia, TeliaSonera and the City of Stockholm. He received his M.Sc. in Computer Science in 1996, his Ph.D. in Informatics in 2000, and became an Associate Professor in Applied IT in 2004, all at the University of Gothenburg.

In his work he has developed many pioneering interfaces and applications in the areas of ubiquitous computing and mobile services, including location-based devices, handheld games, mobile media sharing, visualization techniques, entertainment robotics, tangible interfaces and ambient displays. All of his work has been carried out in multi-disciplinary settings, mixing technology, design and user studies, often in close collaboration with industrial stakeholders.

ACKNOWLEDGMENTS

Although the actual text of this book took exactly one year to produce, the content had been gradually forming for over a decade before I was ready to write it down. During this time I have been discussing, collaborating and fighting with, as well as been influenced, inspired and awed by the best minds in the human-computer interaction and ubiquitous computing research communities. It has been a privilege to interact with so many smart people over the years, and I hope to continue to do so for a long time to come.

First of all, I want to thank Kristina Höök, Oskar Juhlin and Annika Waern who have been my closest academic collaborators for many years. I am proud to, along with them, be founder of what is possibly the most vibrant and exciting research environment in the world right now, the *Mobile Life Centre* at Stockholm University, SICS and the Interactive Institute. All the people and partners in Mobile Life have in one way or another inspired the book, and even though I will be moving on, I count on seeing even greater things from them in the future!

Most of my own research has been carried out in the *Future Applications Lab*, the group I founded at the Viktoria Institute and continued at the Swedish Institute of Computer Science. I thank all the students and researchers who have passed through the lab over the years, in particular Zeynep Ahmet, Sebastian Büttner, Henriette Cramer, Ylva Fernaeus, Lalya Gaye, Maria Håkansson, Mattias Jacobsson, Sara Ljungblad, Mattias Rost, Johan Sanneblad and Tobias Skog, all who made important contributions to the work presented in this book.

I am also grateful to Södertörn University, for having the confidence in me to appoint me Professor, and for being an inspiring workplace with many great colleagues and a vibrant student community.

The funding for this work was provided by many different agencies over the years. I am very grateful for the *Swedish Foundation for Strategic Research (SSF)*, whose *Individual Grant for Young Research Leaders (INGVAR)* allowed me to concentrate on writing this book, as well as partially funding much of the research in it. SSF also funded the *Mobile Services Project*, which supported much of my early research in mobile technology and formed the basis for the Mobile Life Centre. *The Swedish Governmental Agency for Innovation Systems (VINNOVA)* funded some of my earliest work on intelligent environments, as well as being the sponsor of the Mobile Life Centre where much of my recent research has been carried out. *The European Commission* has funded several important projects that produced research mentioned in this book, including *Smart-Its, Embodied and Communicating Agents (ECAgents)*, and *Living with Robots and Interactive Companions (LIREC)*.

I want to thank those institutions and persons who hosted me during important extended writing periods, including Tom Igoe at the Interactive Telecommunications program at New York University, and Bjoern Hartmann at the Computer Science Division and Berkeley Institute of Design at UC Berkeley.

Getting this book published has been a surprisingly pleasant process, and one I hope to repeat someday! The original impulse came from my assignment as fact-checker on Mike Kuniavsky's manuscript, *Smart Things*, also published by Morgan Kaufman. My original acquisition editor, Mary James, was very valuable in the formulation of the original proposal and has since become a good friend. When she left, new editor Rachel Roumeliotis steered me capably through the contract process but has since gone on to new opportunities, replaced by Steve Miller. David Bevans was my trusted support in the year-long process of producing the manuscript, and Danielle S. Miller very helpfully assisted the production of the finished pages, pleasingly designed by Joanne Blank. Thanks to all of you; the book literally would not have existed without you!

I thank my two fact-checkers, Andrew Boyd and Mie Nørgard, for their diligent work and many helpful suggestions, most of which I have implemented to the best of my ability. Any remaining errors are entirely my own fault!

This book is very much a summary of the last ten years of my research, and also represents something of a closing of a chapter. As I am writing this, I am literally in the process of leaving Sweden for a new job in the Bay Area. Therefore I want to thank Elizabeth Churchill for making it happen, and I very much look forward to working together with my new colleagues at Yahoo! Research.

Finally, I thank my many good friends in Stockholm, Gothenburg, London, New York, San Francisco, Toronto, Montreal, Hong Kong, Tokyo and elsewhere, who provided welcome diversions and breaks from the writing and gave me frequent encouragement through the magic of social media. Special notice goes to Larry's Corner in Stockholm, where there was always a sympathetic ear whenever I was stuck.

The people who influenced this book in some way can be counted literally in the hundreds. Therefore, I will stop right here before I run out of space. I just wanted to leave enough room to particularly thank you, dear _____!

Lars Erik Holmquist, Stockholm, November 30, 2011

INTRODUCTION

DA VINCI'S HELICOPTER: IMAGINING WHAT IS NOT THERE

This book is about something very difficult: creating products that do not yet exist. That is not the same as thinking about something that is not here at the moment, but already exists somewhere else, like, say, a helicopter. Chances are, there is not a helicopter with you in the room when you are reading this. But you know enough about the principles of rotary flight, and have seen enough helicopters on television and in the sky to envision what one is like—how big it is, how noisy it is, how it is operated, and so on. You could probably even give a plausible explanation on the principles on which it flies.

What I am talking about is more like what Leonardo Da Vinci did in the 15th century, when he imagined something very similar to a helicopter. Even though it would take several hundred years before the first manned flight, Da Vinci knew enough about the principles of moving air that he could draw a plausible flying machine. However, he did not know quite enough—we now know that the flying machine that Da Vinci drew, and which looked more like a giant screw, could never actually fly. In any case, Da Vinci was apparently too busy with other projects to build one and test it out. It took many centuries of research in aerodynamics before engineers figured out a way that a flying machine could operate in a similar way to the one in Da Vinci's imagination.

What this teaches us is that visionary inventions, like Da Vinci's flying machine, may take a lot of inquiry into the real world before they actually become innovations that can have an effect on peoples' lives. From the first spark, the development of the helicopter took many hundreds of years. Today, with the exploding capabilities of information technology, this kind of process has become more and more compressed. In the last decade we have seen examples where a new technology has gone from a college hack to a billion-dollar business over the course of a few years. Google, Facebook, Twitter and many other online services are instances of this.

We have also seen how devices that were imagined by researchers decades ago have become part of the fabric of everyday life. The most remarkable of these is the personal computer, the principles of which were first developed in research labs many decades years ago. Today, it has not only become a part of everyday life, but its core technology, *information processing*, has mutated to appear in a million different artifacts—from phones and pads to toys, cars and household robots. These *digital products* have already had a profound impact on our existence, and with the accelerated development of processing power, their influence will continue to grow.

To this end, this book is about navigating the process of envisioning products that do not yet exist, but might in the future. It is about how we can dream up these future things in systematic ways, so that they have a greater chance of becoming real. It is about how we can build and test these ideas to see them find their way out in the real world. Finally, it is about how we can use all of the new materials that information technology has made possible, into fashioning wonders that not even Da Vinci could have dreamt of.

HOW TO READ THIS BOOK

This book is divided into two sections: *Methods* and *Materials.*

In the first section, we start by discussing the history and the basic properties of *digital products*—that is, artifacts that rely on digital technology to perform their primary function. We talk about different approaches to innovation from earlier literature and examples. We then introduce the concept of *grounded innovation,* which tries to maximize the innovation potential of an idea. Based on this, we work through a number of concepts and processes that are important for creating successful innovations. These include *inquiry,* which entails finding out about the real-world limitations and potentials; *invention,* which is the process of finding something new; and *prototyping,* where we take these ideas out into the real world to test them. Taken together, this first section will help you to work practically with different aspects of the innovation process.

In the second section, we show how the basic properties of digital products can be used as the raw material for new innovations. This includes *interaction,* which lets users communicate directly with the system; *networking,* which connects products to a larger whole; *sensing,* which allows a product to find out the context in which it is working; and *proactivity,* where the product is acting independently and making decisions on the user's behalf.

The last chapter combines what we have learned so far, and adds recent technology, such as rapid prototyping and mobile mash-ups, to show how development cycles are getting shorter and the opportunity for innovation is accelerating at an unprecedented rate.

Throughout the book are *case studies,* drawn from the author's own research as well as many other sources. These serve to illustrate the book's main concepts with practical examples, based both in academic research and commercial products.

Finally, the book comes with a bibliography, which provides sources to the research and examples cited in the book as well as suggestions for further reading.

PART I

METHODS

CHAPTER 1

UNDERSTANDING DIGITAL PRODUCTS

The most profound technical revolution of the past 50 years is the digital revolution. The theoretical and practical groundwork for computing was laid in the 1940s and 1950s, but the basic building block of computer-based products was invented only a few decades ago. In November 1971, Intel Corporation introduced the Intel 404, generally regarded as the first microprocessor. Integrating all the vital components of a computer's central processing unit onto a single silicon chip greatly reduced the cost of production, paving the way for the ever-increasing speed and ever-decreasing cost of computation that we take for granted today. This is the foundation of *digital products*—products that partly or wholly rely on computer processing to perform their functions, sometimes replacing what was already done by analog technology and other times introducing entirely new functionality that was not possible before. This is the kind of product that we will learn how to create in this book.

Today, countless consumer products include a programmable microchip of some sort. Computer software controls car brakes, heating systems, toys, and kitchen appliances. If something runs on electricity, chances are there is a computer chip somewhere inside it. But do you really think of your dishwasher or portable music player as a computer? Probably not, even though either one contains more processing power and software than was required to run the NASA moon mission in 1969. There is a paradox in that computers have become a vital part of almost every aspect of our daily existence, yet for the most part we don't even think of them.

The permeation of computers all around us has been made possible by an astounding technical development, first predicted by Gordon Moore in 1965 and dubbed "Moore's law." Based on his observations while at computer chip maker Intel, Moore stated that the number of electronic transistors that can be put on a single chip will double every 18 months. This also means that computing power has become very, very inexpensive. A computer processor is literally an everything machine; depending on the code it is loaded with, any chip can perform the same calculations and information processing as any other chip (this property of computing systems was defined by pioneering mathematician Alan Turing as early as 1936). Thus, for control and steering tasks that require some specific steps of logic or switching to be performed, digital circuits can often replace components that would otherwise require custom-made analog wiring. And because the same chip can perform many different jobs, they can be made in large quantities and very cheap. For instance, with different software, the same chip might control the light in a skyscraper, the voice box of a children's toy, and the elaborate program of a dishwasher that makes your dirty silverware come out perfectly clean. Thus, in half a century, we have gone from a world where computers were highly specialized machines, unavailable to the any normal person, to one where it is usually cheaper to put a computer chip into a product than not to.

But there was a time when computation was expensive, and a computer literally filled rooms. In the 1940s and 1950s, computers were huge, expensive, and fragile machines, and only experts in white coats were allowed near them. To perform a computing task you would have to first devise a series of instructions in machine code, painstakingly encode them on a batch of paper cards (so-called punch cards), and hand them over to the men in white coats. If you were lucky, after a few days you would get a stack of cards back with the answer to your problem. But more likely, there was a mistake (a "bug") in the code, and chances were you would have to repeat the whole procedure again until you got it right. In other words, early computers were anything but user-friendly.

It took the visionary mind of J.C.R. Licklider, then head of the American Army's Advanced Research Projects Agency (ARPA), to imagine a better way to interact with computers. In a 1960 article, he suggested *man-computer symbiosis*—the idea of the computer and the human working side by side on a problem. This was a style of working with the machine that was vastly different to the batch processing of early computers, and it seemed way ahead of the technology at the time. But technology moves fast, and only a few years later we started to see actual examples of this man-computer symbiosis. As is often the case, entertainment technology was way ahead of more serious concerns. In 1961 at the Massachusetts Institute of Technology (MIT), a group of science fiction–obsessed hackers created the first real-time computer game, *Space War.* Using a newly acquired (and very expensive) graphics display, they created a system where two spaceships did virtual battle in a computer-generated environment, complete with simulated gravity and hyperspace jumps.

Another groundbreaking effort at MIT was Evan Sutherland's *Sketchpad* in 1963, the first computer-based drawing program. Rather than give the computer a stack of punch cards, or even type into a terminal, users would interact directly with their drawings using a so-called light pen, a pen-shaped input device. This mode of interaction emulated the way we normally interact with drawings while at the same time offering features that only a computer could give, such as effortless "undo" and a hierarchical organization of the components of a drawing. In a contemporary recording, a reporter gushes about how the viewer will see a man "actually talking to a computer"—not with speech, but in a mode that was almost as effortless.

An even more complete vision of this computer future came with Douglas Engelbart's famous demonstration at the Stanford Research Institute in 1968. Here, Engelbart showed what was essentially a functioning version of the *Memex*, a vision of a worldwide information network imagined by Vannevar Bush in 1945. Computer terminals were connected in an information network that could call up information remotely, for instance, by clicking on a high-lighted word in a text—just the way we use the World Wide Web today. The system also included features such as live video conferencing, graphical windows, and a newly invented brick-shaped pointing device nicknamed a "mouse." Although it would take many years to make the technology behind Engelbart's demonstration available for the masses, in many ways it defined how we interact with computers today.

The final pieces of the puzzle came together when Xerox, whose main business was in copy machines, decided to start a research center to figure out its next business model. Envisioning a future where paper would go away (the so-called paperless office), Xerox gave its Palo Alto Research Center (PARC) essentially free hands to come up with the computer of the future. With close ties to Stanford and Engelbart's group, visionaries such as Alan Kay started to not just think of the future but to construct it in practice. Kay had already sketched a device he called the *Dynabook*, a precursor to today's laptops, which he envisioned as a computer suited for nonexpert users such as children and for creative tasks like drawing and music. At PARC, researchers put their minds to building a functioning version of such a system. Thanks to newly emerging technology such as bitmapped displays (which allow for more detail and faster updates than the then-dominating vector displays), laser printers (a Xerox invention), and networking (the Ethernet, the foundation of today's Internet, was also developed at PARC), they had the means to actually do this.

The result was the *Xerox Alto*, a computer workstation complete with a screen, mouse, keyboard, network connection, high-quality printer, and graphical user interface, completed in 1973. Compared to even the cheapest of today's laptops, the system was woefully underequipped—a primitive processor and 128 kilobytes of primary memory—but when it came to interaction, all the pieces were there. With the Alto, a user could sit down with an idea for a document, click on a symbol to start a graphical editing program, compose the document using both text and pictures, and then print it out exactly as it appeared onscreen. This was called "what you see is what you get," and it represented a quantum leap from other digital editing systems, which used command-based input and complicated page description languages. The metaphors used for the interaction with the system were picked from the office environment and dubbed the "desktop metaphor." Individual pieces of data such as documents were called "files" and visually depicted as the file binders in a physical filing cabinet. When users needed to move a block of text from one section to another, they would "cut" and "paste" it, just like if they were working on a regular piece of paper but using pointing and clicking rather than scissors and glue.

Today, the computers that resulted from this development are literally everywhere, woven into the fabric of everyday life. We use Internet-connected home computers to manage our travel tickets, to check what is playing at the theater, to chat with faraway friends. At work, documents are created, calculations performed, and schedules set, all with computers. Thanks to smaller form factors, better batteries, and a pervasive wireless infrastructure of 3G and Wi-Fi, we are no longer tied to the stationary workstations that were prevalent only a few years ago. We can bring laptop computers everywhere—to work at a café during lunch, to read e-mails during a meeting, to cuddle up with a downloaded movie on the sofa, and in some cases even to the bathroom instead of a magazine. The computer has gone from being a work tool closely fixed to an office environment to being something that flows with us through every situation in life.

This development did not pass scientist and researchers by. Having already seen the creation of the personal computer firsthand, around 1990 Xerox PARC chief scientist Mark Weiser and his group at the PARC Computer Science Lab started to think about what would come next. Computers, Weiser claimed, would develop in three stages. The first was the *mainframe* era, where there was one computer for many users. This was the prevalent arrangement up until the early 1980s; each large institution such as a company or university department would have one large computer, which was connected to many different workstations, so-called dumb terminals because they did not have any computing capabilities of their own.

In Weiser's second stage, there would be one computer per user. This is what became *personal computing*, the paradigm pioneered at PARC and made popular by personal computer makers such as Apple and IBM. Here, every user had his or her own computer, which they could employ for whatever purpose they liked without worrying about other users overloading the system. Unlike with the dumb terminal connected to a mainframe, the user now had all the necessary computing power on her own personal desk.

Finally, Weiser claimed that we were entering an era where there would be many computers for every person. He called this *ubiquitous computing*, or *ubicomp* for short. In one sense, this seems like an easy claim to make; after all, already in 1990 it was obvious that microprocessors were replacing analog circuits in many products, and so technically there would soon be more computers than people on the planet. But ubiquitous computing was about more than the number of processors in the world. It was more specifically a reaction to what was seen as the negative effects of personal computers. Here, Weiser and his group were influenced by, among others, Lucy Suchman, a cultural anthropologist who had performed her Ph.D. work studying the automatic help system of copy machines at PARC. Suchman found that the way computer scientists modeled the world did not fit very well with how people actually performed everyday actions. In particular, she argued that even when carrying through a simple task such as copying a piece of paper, we are not following a set plan from beginning to end, but instead we are constantly adapting to changes in the environment and improvising as we discover features in the world around us.

The personal computer of 1990 did not allow for any such situated actions. Instead, it was a highly immobile, rigid device, which required users to sit at a specific desk without any opportunity to interact with each other. This, Weiser claimed, made the computer "isolated from and isolating of" the real world and meant that it "failed to get out of way of the work." As a comparison, he considered another information technology—written language. When learned, a literate person can use writing constantly throughout the day without reflecting on it—taking notes, reading signs, digesting information. This is what Weiser called a "calm technology," which would be well integrated into everyday life, as opposed to the personal computer's rigid set of requirements for where, when, and how we perform our work. He suggested that using future computers should be as easy as picking up a notepad and scribbling on it, and that they would be so cheap that they would be everywhere and you could even discard them when you were done.

To experiment with this idea of ubiquitous computing, Weiser's team constructed three new form factors for computers, based on what they called human measurements, inspired by the traditional American measuring system: the inch, foot, and yard. The inch-size computers were called *tabs;* they were very tiny, fit in the palm of a hand, yet were constantly connected to a wireless network and capable of reacting to changing circumstances in the user's environment. The foot-sized ones were called *pads* and had a form factor similar to a book or notepad. They used pen-based input to facilitate interaction without a keyboard and mouse. Finally, the yard-sized examples were *boards*, interactive wall-mounted screens that facilitated working on shared material in larger groups. All of the devices were connected together in a wireless infrastructure to allow for sharing and collaboration between devices and users.

Today we can see the ideas of ubiquitous computing reflected in many aspects of consumer technology. The tabs have their most obvious heirs in today's so-called smartphone with touch screens, such as the *iPhone* from Apple, the family of phones based on Google's *Android* system, and similar devices from many other manufacturers. The pad has been emulated in a variety of tablet computing devices—keyboard-less PCs with pen- or touch-based screens have been available since the mid-2000s—but has never seen much success outside of specialized applications. There have also been a number of specialized e-book devices such as Amazon's *Kindle*. However, currently the most popular example is a product from Apple, which is not coincidentally called the *iPad*. So far, the interactive wall screen has not seen much commercial success in the consumer market, even though it was the first of PARC's ubiquitous computing technologies to be commercialized (by the company Smart Technologies).

Following Weiser's basic notion of better integrating computing power with human activities, a number of interaction paradigms have been initiated to introduce better alternatives to the desktop-based interaction model. For instance, *virtual reality*, which had its peak in the mid-1990s, would immerse users in an entirely computer-generated world using head-mounted displays or room-size screens, so-called caves. Although computer games based on three-dimensional graphics represent a big area nowadays, immersive computing has so far failed to take off commercially. *Augmented* or *mixed* reality, introduced in the late 1990s and still an active research area, took a step back and tried to mix the real world back in with the virtual—for instance, by using projected overlays on real-world objects. With more capable mobile devices, augmented reality is starting to enter the commercial space with products such as *Layar*, which lets you look "through" the phone screen and see labels and other areas of interest matched up with the video image. Finally, a large effort in the past decade has been to make computer systems that are more integrated with the physical world, often called *tangible* interfaces. Here, the interaction would not use screens but rather physical input and output devices, such as blocks of wood, levers, buttons, and so on. Again, commercial success has so far not been great. Obviously, these genres of interaction and many others often mix so that it may be hard to say if a tabletop interactive music system like the *Reactable* (developed by Pompeu Fabra University in Spain) is tangible, augmented, or something else.

A problem with many of these techniques is that they still take the traditional approach of considering the computer and users as separate entities, connected through an interface. The task of making a computer more user-friendly would then consist of improving the interface rather than considering all the components in the system. This model comes from the original work in human-computer interaction (or HCI), when the field was emerging in the 1980s. In HCI, a number of methods were formulated that made it possible to evaluate the efficiency of interfaces—for instance, by measuring the time it takes to complete a specific task in a lab environment. Although the early methods of HCI served very well for the personal computer and the graphical user interface, the situation today is more complex. Many modern electronic products are "computers" only in the basic sense, in that they perform some kind of information processing to function. Furthermore, it is increasingly difficult to isolate the "interface" component from the overall function of most computer-augmented products, such as a toy or a car. Even accounting for the "human" component is getting tricky if we consider systems interacted with by many people simultaneously, such as in public places, or those that are only "used" implicitly, such as sensor-based systems that control light, air condition, and other environmental factors. Finally, although the methods developed in HCI served well to evaluate particular components of interfaces, the process of developing other products that contain computation is less easy to formalize and consists of many more components than can be captured in a lab study. Therefore, the approach in this book will be to acknowledge that there are a multitude of computational devices and methods to create and understand them, and that the original computer is just one of these.

To this end, rather than talking about a human-computer interface, we will use the term *digital product* to denote *a man-made object that relies on computation in some form to function*. The definition does not say anything about the scale or function of the object. This means that a speaking children's doll is a digital product, because it relies on an embedded microprocessor to produce words. It also means that the automated ventilation system of the Empire State Building is a digital product, because again it relies on computation to shuffle around the air breathed by thousands of people.

Furthermore, the definition does not say the product has to actually have a processor built in. For instance, the radio frequency identification (RFID)–based payment cards used on subway systems in London, Tokyo, and Stockholm constitute digital products. Even a printed paper barcode is a digital product when it is connected to a computerized inventory system. Virtual objects are also man-made objects, so a piece of computer software, such as Excel, is a digital product, as is the pinball game app on your smartphone. Even highly connected and complex online services such as *Facebook* or *Google Mail* are digital products. And, of course, by this definition, a *computer*, with its keyboard, mouse, and screen, is a digital product.

Figure 1-1

A desktop computer is an example of a digital product, a man-made object that relies on computation to perform its primary function. (Stock image)

Looking back at the history of computing that we outlined previously, it is clear that products based on computation have gone through a number of stages in their development. However, at this point, with the computer being just one of many digital products, the measure of simply "counting computers," as Weiser did, does not really suffice. On the one hand, it is obvious that Weiser's prediction

Figure 1-2

Complex online services such as Facebook can also be considered digital products. (Stock image)

was right and that we live in a world of ubiquitous computing, with individual microchip computers embedded in many objects around us. On the other hand, there has at the same time been a trend toward computation and data storage taking place in centralized data centers; the online document suites of Google Docs, the constantly evolving knowledge repository of Wikipedia, and the ever-changing flow of updates, friend suggestions, and games on Facebook all represent a step back to the "one computer, many users" notion of the mainframe era. Similarly, our mobile phones are also spending much of their time connected to online services for photo sharing (e.g., Instagram), location tracking (e.g., FourSquare), and media consumption (e.g., Spotify). Paradoxically, the "personal computers" and "smartphones" of the 1990s have in some respects become "dumb terminals" again! Therefore, although computation is indeed available everywhere, ubiquitous and pervasive, the simple notion of "one user, many computers" is no longer enough to define the breadth of today's digital products.

Instead, in this post-ubicomp era, we need some other way of understanding, decomposing, and classifying digital products. If we can identify some of the essential components or functions that make up such products, it will be easier both to analyze existing ones and to invent entirely new categories. In this, we can be helped by the development of computers mentioned earlier. Working from the first notion of computation, through the personal computer to today's era of ubiquitous computing and beyond, I would like to introduce five *properties* that will be useful to explain the nature of digital products:

- ■ Information processing
- ■ Interaction
- ■ Networking
- ■ Sensing
- ■ Proactivity

The first, *information processing*, which we can also call *computation*, is the most fundamental property of digital products. It is quite simply the notion that some kind of abstractly represented information goes into a machine and then comes back in processed form—the very definition of a computer! Programmable machines were constructed as early as the 18th century; consider, for instance, the *Jacquard loom*, which read instructions from punch cards similar to those later used in early electronic computers. In 1822 Charles Babbage proposed the *difference engine*, a machine that could perform advanced mathematical calculations; however, it was too technically complex to finish at the time. But the theoretical notion of a universal information-processing system goes back to Alan Turing's theoretical system from 1936, commonly known as a *Turing machine*. In Turing's model, the machine is imagined as an infinite paper tape. On this tape are symbols that the machine can read and write, one at a time, using a tape head. Turing showed that by using only a few operators, it was possible to perform all calculations, and that any machine that had this minimal capability would be able to perform the same operations as the ones with the most advanced instruction set, such as today's high-powered microprocessors and graphics chips. Turing's 1936 model along with similar work from Alonzo Church and others around the same time have been the fundament of modern computer science.

The first functional so-called Turing complete computer was constructed by Konrad Zuse in 1941, and in 1945 John von Neumann described the "stored program model" still used in computers today. Despite the fact that the time from asking a question to receiving the results of a computation could be counted in days rather than milliseconds, many extremely useful results were achieved with these first computers, such as the breaking of codes during World War II. However, although a Turing machine running on a piece of paper tape, or even a couple of tons of electronic tubes, is *theoretically* identical to the latest overclocked slab of silicon, if the actual time to come up with a result is included in the equation, these machines would be far from equal. But as we saw from Moore's law, the speed of computation has been increasing rapidly since these early days.

This increased speed of processing was instrumental in making computers *interactive*, as were new forms of input and output devices, such as graphics screens and light pens. Licklider's notion of man-computer symbiosis was realized through pioneering interactive projects such as Space War and Sketchpad, and continues through modern-day digital products. Interactive computing represented a fundamental shift in the relationship with computers, and one that was necessary in order to make computers usable for everyday purposes. As Peter Wegner has pointed out, "interaction is more powerful than algorithms"—meaning that despite the theoretical equalities of all computers, interactive computers can perform many meaningful tasks that batch computers simply could not. This is the fundament of the user-friendly computer, where many applications are not so much computationally complex but instead rely on being time critical and functioning in real time—for instance, games, media players, video conferencing, and so on. Any home computer purchased from the late 1970s and onward had the property of being interactive in this sense.

A further step toward today's computers comes with being *networked*. Networking was demonstrated at Engelbart's 1968 demo, but, of course, there was not much to be networked with at the time! Robert Metcalfe, inventor of the Ethernet that forms the foundation of today's Internet, postulated in 1980 that the value of a telecommunications network is proportionate to the square of the number of nodes—in other words, it grows exponentially with the number of connections. This is also called the "network effect" and holds for telephones as well as computer networks. To take one popular example of the network effect, a fax machine (if anybody remembers those!) is practically useless on its own. Add a second fax machine, and you can send text from one location to another. But as the number of compatible machines grow, the machines become exponentially more useful, until literally every office has one, and they can be relied on for transmitting printed or visual information just about anywhere.

The same has happened with many other technologies, including, of course, the Internet, which had only limited use until it broke out of its original usage domain. The groundwork of today's Internet was laid in the 1970s and 1980s by the U.S. Government's Defense Advanced Research Projects Agency (DARPA), which needed a reliable network for potential wartime communication. The Internet was mostly used at universities until the mid-1990s, when thanks to a combination of cheaper home computers, built-out infrastructure, and technology hype, it took off and entered the mainstream. Today it is almost impossible to imagine a world without the Internet, and every computer bought today will include one or several network connectors as standard. Furthermore, wireless networking has become a standard feature of many public places such as cafés and hotels, and the third-generation (3G) mobile data network covers most of the planet.

If we look at the typical personal computer or laptop today, it is information processing, interactive, and networked. However, one of Weiser's main criticisms of the personal computer was that it had no sense of its surrounding context and thus failed to adapt to the world around it, and this still stands today. It has to do with the hardware design—there simply aren't any ways to allow a standard computer to know very much about the world around it. This is something that can be achieved with *sensing*—something humans are very good at. The right kind of sensor can tell us the location of an object, its temperature, the light conditions, what sounds can be heard around it, if it is moving or resting, and much more. By applying additional information processing it is even possible to turn simple sensing readings into more complex information about the world—for instance, if a person is walking or running or if the surrounding noise consists of conversation or traffic. Although sensing is not yet common in computers, it is used in many other digital products and will form an important part of future technology.

Although interaction and sensing are defining factors, some digital products go even further and are *proactive*, meaning they respond to users' needs or their environment. In the late 1990s there was a debate in human-computer interaction between those proposing *direct manipulation* (i.e., interfaces where the user could clearly and graphically control all functions) and *agents* (which would use artificial intelligence techniques to assist the user without needing any direct instructions). An example of the former would be a movie selection interface, where the direct manipulation version would present all available titles sorted according to different criteria to let the user make her or his own pick, whereas the latter would suggest new titles based on the user's previous viewing habits (we can think of it as browsing a video store on your own versus getting recommendations from one of the clerks—both have their advantages and drawbacks). The opposition between these views was largely a construction, and today it makes more sense to combine them, such as the interactive word processor that automatically corrects words as you type.

Armed with these five properties, we can now examine some common digital products to see what they have in common and how they differ (see Table 1-1 for a summary). For instance, original batch-processing mainframes of the 1950s did computation but nothing else, whereas pioneering systems like the Sketchpad introduced interactivity. The Xerox Alto added networking

	Information Processing	Interaction	Networking	Sensing	Proactivity
Mainframe (1950s)	√				
Sketchpad (1960s)	√	√			
Xerox Alto (1970s)	√	√	√		
Apple Macintosh (1980s)	√	√			
Word processor with automatic spellchecker (1990s)	√	√			√
Internet PC/laptop (1990s)	√	√	√		
Car with ESC (1990s)	√			√	√
Adidas_1 (2000s)	√			√	√
Nike+ (2000s)	√			√	√
Suica card (2000s)		√	√		
Smartphone (2000s)	√	√	√	√	√

Table 1-1

Summary of the properties of some digital products.

Figure 1-3

A "smart card," such as the Suica ("super urban intelligent card") used for public transport and payment in Japan, does not perform any computation of its own yet is a digital product because it is part of an information processing system. (Stock image)

with other computers to the mix. Curiously, the Macintosh seems to represent a step back in that Apple decided not to include a network adapter—it was too expensive and the company simply did not see any use that could motivate the cost. However, as a personal workstation the Mac became very influential, and unlike Xerox' attempt at a similar commercial product, it became a standard tool in everyday practices such as desktop publishing.

Going beyond the traditional computer, a lot of other objects fall under the header of digital products. Interestingly, some of them do not actually do any information processing of their own! For instance, a "smart card," such as one used for opening office doors, is often not actually smart at all—it simply contains a unique code embedded in a radio frequency identification (RFID) tag. A sensor on the door picks up the code, the identification number is looked up, and if it matches the list of allowed codes, the door opens automatically. Thus, although the whole system relies on information processing, the actual card is completely passive; yet it is a digital product because it relies on computation to perform its function. Other examples of "passive" digital products are subway payment cards and even products equipped with printed barcodes in supermarkets, which are registered at the till.

Many digital products simply use a processor to replace a function that was previously performed by mechanical or analog means; for instance, a modern "analog" watch, which even though it has physical hands to show the time, will most likely be controlled by a computer chip. More interesting are cases where an entirely new function is created or added to an existing object. One example would be those products where technology is embedded in clothing or other everyday items—a scenario that still seems somewhat futuristic. For instance, the *Adidas_1* shoe, introduced in 2005, was one of the first commercial examples of *wearable computing*, where digital technology is worn like clothing. What looks like an ordinary running shoe has a compression sensor embedded in the heel that continuously senses the running style of the user. This information is passed on to an onboard microprocessor that computes the ideal stiffness of the heel for any particular moment. The shoe contains a solenoid, a sort of memory metal that changes it stiffness according to how much current passes through it. As the current changes, the shoe can adjust its stiffness to exactly the right degree required for the current running, giving the user a shoe that continuously updates its physical properties to suit the current situation, literally providing the possibility of being a different shoe for every step. Looking at the properties, the Adidas_1 is thus information processing, sensing, and proactive; on the other hand, it is not interactive because it does not respond to any direct commands, and it has no network connection. Although not yet a big commercial success, it is a nice example of how proactivity can be embedded in an everyday situation.

The mobile phone is one of the most ubiquitous digital products today, and arguably the most complex. If we look at a modern smart phone—for example Apple's iPhone or one based on Google's Android operating system—much of its functions have a direct predecessor in the desktop computing world, such as e-mail or web browsing. What the phone has that a computer does not is an advanced set of sensors, including a microphone, a camera, an accelerometer, and often a high-precision location sensor through the global positioning system (GPS). Most phones without GPS can also roughly determine their location through the configuration of the cell network. This is clearly a lot more to work with than the standard desktop, and the smart phone can in many ways be considered the first true ubicomp device. In fact, as we shall see later, many of the early and highly advanced experiments in ubiquitous computing technology can now be repeated effortlessly on a standard mobile phone.

Figure 1-4

The Adidas_1 shoe is an example of a digital product where information processing is used to provide a function that is not available in any analog counterpart. (Image courtesy of Adidas)

The next step of digital products might look more familiar than we think, as computation becomes ever more embedded in everyday objects. In 1999, researchers at the University of Karlsruhe produced the *Media Cup*, a seemingly ordinary coffee cup that in fact was equipped with a lot of advanced technology, including computing, sensing, and networking. Each Media Cup had an accelerometer for sensing its movements, a thermometer for determining the temperature of liquids inside it, and an infrared transceiver for communicating with a network as well as for determining its position in the building. If we imagine a set of such networked cups in an office, all connected to a central server, it suddenly becomes possible to tell a lot about the activities that are going on. For instance, if a number of cups are gathered at the same time in the meeting room, the accelerometers are sensing that they are all in occasional movement (because of people drinking from them), and the liquids inside are hot according to the thermometer (from hot coffee or tea), then we can deduce that there is a meeting going on in this room. This high-level information comes as a side effect of what we learn from the cups, without us actually knowing anything more about the people involved. If we then look a few hours later and the same cups are still there but now they are not

Figure 1-5

The Media Cup, *invented at the University of Karlsruhe, augmented a common household object with information processing, networking, and sensing, thus providing entirely new functionality. (Image courtesy of TECO, www.teco.edu)*

moving and the liquid inside is cold (or gone), we can assume the meeting is over—and it is probably time to go there and clean up!

This vision of a world where everything is sensing and everything is connected is sometimes called *the Internet of things,* and it might be the next big thing after mobile phones. Several large companies are banking hard on this coming true. For instance, Ericsson has introduced a vision of "50 billion devices," distributed all over the world and connected through a wireless network, constantly sharing information between each other and with users. Of course, the hope is that most of this data traffic will go through networks constructed by Ericsson! Similarly, Intel, maker of the first microprocessor, sees a vision of *pervasive computing,* where just about everything has a processor of one kind or another inside, presumably made by Intel. This kind of technological push is shaping the future of digital products, but it seems that there is more technology than ideas for how to actually use it. Despite some 10 years of research since the Media Cup, the fact is that we have still not come up with a use for a smart coffee cup that would even remotely justify the cost.

So what is the real future of digital products? Moore's law tells us that microprocessors will continue to become cheaper and more capable. For the ordinary computer on our desk or in our lap, this is not really very interesting anymore—the truth is that most of us already have more megahertz than we know what to do with. But for other digital products, this means that we can continue to embed more and more processing power into objects at an ever-lower price for the consumer. We can enhance both existing and completely new objects with any combination of information processing, interactivity, networking, sensing, and proactivity. We will see not just shoes, clothes, and other objects with embedded computing, but functions and opportunities we cannot even begin to imagine. But creating these new digital products is a complex process and requires us to understand how to generate new ideas that are realistically constrained both by the capabilities of technology and the context of use, and we need to systematically test them in the real world to understand their properties. In the following chapter, we will get a better understanding of what it means to go from simply thinking of something new—an *invention*—to actually creating something that has an effect on the world—which is what we call an *innovation*.

CHAPTER 2

INNOVATION: MAKING A CHANGE IN THE WORLD

As we have seen, the microprocessor has enabled a multitude of digital products—from interactive computers to mobile phones, toys, kitchen appliances, and much else besides. Information processing, the most fundamental property of digital products, has become a new material with which it is possible to build a seemingly unlimited number of functions, many of which were unthinkable with only mechanical and analog technology. And given Moore's law, the best may very well be ahead of us; as chips become ever smaller and cheaper, it becomes feasible to build artifacts that provide functions that would have been impossible only a few years ago.

But who comes up with these new functions anyway? And why are some digital artifacts wildly successful, whereas others fail utterly? For every runaway success, for every iPod or Facebook, there are literally thousands of other products that never gain any traction or have any impact on the world. Strangely, many of these failed attempts seem to be, at least on paper, as good as or better than the successful examples. When reading research papers, studying startup ventures, and going over corporate histories, it is striking to discover how many seemingly great and original ideas never actually made it out of the lab, college dorm, or high-profile design department.

A problem with coming up with entirely new product concepts is that it is essentially a *design process without a goal*. This goes against the traditional view of design. Nobel laureate Herbert Simon claimed that to design means to devise "courses of action aimed at changing existing situations into preferred ones"—in other words, taking the steps of going from a current state into another, better state. This is a highly instrumented view of the design process, suggesting that it is a rational search for a solution and that it can be formalized in a set of rules or even a computer program (in the 1960s, Simon was influential in the formative field of artificial intelligence). This view is also reflected in models of software engineering, such as the *waterfall model*. Here, the whole process of building a large-scale software system is highly regulated with a series of stages that are not reversible. A similar model was called the *spiral* and allowed for a more iterative approach, where the design brief could be updated in stages, but still followed a rigorous schedule. However, it turns out that the process of designing software is much more complex and does

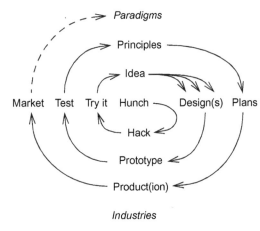

Figure 2-1

Verplank's spiral offers a way to understand the product development process, from the first hunch to products on the market. (Image courtesy of the author)

not lend itself very well to rigorous routines. After many spectacular failures in building large software systems, recently more dynamic methods have become popular, such as *extreme programming*, which emphasizes continuous refinement of goals during the development process. However, all of these processes still assume there is a preferred state to be reached, usually determined by an external factor such as a customer.

But what if the goal is not to fulfill a certain specification but much more fuzzy—say, to come up with a new digital product? One way to understand a design process without a clear goal is to consider Bill Verplank's spiral. Instead of being a strict progression from one stage to the next with a clear end point, this model emphasizes iteration. Verplank's model (Figure 2-1) is placed on a continuum where the vertical axes are the dimension of *paradigms* versus *industries*. In this model, a project typically starts out with a *hunch*—a vague notion of what to do. This leads to a *hack*—a first, primitive technical demonstrator of some kind. (This could also be thought of as a first *sketch* of an idea, but it is executed in a functioning format rather than just on paper.) The hack makes it possible to see if the hunch is valid, and this in turn leads to an *idea*. At this point, the hunch has been transformed into something much more concrete and can be verbalized as a hypothesis or, in other words, a potential goal or state.

Thus, the idea leads to one or more *designs*. This is the place in the spiral where several alternative avenues present themselves, as it might be possible to devise more than one design from the same idea. The designs are then fashioned into *prototypes*—working instantiations of the design. The prototypes can then be tested, and this in turn leads to a set of *principles* arising from the tests. These principles can then be fashioned into *plans*, which are specific enough to be used for production of actual *products* that can reach the *market*. Finally, if the product is successful it might give rise to a new *paradigm* that might even become an integral part of our lives (this would presumably happen rarely, and I have chosen a dashed line to indicate this and also to acknowledge that it is not absolutely clear to me whether Verplank meant a paradigm to be an actual design goal as well as an underlying dimension). By applying this model, we can see how the major technological innovations of our time, from the printing press to airplanes, from television sets to the desktop computer, fit into this cycle from hunch all the way to paradigm.

Verplank's model takes into account that there are many potential sources of innovations and that the process of going from idea to successful product involves a number of steps of very different quality—and that more often than not, it stops well before there is actually a successful product. In fact, one of the most useful aspects of this model is that it lets you verbalize exactly *where* in the process you want to start and end. For many researchers, it is most productive to end at the *principles* stage, because they are more effective in going back and working on new hunches rather than taking them all the way to industry. On the other hand, a venture capitalist might only become interested when the concept is already at the *plans* stage, when there is a clear path to production and market.

But what are the steps and decisions that can turn a hunch into a product that is actually taken up and used by a large number of people, like, for instance, the personal computer? The key to distinguishing failures from successes lies in understanding the nature of innovation. When I am teaching this topic, the first thing I ask students is what they think innovation means. The first responses always have to do with "something new," "something nobody has yet done," "a new thing." But when I am not satisfied with these responses they start pondering and soon come up with more complex answers. "Something that works better," "is a product," "is useful," and so on. There is more to being innovative than just coming up with new ideas, but at the same time, the newness is an intrinsic part of the concept.

Computer scientist and innovation writer Peter J. Denning has given some helpful definitions of innovation and related terms. He first makes a distinction between innovation and invention: "*invention* means simply the creation of something new," he says. Innovation, on the other hand, means "the adoption of a new practice in a community … [It] requires attention to other people, what they value and will adopt." In other words, an invention does not become an innovation until people actually start to use it. To achieve this, it is not enough that something is new; it is necessary to understand the prospective users and what they want.

Furthermore, research on innovation teaches us that not only is an invention not the *only* thing required for an innovation, it is not even the *most important* thing! This might fly in the face of those researchers and inventors who strive so hard to come up with a brilliant idea without giving much thought to how it will be used or what its effects will be. In a study of successful entrepreneurs, writer and management consultant Peter F. Drucker found that contrary to popular belief, such people are not risk takers who simply go out on a limb for an exciting idea. Instead, they work systematically in a process to reduce the risk of failure.

From his empirical data, Drucker identified five elements in the process of innovation:

1. Searching for opportunity—from one of seven innovation sources
2. Analysis—risks and benefits
3. Listening—to the community

4. Focus—on a simple articulation
5. Leadership—mobilizing people and a market for the product

The full process of creating a successful business from these steps is beyond the scope of this book; I recommend the literature on entrepreneurship (including Drucker) as an avenue for that research, as well as consulting with successful entrepreneurs and investors. Here, our main interests are the opportunities and sources of innovation that Drucker identified. This is typically what happens *before* the decision to go forward to start a company or launch a business is made. This is the closest to what takes place in graduate programs, research labs, design studios, and startup factories aimed at producing ideas for new digital products.

In his studies, Drucker found seven sources for innovation opportunities. The first four sources that he identified are internal to a business and can usually be pursued without worry about external competition:

- *The unexpected.* An unexpected success, an unexpected failure, or an unexpected outside event can be a symptom of a unique opportunity.
- *The incongruity.* A discrepancy between reality and what everyone assumes it to be, or between what is and what ought to be, can create an innovative opportunity.
- *Innovation based on process need.* When a weak link is evident in a particular process, but people work around it instead of doing something about it, an opportunity is present to the person or company willing to supply the "missing link."
- *Changes in industry or market structure.* The opportunity for an innovative product, service, or business approach occurs when the underlying foundation of the industry or market shifts.

The following three sources are dependent on changes in the outside world and are thus also available for competitors to take advantage of:

- *Demographics.* Changes in the population's size, age structure, composition, employment, level of education, and income can create innovative opportunities.
- *Changes in perception, mood, and meaning.* Innovative opportunities can develop when a society's general assumptions, attitudes, and beliefs change.
- *New knowledge.* Advances in scientific and nonscientific knowledge can create new products and new markets.

All of these are useful to identify and can be harnessed to come up with potential innovations. But note that "new knowledge"—the product of almost all activity in academic and industrial research labs—appears as number 7 (last) in Drucker's original list! It seems that the studies in entrepreneurship tell us that there is little chance that a new scientific result, no matter how exciting, will ever make it into the real world. Or more generally, of all the inventions produced in science labs and graduate schools, almost none will become actual innovations in Denning's sense.

This is not as depressing as it may sound. First of all, researchers are already aware of this; most of what they do adds to an existing knowledge base even if the results are not directly useful in the short term. But second and more important, for those who do want to produce lasting innovations, there is a whole wealth of other opportunities to pick from that can help propel their results into the mainstream. To give a popular example, in 1968 Spence Silver, a researcher at 3M, was interested in producing a better and more long-lasting glue for the company's products. Unfortunately, what he came up with turned out to be the opposite—a glue that was so weak that a paper treated with it would peel off the surface it had been attached to without leaving any trace. He ransacked his brain for years trying to come up with a use for this new invention. Another 3M employee, Art Fry, finally came up with the idea of applying the glue to small pieces of paper that could, for instance, be used to save one's place in a book without leaving a mark on the pages (he got the inspiration when the paper bookmarks in his church choir book scattered to the wind when he stood up to sing). The product, *Post-it Notes*, was finally launched in 1980 and is now a mainstay in offices and homes around the world. Technically, Silver's invention was a complete failure considering what the goal was. But by considering the result and combining it with other activities, the researchers came up with another use for it. It is quite likely that every research lab houses a multitude of such seemingly useless results that could be turned into products.

In addition to the sources that Drucker identified, Denning suggested a final source of innovation:

■ *Marginal practices.* A different field offering a novel solution.

This is a way of harnessing innovation by looking at what other smart people, those outside of one's own immediate surroundings, are already doing. A practice that may seem irrelevant in your field might in fact offer a solution to a problem. In a similar vein, Erich Von Hippel coined the term *user-driven innovation*, which is based on the idea of *lead users* who are ahead of the curve with a given technology. By finding somebody who is already an advanced user of a technology, a company can find uses that it did not think of. For instance, 3M used this method to develop a breakthrough surgical drape product; the company assembled a team of lead users, which included a veterinarian surgeon, a makeup artist, doctors from developing countries, and military medics. It is also possible to go out in the field to get inspiration from how the advanced users are already using the product.

Case Study: The Personal Computer

When it comes to digital products, the desktop computer is a striking example of how hard it can be to turn even the best invention into a successful product. It seems that as early as 1974, the Alto workstation developed at the Xerox Palo Alto Research Center (PARC) already contained almost all of the vital components of today's computers: a user-friendly interface based on the desktop metaphor, powerful document editing complete with high-quality laser printing, and networking capabilities to tie it into a larger web of information. Clearly, the Alto was so way ahead of its time it would take the rest of the world decades to catch up.

Yet when Xerox turned its technology into a product, the Star workstation, the result was a failure. Why? Not because of the inventions contained in the Alto; history has confirmed the company got almost everything right in that respect. Instead Xerox failed to exploit any of the other opportunities for innovation. Many accounts simply point to the high price of the Star as the deciding factor ($75,000 for a basic installation), but that is only part of the problem. What Xerox failed to do was to provide a use case that motivated the price. Corporations were already buying highly capable business computers at a similar price point, such as PDP and VAX machines, which performed similar functions. The problem with the Star was that the additional selling point—user-friendliness—could not be accounted for in business terms. Even worse, the Star was not really as user-friendly as it should have been. When designing it, the engineers went for a "more is better" approach and included every advanced user interface feature they could, making the graphics pretty and the interactions a wonder of intuitiveness. Unfortunately, the Star's hardware simply could not cope with all of these features. In real-world conditions, the Star operated so slowly that it was practically unusable.

When Steve Jobs visited PARC, he saw all the inventions embodied in the Alto, but he also clearly understood the opportunities for innovations. Apple was at the time selling computers to hobbyists; the company's products were far less capable than business machines, but they were also much less expensive. Apple was used to selling not a handful of machines to big businesses for a very high price at high margin, but large numbers at a more compressed price point. Furthermore, working with limited resources, Apple's programmers were good at squeezing performance from existing hardware. Unlike the engineers at Xerox, who would simply devise a faster processor or add more memory if a program ran too slowly, the engineers at Apple had to optimize the software until it worked.

When creating the Macintosh, Apple exploited a number of opportunities for innovation that had eluded Xerox. First, Apple exploited a change in the industry, where computers went from being sold to large corporations to also being sold to hobbyists and small businesses. To do this the company had to adapt its product to the new market. This included setting a much lower price point. Whereas

Xerox was intent on producing the "best" desktop computer with the most advanced user interface, Apple worked within the limitations of existing technology to produce the best computers that could be affordably produced. This meant stripping out some of the more advanced features of the Alto and making a less pretty, but still functional, experience. However, the result was that unlike the Star, the Macintosh "felt" more usable, because it responded faster and was optimized for speed rather than appearance. Apple also excluded hardware features that could not be easily justified, such as networking. This in turn meant that the Macintosh was a stand-alone system rather than one that had to rely on a network of devices; this brought the price of the installation down even more.

The Macintosh also had a clear use case. In contemporary advertisements, Xerox claimed that with the Star you could "create documents with words and pictures." However, the corporations that they hoped would buy their machines already had advanced systems, attended by highly skilled workers, that let them do exactly that. This was done in advanced page description languages and editing facilities and was far from "what you see is what you get" (WYSIWYG), but that did not really matter because the end result was the same. However, Apple set its sights on small businesses that could not afford to hire dedicated personnel to create their printed materials. By providing a user-friendly computer, Apple let the same person perform many different tasks with little or no training. For a small company, it was suddenly possible, with an investment of a couple of thousand dollars (for a Macintosh and a laser printer), to perform a job that previously would have gone to an external company. Of course, quality suffered somewhat—there are many examples of amateur designers going overboard with the new possibilities in the early days of desktop publishing. But the results still looked infinitely more professional than what previously was created by hand, and in the long run they were much less expensive than having the work done by an outside contractor.

However, despite this success, the Macintosh was never the dominant personal computer when it comes to market share. It was IBM, one of the dominant makers of large business computers, that first popularized the idea of a computer on every office desktop. Before IBM released the IBM PC in 1981, there was a perception among many businesses that microcomputers were only suitable for home use—which mostly meant games, since nobody had really been able to figure out any other practical use for a home computer. When IBM threw its weight behind the PC, it effectively legitimized the idea of a personal computer. However, IBM made some interesting decisions when constructing its computer; the company used off-the-shelf components to keep costs down and outsourced the software operating system to another company, Microsoft. Soon IBM discovered that because of this decision, any manufacturer could put together a "PC-compatible" machine from readily available components, undercutting IBM's business. Furthermore, Microsoft had kept the copyright on the Disk Operating System (DOS) operating system, which was required to run PC software, thus effectively removing the whole PC business from IBM's control. By the time the company tried to launch a new operating system, OS/2, the Microsoft DOS-based PC was already too entrenched to be supplanted.

Microsoft is another interesting example of an innovative company, because unlike most of its successful contemporaries, Microsoft's whole business at the time was software, not hardware. Of all the competing personal computer brands of the early 1980s—Commodore, Atari, Tandy, and so on—most are gone, and almost none of those remaining manufacture hardware anymore. Microsoft's key insight was that since it was built on common components, it was the software, not the hardware, that defined the PC. And of course, neither the marvels at Xerox PARC nor the relative success of Apple had passed Bill Gates and his company by. Microsoft started to extend its text-based operating system with a graphical user interface (GUI), named Windows. It was an uphill battle, because Microsoft did not have the same tight control of hardware as Apple did—the original PC specification did not include any high-resolution graphics, and add-ons such as mice were not standardized. Apple actually sued Microsoft in 1994 for replicating the "look and feel" of its interface with Windows, but the judge decided that by this time the components of the GUI were already in the public domain and could not get patent-like protection (there were several other machines that also had GUIs, including Commodore's Amiga and Atari's ST). In 1995, Microsoft launched the successful Windows 95 operating system, which to all intents and purposes replicated the interfaces of the previous GUI systems to a T. Thus, more than two decades after the first Alto, thanks to a number of other companies exploiting a variety of opportunities for innovation, the inventions of Xerox PARC and its predecessors had finally become truly mainstream.

We have now seen how entrepreneurs can work with a set of risk-reducing factors and opportunities to create successful innovations. But let us try to tease out a few aspects of innovation that previous analysis has not covered.

First of all, remember the distinction between *innovation* and *invention*. Whereas a great invention is not enough to produce a successful innovation, it is a necessary component of the process. Inventions can have many different forms, from the vaguest notion of a concept that might or not might not be doable ("Wouldn't it be great to have a flying car!") to a fully working instance of the concept—which still might not have a realistic chance of being used (in this case, any flying car prototype or product actually produced). Ideas for inventions can come from many sources—observing the world around you, consuming popular culture, reading about new scientific breakthroughs, and so on. Although sometimes idea generation is seen as a "black box" process, there are actually a number of methods that can increase the quantity (and sometimes quality) of new ideas.

Using such methods does not in any way guarantee the quality of new ideas. Many methods that aim to generate novel solutions to problems, such as brainstorming, include an idea generation phase where the important factor is not the quality but the quantity of new ideas. It turns out that generating new ideas can be quite easy under such circumstances. However, this also means that the real work comes later, which is selecting the useful ideas. Brainstorming techniques usually include several phases for sorting and selecting ideas.

But a successful innovation also has to provide a useful function in the real world. To distinguish those inventions that are simply blue sky from those that actually have a chance of working, we need to perform *inquiry* in order to understand the world better. Inquiry can include many different domains and methods. For instance, if the goal is to create a solution to a specific problem at a workplace, it is often useful to spend some time at the actual site or talk to people involved in the work. On the other hand, if it is important to use a particular emerging technology, it is a good idea to understand as much as possible of what the technology is capable of.

When it comes to user-oriented inquiry, there are many established methods for gathering data on what users need (or think they need), such as utilizing questionnaires, interviews, focus groups, and so on. In human-computer interaction research, it has become popular to adapt observation and analysis methods from social science, in particular, ethnography and ethnomethodology. Here, in order to identify problems encountered in a workplace or other situation, the researcher observes it from outside, without interfering. The idea is that this will give a truer and less prejudiced picture of the setting, which can then be turned into system requirements.

However, although both invention and inquiry are necessary components, they both also present problems. Even considering brainstorming methods and other methods that include a selection phase, with blue-sky idea generation, there is no guarantee that the inventions that arise are actually realistic or have any bearing on reality. Anyone can sit down for an hour and produce a dozen ideas for seemingly great new products, but most of them will either be impossible to realize with today's technology or have no actual value to consumers or corporations.

On the other hand, inquiry does not guarantee success either. It is entirely possible to spend months or even years of study getting to know the minutiae of a workplace setting, but this does not mean that the product will be ideas that can actually change or improve the situation. Rather, it is possible for researchers to become so entrenched in the current situation that they find it difficult or impossible to look beyond it to new solutions. The fact is that the people performing the work might not even be the right ones to ask; if given the opportunity to wish for a new technology, they will usually ask for something similar to what they already have. Thus, the risk is ending up with technologies that support existing work practices with little additional benefit that the workers could have had with the introduction of new technologies and ideas.

In reality, most methods that are commonly used in research and product development today are situated in the middle ground, drawing on both invention and inquiry. With more or less success they attempt to combine both idea generation and user studies to produce novel or useful systems and products. But different methods and techniques emphasize invention and inquiry to different degrees. Some are firmly rooted in the data gathered from users and strive to design systems that address specific problems; others take this information as just one of many inputs to the design process. Approaches that try to involve users more creatively in the process, and thus might include a higher level of invention, can be found in the area of *participatory design*. Here, the prospective users are involved in the system design from the start, not just as study objects, but they are on equal footing with the designers. This practice springs largely from the so-called *Scandinavian school of systems development*, which was formulated in the 1970s with a clear agenda of democratizing the introduction of new technology, specifically by involving labor unions. Participatory design has come to be used as a product development strategy, and participatory design projects with a high level of user involvement have produced innovative results in areas ranging from home electronics to wastewater treatment. Various techniques can be used to improve the collaboration between designers and users; for instance, the users can act out and film videos of different scenarios for technology use. This method can be used to encourage a creative dialogue between designers and users and help formulate inventive ideas that are rooted in the users' own experience.

If we map the axes of innovation and inquiry in a two-dimensional field, we can start identifying where different approaches and methods appear. The user-centered design methods all fall in the center of the diagram; they include a modicum of both invention and inquiry. Pure idea generation, such as brainstorming and conceptual art projects, typically strive for a high degree of originality and invention but little in the form of inquiry. Pure studies, on the other hand, whether it be engineering feasibility to test out a new technology or long-term ethnographic studies to investigate a setting, score high on inquiry but have little or no ambition for invention.

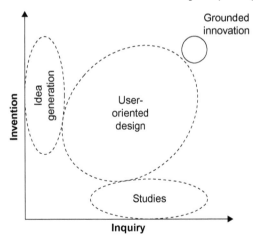

Figure 2-2

Grounded innovation *represents an attempt to maximize the degree of both inquiry and invention that goes into the creation of new product concepts. (Image courtesy of the author)*

It would seem that to produce great innovations we would need to have both a high level of originality and invention (to come up with something genuinely new) and a strong grounding base of inquiry in the real world (to know what the possibilities and opportunities really are). If we sketch out this "ideal" method, it would fall in the top right-hand corner of our diagram, where both axes are at or close to their maximum. This is what I call *grounded innovation.*

So how can we achieve grounded innovation, where we maximize the impact of inquiry and invention? In reality, even with the best methods this is not a state that can be realistically achieved—if so, everybody would already be producing world-class products! And even if we could formulate a method that captured this state, the results of any such method would only be as good as the people who were carrying it out. But by being aware of the potential that is there and by consciously adapting our methods to get closer to the desired state, I argue it is entirely possible to systematically work in a way that has a higher chance of producing innovations than other methods. This is a bold claim and we will need the rest of the book to work it through fully, both by understanding the components and how to test ideas in the real world and then by showing how different materials can be used in different ways in the process.

Case Study: Transfer Scenarios

To clarify what we mean by grounded innovation methods, let us take a concrete example of how my group has strived to achieve this goal. I collaborated with other researchers in developing the *transfer scenarios* method, originated by Sara Ljungblad. It provides a way to transfer grounding from one domain to inspire inventions in another. As part of a large European project, we were given the task of coming up with ideas for what future robot technology might look like. Robots are a complicated class of digital artifacts; per definition, a robot is any machine that has the possibility of autonomously acting on the physical world (using the properties of *sensing* and *proactivity*). But in the public mind, robots are much more narrowly defined. Ask anybody to draw a robot, and most will come up with a mechanical, humanoid, perhaps somewhat menacing science fiction–inspired image. If you ask people what they would like a robot to do if they had one, they will typically ask that it do human tasks, such as doing the dishes. In our early work with robots, we tried various ways to break this image, including brainstorming sessions such as the bootlegging technique described in a following chapter. However, it was clear that the ideas we came up with were not well grounded in reality. They were too far out to be implemented technically, and they did not provide any actual use or fulfill any human need that would make them attractive in the long run.

We first decided to attack the latter problem, of envisioning compelling functions and roles for robots beyond the science fiction scenarios. However, the problem with finding any kind of use for a robot is that people have no idea what they would do with one! It does not really help to ask prospective users what they want, because the answers will be just as unrealistic and ill grounded as whatever researchers can come up with, if not more so. And there are few situations to study in which robots are part of everyday activities, outside of highly controlled factory environments and clearly defined tasks such as vacuuming (for which iRobot's Roomba has become one of the few successful household robot products). It was obvious we needed a new approach to our methods of inquiry, one that would inspire design without fettering us to existing preconceptions.

One of the opportunities for innovation identified previously is the concept of *marginal practices*. By looking at user groups outside of your own general experience, it might be possible to come up with solutions to problems that you would otherwise not think of. A potential marginal practice for robots might be robotics researchers, who are already living with various robot prototypes of some sort. However, we realized that the grounding in an innovation process does not necessarily have to come from the same domain as that of the technology—it might even help if they are different. Instead it could be useful to find some activity or group that has properties that are similar to the one we are innovating for—we can call that *analog practices*. Sara Ljungblad, who was then a Ph.D. student in my group, set out to find an analog practice that was suitable for robots. We based the search on the properties that we had identified for robots, including the following:

- Autonomous
- Emerging behaviors
- Taking advantage of the physical world

Several previous robot designs have been based on common household pets, such as dogs (e.g. Sony's *AIBO*). However, compared to current digital products, dogs are in fact extremely complex, and even the most basic dog behavior is almost impossible to replicate with today's technology. Instead, we found that another group of animals also matched the set criteria, but with less complex behaviors. It turns out that exotic pets such as insects, spiders, and reptiles have very devout owners, but their overall behavior is significantly less complex than that of a dog. Furthermore, most people do not have any experience with these types of animals and would have fewer preconceptions of what they could do. Finally, as with many marginal practices, it turns out that although the group that owns these kind of animals is quite small compared to those who own more mainstream pets, these owners are also often highly articulate and happy to share their reasons for owning these animals.

Figures 2-3–2-5

For inspiration, we interviewed passionate owners of unusual pets, such as spiders and lizards.

Supported by her research assistant, Katarina Walters, Sara set out to gather information about owners of exotic pets. Through various organizations, they found 10 owners of lizards, spiders, snakes, and other animals who were willing to share their experiences. The data gathering was performed as semistructured interviews, where the interviewer had a set of guiding questions to keep the conversation on track but the interview format also allowed for detours along the way if something of particular interest arose. Examples of the questions were as follows:

- What do you consider important qualities of your pet?
- Why are you interested in this kind of animal?
- What do you do with your pet?
- What does the pet do?
- Do you have any social interaction with other pet owners?

These interviews produced a rich set of statements about why people keep these unusual pets, what kind of activities the pets perform, how the owners interact with others regarding their interest, and so on. In other words, this was real *grounding* in actual experiences. What made it useful for us was that these people owned something that had at least some analogous qualities to the robot technology we were ultimately interested in.

The subjects had many different motivations for owning and enjoying their pets. For instance, one saw them not so much as pets but as an object of a more distanced interest, acknowledging that you cannot interact with a snake in the same way as with, for instance, a dog:

> I mean the snakes are constructed in a specific way and if you get them you have to accept that they aren't any cozy pets or alike, you have to have them as your interest.

Another owner had a more instrumental and activity-centered way of approaching the pets, being interested in the challenge of breeding:

> Yes, well, it's mostly that it is exciting and a challenge to develop certain colors and things like that.

There were also many stories about the personal relationships that would develop between owner and pet, even though the interviewee was, of course, fully aware that in reality a lizard does not really form actual relationships with people:

> Eh... here is a leopard gecko. It is partially sighted, so I have fed it with tweezers since it was small, and now it is a bit over a year, so it is pretty special to me.

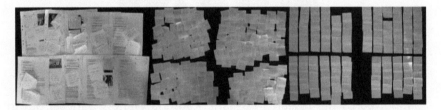

Figure 2-6
The raw material from the interviews was first organized into clusters of similar themes, and then overlapping statements were grouped together to avoid repetition.

The next step was to organize all of this material into a form that would make it useful for design purposes. First, all references to particular types of pets were removed and replaced with the neutral word "agent" (we did not want to use "robot" because of the connotations mentioned previously). With this neutralized data, where a leopard gecko lizard was on equal footing with a black widow spider or any other kind of exotic pet, it turned out that many of the statements fell in the same general area. For instance, there was a group of statements that had to do with how owners care for and relate to their pets in their environments:

> Partly it is fun to build these environments, and partly it is that I can spend hours to just sit and look at them when I have fed them or something like this.

> Well, it should be... be like a furniture preferably—nice to look at and at the same time easy to care for.

> Well, I have had it [the terrarium] in the living room, and then... well it's like a little extra furniture piece with a jungle theme.

What came out of this process were four rough groups of different ways to relate to the agents. The next step was to turn these groups into more concrete cases. For this, we used a technique called *personas*. This was originally created to make it easier to envision use cases for products such as web pages. A persona is a fictive person created to illustrate a particular kind of user. A persona can be quite elaborate, complete with a full name, work history, family background, hobbies, personality traits, and so on. Personas are often based on material from user studies, but they serve to focus more general findings into very specific use cases. The idea is that by using the persona, it is easier for a designer to imagine different functions and obstacles that might occur. For instance, on a shopping website it might be very useful to distinguish between "single father with two kids shopping for sports clothes" versus "fashion-conscious teenager looking for something to wear over the weekend." The two cases may have very different needs, and this can expose flaws in a design without the need for a complete user study.

We used the material from the interviews with pet owners to create personas for users of future embodied agent technology. But rather than explore specific use cases in a product that had already been largely decided on—as is the case with personas used in web design, for instance—the idea here was to paint a picture of a future technology that did not yet exist. These personas were thus "imagined use cases" for a technology that had not yet been invented. At the same time, because the personas were drawn on real-world data, the way the people in the scenarios related to their "agents" was grounded in reality. The persona descriptions were quite elaborate, with full names, occupations, backgrounds, and other specifics, and illustrated a variety of ways that each person related to some technology. However, there still was no description of exactly what that technology was, only the word "agent." The idea was that the object of interaction would be neutralized, effectively leaving a hole that could be filled with technology of our own design.

There were four personas in total, each based on one of the four groups that were found in the data. The four personas that emerged were Nadim, who considered his agents a hobby; Anne, who considered them as a part of her interior design; Magda, who viewed them as an extension of her identity; and Christopher, who used them as a contact mediator. To give a flavor of what the personas looked like, here are some excerpts from two of them:

Anne is a 41-year-old physiotherapist. When she is not working, she enjoys getting together with friends and family. She lives with her boyfriend in a one-bedroom apartment in the suburb of a small city. She is interested in interior design and has a wall off the living room that is occupied with agents. Her fiancé is not so fond of the agents, but he is of Anne, so the agents can stay. Anne had the agents a long time before she and her boyfriend got together, and she is never going to get rid of them. Anne is fascinated by the feeling the agents give the interior. She believes they create pleasant surroundings to live in, as the room feels more alive and dynamic.

Nadim is 32 years old and works as a network engineer. He lives alone in a two-bedroom flat in a small town. One of the rooms is Nadim's hobby room, and this is where he keeps his agents. Most of the people in Nadim's hometown do not know he owns agents; it is not something he talks about. He has always had a great interest in collecting and exploring various things, and as he got older he became fascinated with having agents as a hobby. Nadim finds it exciting to try to understand their behavior and sees his agents as an area of research where there is always something more to learn. He specializes in a type of agent that communicates through colors. He enjoys watching them communicate with each other and change their patterns.

The next step in this process was to fill the "holes" in the personas with actual technology. It is important to consider that at this stage, the scenarios were still very open-ended; there were many ways in which we could imagine technologies that could provide the kinds of interactions the personas suggested. However, at this point we also introduced some technological constraints. We wanted the final designs to be something that could actually be built and demonstrated with the resources available in the project, rather than some science fiction vision that might never see the light of day. This meant working with technologies that the team was already fairly familiar with, such as mobile phones, projected displays, and existing research robots that could be easily modified.

The final designs were the result of a tight interplay between the interactions described in the personas and the technology we had to work with. The first scenario, with Nadim and his hobby agents, resulted in a system we called *GlowBots*. Inspired by the idea of agents that could "breed" to somehow create new patterns, we imagined a collection of small autonomous robots that could change appearance by means of a colorful display. When the robots were placed next to each other, each one would be inspired by the pattern shown on its neighbors and create a new pattern that was a mix of the existing ones. For the actual implementation, carried out by Mattias Jacobsson and Johan Bodin, we used a small educational robot platform called the *E-Puck,* which was developed by one of the

Figures 2-7–2-9

One result of the transfer scenarios was the GlowBot, a small autonomous robot that communicates its state through dynamic patterns on a custom-built LED display. Users could tell the GlowBots how they liked the results by picking them up and shaking them—up and down for "good" and left to right for "come up with something better!" (Images courtesy of Viktoria Institute)

other partners in the project, EPFL in Switzerland. This coffee cup–sized robot provided most of the necessary technology to realize the scenario, including wheels for moving around and a set of infra-red receivers and transmitters to communicate between the agents. However, the E-Puck did not have any visual display, so we needed to design and produce a round LED display that fit snugly on top of the existing robot. With that in place, we wrote custom software to control the E-Pucks to exhibit the new behavior.

Figures 2-10–2-14

In the Flower Wall, pictures sent from a mobile phone become visual "seeds" to virtual flowers growing on the wallpaper. The user first finds an interesting image—say, a yellow house (Figure 2-10)—and takes a photograph with her mobile phone (Figure 2-11). When she arrives home, the photo can be "planted" on the wall (Figure 2-12), where its characteristics are reflected in the new flower images that are created—other images create different effects (Figure 2-14). (Images courtesy of Viktoria Institute)

In the second scenario, Anne used her agents to make her living room feel more alive. To achieve this goal, we wanted a large display that could cover an entire wall. In the future, this might be possible to realize with technologies such as electronic ink or textiles, but for this implementation we settled for a data projector. To make the display dynamic, we used algorithms that can create lifelike simulations of plants that grow and wilt away over time. Because we wanted the display to somehow reflect Anne's everyday experiences, the system can receive images taken by a mobile phone camera; the colors and shapes extracted from these images become the basis for the appearance of the plants. *The Flower Wall* (software implemented by Marcus Forsmoo) allows users to send pictures from their phones (using Bluetooth or e-mail) to the system, and every new picture will be turned into an attractive flower that grows and wilts away over time. For demonstration purposes, this process is quite fast, taking place in minutes. However, the intention is that if this system would be installed more permanently, the flowers would take weeks or months to grow and eventually disappear, creating the impression of a true "living" wall in the living room.

We do not yet know if these particular examples are innovations that could be turned into successful products, because the technology that they require (robust autonomous robots and large, unobtrusive displays) is still too expensive to make them viable for the mass market. However, both systems have been demonstrated for many thousands of people in various settings and have received a lot of positive feedback. Both illustrate unique properties of autonomous agents that we would not have come up with without the transfer of qualities from exotic pet owners to novel technology. Thus, they point toward potential future digital products, and even if all the pieces are not yet in place to make them real, it can be argued that these concepts are both grounded and novel enough to become actual products somewhere down the road.

This example shows how it is possible to have a creative interplay between inquiry and invention, which is necessary to achieve grounded innovation. The inquiry was both user oriented and technical; the interviews with owners of exotic pets gave us grounding in real-world practices, whereas a careful consideration of available technology ensured that the results would be possible to implement. But the technology also directly inspired the results—the GlowBots might have been entirely different if we had used another robot platform, and the Flower Wall was directly affected by our experience with camera phones as well as experiments with other forms of dynamic decoration. Most important, the fact that user studies and technology from totally different domains were combined provided a creative spark that could not have been achieved otherwise. These kinds of forced combinations have proved to be extremely effective in providing design inspiration—for instance, in idea generation methods such as *bootlegging* and *extreme characters*—and will be further explored in a coming chapter.

Of course, transfer scenarios have their caveats, as do all methods. It is not always easy to find a suitable practice to match a particular technology, and it is hard to provide any guidelines except to rely on intuition and trial and error. The final outcome is very much dependent on the skills and technical knowledge of the designers; given another set of people, the results could be completely different, for better or worse. But the idea of taking a marginal practice as inspiration and the method of turning raw data into personas are solid processes that can be easily replicated. No method can completely guarantee the quality of the results—that ultimately depends on the skills of the people who actually perform the work—but this method can at least provide a combination of inquiry and invention that takes us one step closer to grounded innovation. In the next chapter, we will look at some ways that innovation can be grounded in *inquiry*, which entails finding out about people and what they value, as well as understanding the limits and possibilities of technology.

CHAPTER 3

INQUIRY: FINDING OUT HOW THINGS ARE

The first component in grounded innovation that we will talk about in more depth is inquiry. With that, we mean any kind of investigation into how the world is. This is an essential part of the grounding of the innovation process, since it provides a solid base for the inventions to stand on. Without inquiry, it is difficult to know if an invention will have any use in the real world, or even if it will be possible to implement, either technically or socially.

At the same time, coming up with new ideas is always an essential component for innovations. Therefore, it is also important to be able to go beyond the results of an inquiry and introduce new elements. While there might be no such thing as too much grounding for an innovation process, it is necessary to be able to break free from it in creative ways. This also means that we have to balance how much effort and time is given to the inquiry, compared to other elements of innovation.

With some simplification, we can divide the inquiry into two main categories: user oriented and technology oriented. Both are equally important! Without a strong grounding in potential users' desires and needs, it is unlikely that any new idea will gain traction. But at the same time, an invention may be ever so desirable, but if it is not actually within the possibilities of existing or future technology, it will simply never be realized. The latter is of particular importance when working with digital products. Because development since the 1960s has been so fast, it is easy to imagine that basically everything we can dream up will be possible given the ever-increasing processor speed and storage space promised by Moore's law. However, this is far from always the case; not only do other factors in addition to Moore's law limit digital artifacts (such as the cost and size of sensor and actuator technology), many information processing problems are intractable even with today's fastest computers. We will discuss technical grounding later in this chapter.

USER INQUIRY

User-oriented inquiry has a long history in the design of digital artifacts. User studies contributed greatly to the influence (if not immediate commercial success) of the user interface of the Xerox Alto and Star workstations. When designing it, Xerox imagined that its technology would be used in businesses that traditionally handled a lot of text, such as book publishing. To make its system better suitable for this audience, rather than just asking those in high levels of management what was necessary to make a good system, Xerox sent a team to do studies at an actual book publishing company. The team members spent time observing everyday work practices, and elements of what they found were introduced in the interface that they then designed. In particular, in the days of publishing before computers, the typeset text would arrive on large rolls of paper, which the employees would then cut into suitable pieces and paste onto single sheets of paper to make up a book. Inspired by this observation, the designers of the Xerox publishing interface introduced a similar system to "cut" and "paste" text from one place to another—the same commands you can find on your computer's menu bar today, as well as on many other devices. Today this idea has been generalized so that we cut and paste not just text but all types of media, even sounds and moving images. In other words, a vital part of the interaction in every current graphical user interface—whether on tablets, computers, or smartphones—is still based on a metaphor that came out of a specific practice in the book publishing industry and one that existed long before the introduction of graphical layout software!

The power of something like the cut and paste command was its transferability (consider the transfer scenarios discussed in the previous chapter). By looking into a marginal practice, in this case the publishing industry, Xerox created something that had universal appeal. With this practice, the company found a simple metaphor for something that could be used not just for moving blocks of text but also for moving images, sounds, files, and so on. Although every book publisher indeed does use WYSIWYG editing software today, the number of user groups who have benefited from this innovation is much, much larger. Therefore, a crucial lesson from this example is that while user inquiries may be the source of innovations, they may also become much more powerful when they go beyond the original user group. A goal with grounded innovation should be to incorporate this possibility from the start.

As computer use became more widespread in the 1980s, it became apparent that it was necessary to make computers more usable for nonexperts. This led to the inception of the field of human-computer interaction (HCI). This field originally has its roots in a combination of computer science and cognitive psychology, as well as cognitive ergonomics. Based on theories of how the brain works, HCI researchers attempted to find systematic ways of evaluating the usefulness or usability of computer interfaces. A popular way to do this has been through laboratory studies, where all aspects of an interaction can be controlled.

A typical example would be to measure the time it takes for a number of users to complete a specific task given a new interface technology, as compared to a control group. More recently, and as the use of computers has spread to all walks of life, the limitations of controlled studies have become more apparent. Most computers and other digital products are now used in settings that are far beyond the comparatively stable desktop environment of the original personal computer. Therefore, many recent evaluations of new interface technology attempt to perform more naturalistic studies, where the technology is used over a longer period of time in more or less realistic situations.

Furthermore, HCI has become influenced by fields such as sociology, as well as more open-ended methods for study including ethnomethodology. The latter is an approach to observational studies of human activities where researchers have few or no preconceptions of what these activities mean or what motivates the people performing them. So-called ethnographic studies have become a de facto method in collecting data about user settings, both as evaluations of technology that has already been deployed and as input to future design. Using ethnography in designing new technology has an advantage: rather than asking users or management what they need to improve a particular work process—something that could clearly bias the resulting designs and lead to the discarding of potentially creative solutions—the researcher can collect unbiased data about the actual setting. These data can then be presented as implications for the design of new systems.

Ethnographic studies have the advantage of giving an uncolored view of the practices of a particular setting, whether it be a busy factory, an open-plan office, or a subway where teenagers are sharing data on mobile phones. However, even if it is more unbiased than other methods, just knowing a lot about a setting does not guarantee that this knowledge can be turned into a successful innovation. Some even argue that this should not be the goal of ethnographic studies in HCI; for instance, UCI Professor Paul Dourish emphasizes the quality and value of a study itself over the often tacked on "implications for design." There is also a tension in the HCI field regarding whether the same team should do the studies *and* design the new technology; it can be argued that it is difficult to be an expert on both. Furthermore, compared to other methods, ethnography is comparatively expensive because it requires a lot of study time and analysis to do properly. This has led to the "quick and dirty" approach to ethnography, where the study is less formally correct but the results come out quicker and thus have more potential to be useful in the short run. In any case, there is no question that ethnography is a powerful tool for delving into a complex setting and that when approached in the right way it can give rise to solutions to problems that would otherwise be hard to identify.

Other methods of HCI have attempted to engage users in a more direct fashion in the design of new technology. Participatory design, which grew out of the politically influenced *Scandinavian School* and other movements for including workers' input in the production process, is one example. Here, the people who are the actual recipients of new technology are invited to take part in its creation. This has led to many well-documented instances of improved design for new work-oriented technologies and has the added advantage of making the users feel more invested and supportive of the introduction of new technical solutions at their workplace.

However, if we look at producing innovations, it turns out it is not always a good idea to ask directly what the users want. Chances are the answers will emphasize the preservation of existing practices or be technically unfeasible, rather than introduce new inventions. To mitigate this outcome, participatory design includes a number of methods to let researchers and users work together to create new solutions. For instance, with so-called *video prototyping*, users can act out different scenarios of how they imagine a new technology could help them do their work. This kind of acting out makes it easier for users to see the real-world issues that arise. The researchers and users together can then study and analyze videos, and the results can be used to create new technology. This is a good example of a method that combines both inquiry and innovation. However, in video prototyping and other participatory design methods, the emphasis is clearly on creating solutions for well-specified problems in a specific setting, rather than coming up with innovations that have more widespread potential.

The HCI field is unique in how it takes influences from different disciplines and combines them to develop and evaluate new technology. But in essence it is also a very technical field. Parallel to the evaluation and study of existing artifacts, HCI has also pioneered many new types of digital products, including those that go beyond the desktop computer. These ideas often start with what Verplank called a "hunch" (see the previous chapter), which then has to be evaluated. When exploring a new concept, researchers often go through a series of iterations of prototypes that are evaluated in lab studies or naturalistic settings. The field's emphasis on this kind of prototyping and testing cycle concerning new technology means that it lies in the middle field of the innovation space that we sketched out in the previous chapter. It has also had a methodological influence on practices used in other fields, including product design. Many of the HCI methods discussed here, as well as many others that we do not have time to go into, are applied heavily in the development and testing of established digital product categories, such as web pages and mobile phones.

However, it also seems that for the most part current HCI research has failed to create the kind of breakout innovations that, for instance, were represented by the personal computer developed by the Palo Alto Research

Center (PARC). In fact, the influential HCI researchers Bill Buxton and Saul Greenberg have claimed that the field's emphasis on evaluation means that it would not have been accepting of inventions that we now know were groundbreaking, such as Bush's Memex or Sutherland's Sketchpad. This may indicate that while HCI methods are well developed for solving certain issues, they often fail to provide the grounded innovation that would result in new technologies that could have an impact on society at large.

An explanation of HCI's relative failure to produce lasting innovations when it comes to actual digital products may lie in the field's historical emphasis on validation over invention. Controlled laboratory studies can provide post hoc evaluations of inventions, but they give little guidance as to how they are produced in the first place. Further, as mentioned earlier, studies in strictly controlled environments with comparatively few users may be scientifically valid but do not always indicate the real value of a new product. Naturalistic studies, on the other hand, are hard to perform in a controlled manner. They usually require that users actually use an artifact over an extended period of time. This puts high requirements on the technology; it has to be both robust enough to withstand extended use and provide a compelling enough use case that people actually make it part of their daily routine. It might be possible to use an incentive such as money or goods to encourage extended use, but doing so might skew the results. Instead of relying on a fully natural environment, a middle ground position might be to perform demonstrations for the general public in a public space, such as a museum or a technology fair (as was done with the GlowBots and Flower Wall, discussed in the previous chapter). This option would provide a seminaturalistic setting, because the visitors have come of their own accord and can offer an unbalanced view when they interact with the technology. On the other hand, it is difficult to obtain any extended use in such a situation, as visitors typically move from exhibit to exhibit.

Case Study: Dressing Up Robots and Phones

So what can we do if we want a better grounding in how a new technology is used, but the technology is not mature enough? One solution can be to find a commercial product that is close to what we are interested in, but more robust. For instance, in another project, we were interested in exploring the long-term effects of having a robot as an everyday companion. In particular, we wanted to see how robots could be incorporated in everyday family life. However, the robot prototypes we had developed ourselves, such as the GlowBots, were not robust enough to put into a family for an extended period of time. Advanced research robots, such as Sony's AIBO, a robotic dog, were very expensive and not suitable for everyday use. Instead, we settled on using an advanced toy, the *Pleo*, a commercial robotic product that resembled a small dinosaur (that was released in 2007). This had the advantage of being mass-produced to high enough standards that it would not break easily, and the price was relatively low (about $200). Although it was a commercial product, it was also ahead of its time, and the company behind it, Ugobe, introduced it as an "artificial lifeform" rather than a toy. In advertisements, the Pleo promised to behave almost like a pet and be a toy that would develop over time and grow together with its owners. Unfortunately, the Pleo failed to live up to its promise, and the company went bankrupt soon after it was introduced.

A group of researchers from my lab, including Ylva Fernaeus, Maria Håkansson, Mattias Jacobsson, and Sara Ljungblad, recruited a number of families that would "adopt" a Pleo for several months. The intention was that they would live with the technology as a natural part of their life and document their experiences through photography, video, and blogs. In their studies of the Pleo toy, the researchers found that the families had much higher expectations on the Pleo than it could deliver. For instance, they hoped it would develop and become smarter over time, but in fact, the Pleo's virtual intellect stopped advancing after about two weeks. The families also had expectations of how the Pleo would react in its environment; because it looked like a small animal, children would try to make it fetch and do other tasks that a dog could do, but the Pleo was incapable of performing these tasks. Also, maintaining the Pleo required a lot of work; it had to be recharged every couple of hours, and when its batteries ran out it would simply stop working midmovement without any warning. Finally, one reason that the Pleo was abandoned was that children typically go through various play stages and will eventually discard most of their toys in favor of something new. The Pleo was great for a kid interested in dinosaurs (as many are), but when that phase passed (as it inevitably does) it would have much less value in the ecosystem of toys in the child's home. This apparent mismatch between technology and expectations might have been avoided had the developers spent more time grounding their ideas in user studies.

Some of the people behind the Pleo had previously developed the *Furby*, a similar but much less technically advanced toy that became a commercial success for a short period in the late 1990s. It is illuminating to compare the failure of the Pleo with the success of the Furby. The Furby was much simpler mechanically (it only had one motor, versus the Pleo's 14), in terms of sensing capabilities (it had only an accelerometer and several touch sensors, versus the Pleo's 35-plus sensors for sight, sound, and touch), and in software complexity. There was even less development of the Furby's vocabulary and behavior. Yet the interaction with the Furby was more *compelling*—even in the long term. A lot of this comes down to the simplicity: you could pick a Furby up at any time and it would immediately wake up and start speaking or making facial movements. It reacted quickly and in a direct manner to input such as shaking it, "feeding" it by putting a plastic spoon in its mouth, or pressing one of the sensors on the front or back.

The Pleo also did these things, but because it gave the impression of being capable of much more advanced interactions (and cost many times more), this was simply not enough. This potential mismatch between the expectations and capabilities of a system is well known in the HCI community. As early as 1990, researchers at Apple found that people would start to treat a virtual guide more like a real person and expected more intelligent answers the more real it looked. Thus, if a robot or agent looks cartoonish, like the Furby, the expectations for its capabilities are low; but the more real it looks, the higher the expectations are. The Pleo looks similar to a real animal, like a dog or a cat, and thus the expectations (even more supported by the way it was marketed) were way above its real capabilities. In other words, by creating a more complex interaction, the makers of the Pleo had actually made their product less compelling.

Despite the Pleo's failure as a product, our studies did lead to some potential innovations. When studying the Pleo owners, Ylva Fernaeus and Mattias Jacobsson found that they would often adorn the toys with different types of clothing and decorations. For instance, the owners would put a hat or a dog collar onto their Pleo, and then they would create stories of how the toy felt or behaved when it was wearing these items. (This behavior has also been observed with owners of consumer robots, such as the Roomba vacuum cleaning robot.) Of course, the owners were well aware that an electronic toy does not have real feelings, but what if the clothes would actually change the behavior of the robot? This led to a new interaction concept, *ActDresses*. The idea is simple. A problem with robots is that it is hard to determining which "mode" it is in, in other words which program it is running, if there are no clear indications. But say that you put a studded collar, like that of a guard dog, on your robot; then its behavior would change into "guard" mode—perhaps it would be more vigilant and give a signal if something approaches. Put on a Santa hat and it starts to sing Christmas carols, or put on pajamas and it goes to sleep. This turns out to be a useful way of interacting not only with robotic pets but with many types of digital artifacts. One example is to put a hat on a Roomba that would indicate different cleaning behaviors.

But the concept does not stop at robots—which is still a fairly limited market. Another interesting opportunity for this idea could be to change the behavior of mobile phones. We usually carry the same phone to work, to family outings, to parties, and to other activities, but the function of the phone might be vastly different in these settings. (In Japan, it is common to carry several different phones for exactly this reason.) Mattias Jacobsson and Ylva Fernaeus developed

Figures 3-1–3-2

Owners of robotic pets, such as the Pleo, often dress their toys in different clothes to mark different activities. For instance, an owner might put pajamas on the Pleo before making it "go to sleep" in the evening.

Figures 3-3–3-4

The study of Pleo inspired ActDresses, where users could change the function of a robot by altering its attributes, such as activating different cleaning behaviors by "dressing up" a Roomba vacuum cleaning robot with different dresses and symbols.

Figure 3-5

Mobile ActDresses *adapt the interface of a phone when the physical cover is changed; they were inspired by the same study as the robot system. (Images courtesy of the Swedish Institute of Computer Science)*

Mobile ActDresses, inspired by the mobile phone charms jewelry that is common among young users, especially in Asia. In this case they built the functionality into the detachable back cover of a standard phone. By changing the cover on your phone, you would not only change its color but also its behavior. For instance, at work you might use a gray shell with the corporate logo; then the phone's interface would sport a strict worklike background, it would give quick access to your meeting schedule and corporate e-mails, and it would prioritize calls from your boss. After work hours, you could change it into a personalized cover with a drawing made by your daughter. Now the phone has a warm and friendly theme, gives you instant access to family photos, notifies you of upcoming birthdays and events, and sends work calls directly to voicemail. Although most phones offer the opportunity for some personalization, this feature is hard to access and there is no way for an outsider to tell which "mode" you are in. Another way of implementing this idea would be to make use of those popular mobile phone charms. By attaching several charms to their phone at the same time, users would have access to multiple functions. This idea is still in the prototype stage, but it could easily be developed into a product and is a great illustration of how an innovation that started with user inquiries in one domain (pet robots) can be transferred to another (mobile phones).

TECHNICAL INQUIRY

Although user-oriented inquiry is vital for producing innovations, a solid technical grounding is equally or more important. If a new idea lacks fundamental technical feasibility, it will never make it into the real world, no matter how well grounded it is in user need. Technology is also a source of innovation in itself, and it can often be fruitful to play around with the possibilities afforded by emerging technology. The process of inventing new interfaces and applications from technology can also be systematic, and here technical inquiry is key. Knowledge of emerging technologies and their limitations can come from many different sources: technology blogs, technical conferences and journals, popular magazines, exhibitions and fairs, and so on. Anyone with the ambition to create innovative digital artifacts should keep up with as many sources as possible to keep a steady influx of new technical ideas. Some of these are listed in the appendix.

However, despite its reliance on technically advanced digital artifacts, the human-computer interaction community offers fewer examples of methods for technology-driven innovation than for user-oriented approaches. In fact, for the most part, technical inventions in HCI do not seem to be created with any systematic approach at all, except the general scientific principle of building on previous work. Instead, as mentioned, the bulk of the methodology lies with either user-oriented inquiry a priori to creating a design, or with post hoc evaluations of interactive systems. The most systematic approaches to blue-sky invention, such as brainstorming, are the methods taken from or inspired by the design community, which we will talk about in the next chapter. There are also many technical subfields where technical inquiry is more immediately obvious, such as ubiquitous computing. However, for the most part, such inquiry will lead to improvements of existing technologies rather than new innovations. For instance, there has been a lot of study on location awareness, and many techniques developed at research labs have made it into the mainstream, such as Wi-Fi positioning (see Chapter 7 for more information); but as to how we can create new applications that make use of positioning, there is little methodological guidance.

This does not mean that technical inquiry is absent from HCI and other fields concerned with the design of digital artifacts, far from it; but it is perhaps more internalized. However, the scientific method that is required for publishing is not always the best format for fostering innovation. To be accepted as science, an academic project should follow the format of hypothesis–experiment–result. This means that the researcher first establishes a prediction of what will happen, such as "this new interface will make window switching 30% faster." Then an experiment is performed to test the hypothesis. Finally, the results are presented (papers rarely are published if the hypothesis is wrong, even though this might be just as valuable). For an open-ended problem, which is what we encounter in the innovation process, this is a bit like putting the cart before the horse. If we already have established a hypothesis of what a good solution might be, there is little room for new ideas to emerge during the process. In reality, of course, this is not what happens. The development of new digital artifacts is in reality more a form of what Bruno Latour calls tinkering, a constant cycle of messing about with the materials until something of value emerges—but of course, this does not sound very scientific! It is also close to the prototyping approach that we will discuss in Chapter 5.

Case Study: Smart-Its Friends and Bump

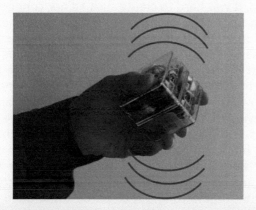

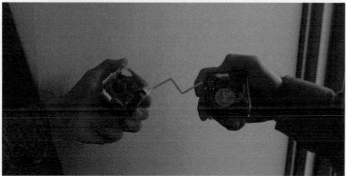

Figures 3-6–3-7

In 2001, with Smart-Its Friends, *we implemented a method for users to associate objects with each other by shaking them. (Images courtesy of TECO and Viktoria Institute)*

It is not just user-oriented studies that may be the subject of transfer, such as the cut-and-paste command that made its way from book publishers to the general audience, or the studies of exotic pets that were turned into new applications. Sometimes inventions that arise from technology make the transfer to a completely different technical solution. Around 2001, I was working on a project to develop a wireless sensor device, the Smart-It (more on this in the Materials section in Chapter 8). The idea was that by attaching a Smart-It to an ordinary object—say, a coffee cup or a shoe—we could instantly turn it into a digital artifact. However, this new kind of object provides some serious user interface problems. How do you give user commands to a device that has no buttons, screen, or other input/output devices? For instance, say that you want to tell some objects that they "belong together," such as your wallet, your keys, and your phone. You hardly leave home without all three of them, and if one is missing from the assembly, this would be a cause for sending an alert. It might also be useful for them to be able to communicate securely, for instance, to exchange a payment between an electronic wallet and a shop stall. But with no obvious input method, it was hard to create such ad hoc connections.

When thinking about this problem, I realized that one way to create this connection would be to make it so that the objects all would experience the same sensor data at the same time. One of the sensors on the Smart-It was an accelerometer, which can be used to precisely measure movement and orientation. It was easy enough to set the built-in radio in the Smart-It to transmit the accelerometer data of each device that had a Smart-It attached. If we now would take two objects and hold them together and shake them, chances are there would be no other objects within radio range that had the same movement signature. By looking at the exact time of the shaking movements and considering the fact that the objects were close enough to be within radio range, it could be established with almost 100% accuracy that they were being held and shaken in the same hand. Thus, this would be an excellent way of telling the objects that they belonged together. Excited by this idea, some of the other partners on the project put together a proof-of-concept prototype of this idea, which we called Smart-Its Friends, and published it. Other researchers, including Ken Hinckley at Microsoft, built similar systems, including a system where one could bump two objects together rather than shake them (which fit better for larger form factors such as tablet PCs). But we did not really see any use of the technique outside of these research experiments.

Fast-forward 10 years and I'm in a bar in Tokyo. Somebody I just met wants to send me a photograph, but because we have no shared Internet connection and different brands of smartphone, it is not exactly easy. However, my new friend pulls up an app on his phone called Bump, and to my surprise it uses exactly the same sharing method I suggested a decade ago! If two phones run the Bump software (they do not have to be of the same brand), you can "bump" them together, and they will be put in a state to transmit data between each other. It works; after I download the app, we bump our phones together and are effortlessly sharing photos and other information over the mobile phone network, with no need to set up any

Figure 3-8

The Bump application lets users exchange information, including contact data, photographs, and music, between phones by bumping them together. It has been downloaded more than 45 million times. (Image courtesy of Bump Technologies)

addresses or protocols. As an experiment, I hold our phones together and shake, instead of bumping, to create a connection. It works just as well as bumping them, although the social protocol is somewhat more awkward because I need to briefly take possession of my new friend's phone!

A few months later, I got to meet one of the co-founders of Bump, David Lieb, and he explained how he and his colleagues came up with the idea. Unlike my research projects, they had come at it from a purely utilitarian angle. They had been at a function where a number of guests wanted to exchange contact information. However, despite owning some of the most advanced mobile phones in existence, it turned out to be very hard for them to do this in practice. The phones used different operating systems, different data formats, and even had different communications hardware such as Bluetooth radio or infrared light. While thinking about this problem, Lieb and company came up with the simple idea of bumping two phones together to exchange data. Unlike in 2001, this would now actually be possible on a mass-market scale.

What had happened in the intervening years was that technology had grown up. While the interaction looked the same as Smart-Its Friends, the people behind Bump had in fact used a completely different set of technologies to realize it. This is what turned my idea from an invention with no clear purpose to an innovation that today has users numbering in the tens of millions (Bump is currently one of the top 10 downloaded apps of all time for iOS and Android). First of all, Bump observed that every smartphone, such as the iPhone and Android, now has an accelerometer of at least the same precision as we used in Smart-Its. This laid the foundation for using a "bump" between two phones as a way of establishing a connection. However, instead of relying on a direct radio connection between devices to transmit the sensor data, Bump establishes a connection over the mobile 3G Wi-Fi network using standard Internet protocols. This is a much more reliable mode of communication than trying to negotiate the many different types of ad hoc infrared and Bluetooth protocols that different phone models may come equipped with. The system then transmits the bumping data from my phone's accelerometer to a central server, where it is collected along with the bumps of all other phones happening at the same time. But without being in direct radio contact, how does Bump know I bumped my bar neighbor's phone and not one in Kuala Lumpur or Bergen that somebody happened to be bumping at the same time? It does this by using another standard sensor in modern phones: location. Even though thousands of bumps may be happening at the same time all over the world, chances are that the one I am interested in is the one that just bumped in the same place. Even though one's location sensing capability indoors may be coarse, it is usually sharp enough to determine location within a couple of hundred meters so that it can successfully differentiate yours and your buddy's bump from those happening somewhere else on the globe. Finally, when you wish to transmit some data such as a photo, Bump does this over its own server through an Internet connection.

It turned out that the inventors of Bump had not heard of Smart-Its Friends when they constructed their system but came up with it independently; in any case, we never bothered to patent the idea. The interesting thing is how researchers could come up with a perfectly valid idea for interaction based simply on the available technology. However, to transform that idea into a useful product, almost 10 years of technology development was necessary before the requisite sensors and networks were pervasive enough to provide it with enough critical mass to become an actual innovation.

THE TECHNOLOGY HYPE CYCLE

This kind of trajectory is true of many other technologies, both newly emerging and those that have been around for a long time. Often, new ideas can come from looking at technology that is already available but not yet ready for prime time. In such cases is important to understand the limitations of the technology and the timeline that can be expected for how fast the ideas will become cheap, small, or robust enough for use in actual products. Several examples of such technologies have appeared to much fanfare, but disappeared from view when it became obvious that they were not ready or that the use cases simply were not compelling enough. But sometimes, a technology will overcome this first wave of disappointment and emerge years or decades later as a vital component of new innovation. The information technology analyst firm Gartner formalized this process into a "hype cycle" with five

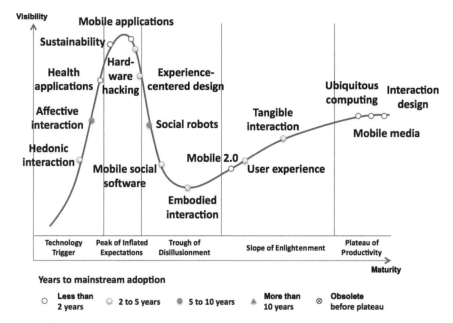

Figure 3-9

An example of a "hype cycle," constructed by the author and colleagues in 2009 to identify established and emerging interaction technologies. It is interesting to see what has happened to our predictions a few years later! (Image courtesy of IDI Lab, Swedish Institute of Computer Science)

stages: an initial technology trigger; a peak of expectations; a trough of disillusionment; an upward slope of enlightenment; and finally, a stage of productivity, where the technology is actually used. It is a vital part of technical inquiry to be aware of not only where a technology is during this stage of development, but also as far as possible predict whether it will have a chance of passing through the inevitable disappointment after the first hype. Examples of now-established technologies that have gone through this cycle include the Internet, radio frequency identification tags (RFID), and automatic text translation. On the other hand, many technologies have yet to achieve productivity despite years of hype, such as fuel cells, nanoscale machines, and immersive virtual reality.

Case Study: Electronic Ink

One interesting technology that has passed through the whole curve is electronic paper, also known as electronic ink or e-ink. I first saw a demonstration of this exciting technology in 1997 at the Massachusetts Institute of Technology (MIT) Media Lab, but at that point it had already been around in various forms for almost a decade. Electronic ink technologies promised to provide a new form of display that is closer to that of ordinary paper than it is to traditional computer screens. Originally, commercial computer screens were based on a single ray of light, a cathode ray, that would scan the display and light up pixels in turn, forming a display. Later the cathode ray tube (CRT) display was replaced with backlit liquid crystal displays (LCDs), where a matrix of microscopic gates would open and close to let light out from a single stationary lamp. Both CRT and LCD displays are light emitting, and this means that they work badly in bright light such as outdoors—the exact opposite of a printed page. Furthermore, they consume a lot of energy to keep the light bright enough for reading. Electronic ink displays, on the other hand, behave like print and rely on external light, making them easy to read under a lamp or in the sun. Thus, they offer more natural reading conditions than the flickering of a backlit display.

One form of electronic paper was developed at Xerox PARC in the early 1990s and called the *Gyricon* display. Microscopically small balls, black on one side and white on the other, were embedded in a clear substrate; by changing their direction with a magnetic pulse, they could be made to show either black or white. Another form, *electronic ink*, was later developed at MIT. Instead of small rotating balls, this version contained electrically charged microscopic sacks of particles in a fluid, half black and half white. By applying a positive or negative external charge through a magnet, either the black or the white particles could be made to rise to the surface. An advantage of electronic ink is that the display can be printed on an opaque substrate, even on a thick piece of paper. Both of these techniques have several advantages over traditional displays, such as offering a more booklike reading experience and consuming much less energy (they only require energy when the display is changed; during the rest of the time, the image stays without consuming any energy). Several commercial companies, including Philips and Sony, developed similar technologies.

When electronic ink technology emerged in the public eye in the late 1990s, the hopes were high. However, the technology was no immediate success. Even though e-ink could be printed on many different substrates, it still required supporting electronics to actually work, and this added greatly to cost and size. Furthermore, the resolution was quite low—again, not so much because of the ink itself but because of the limitations of the electronics that controlled the forces that made the ink change color. For a time, it seemed that electronic ink would only be practical for large installations such as signs, where the cost and size of the required electronics would be offset by the savings in energy and improved readability compared to traditional electronic signs. Electronic books seemed very far off, and many wondered if the promise of those early demos would ever be fulfilled.

The technology continued to be developed and finally appeared in a few e-book readers, such as Philips' *Iliad* in 2005 and the *Sony Reader* in 2007. By this time, electronic ink technology was actually good enough to provide an acceptable reading experience (though it still did not quite match that of a printed page). But e-books were for the most part an unknown quantity with no clear distribution channel, and these hardware companies could not supply their readers with compelling content.

However, one company that could provide content was Amazon, the world's largest online seller of paper books. Although it was not a hardware developer, in 2009, Amazon introduced its e-ink–based reader, *Kindle*. Unlike the previous examples, the Kindle was an immediate success—not because of the e-ink technology, as many other companies could do an equally good job of that. Instead, it was the entire ecosystem that Amazon put into place—with an established channel for selling books and a large established customer base—that made its e-book reader a viable proposition. This is similar to how Apple built an ecosystem around its iPod music player, which subsequently benefited other Apple products such as the iPhone and iPad. But interestingly, Amazon's business model is essentially the opposite: whereas Apple makes its main profit off of hardware sales, with other content mainly acting as an incentive to buy and use the products, Amazon makes very little money from the sales of the Kindle and instead earns most of its income from selling books.

To facilitate distribution, Amazon also put a mobile 3G connection into the Kindle, which meant that books could be bought and downloaded anywhere, without relying on a local Wi-Fi network. This seemingly "free" network access (in fact subsidized by the book sales) was another important part in the puzzle of making the Kindle a success. To date, Amazon has updated the Kindle multiple times, and some new titles now sell more in Kindle format than in hardcover. The major competition does not come from the hardware companies such as Sony and Philips, but from devices developed by booksellers, like Barnes and Noble's *Nook*. Creating a successful e-reader thus seems to have more to do with designing a *service* that provides content, rather than developing the best e-reading technology, whether based on e-ink or something else.

One lesson of the e-ink story is that just because a technology shows great promise, does not mean that it is ready for prime time—but if you are convinced that it will get there at some point, you can be prepared and jump on the train when necessary. Also, it is not necessarily the traditional hardware and device manufacturers that will benefit from new technical inventions—it might as well be those who have an existing ecosystem in place where the technology fits in. Amazon is not interested in selling Kindles or other hardware of its own making; the company wants to sell books. But as long as nobody else was offering a viable platform for e-books, Amazon had to provide one itself. And in fact, right now Amazon is essentially liberating itself from its own hardware by offering Kindle as a pure software solution for other platforms, including tablet devices such as Apple's iPad as well as generic Android-based devices (including some manufactured by Amazon). This means that the company can essentially sell its books to readers who are using devices made by any number of different hardware manufacturers—based on e-ink or some other technology. Meanwhile, the original e-ink technology is constantly being developed and will certainly turn up in many other products beyond book readers.

Ultimately, both user-oriented and technology-oriented inquiry can be considered *raw materials* for innovation. By relying on this material in creative ways, we can fashion new inventions that have a better chance to be grounded and turn into actual innovations. However, it is important to not be stuck by the results of the inquiry—that will never let us lift our gaze from the obvious solutions and create unique new ideas. But how can we encourage inventive thinking that goes beyond the established grounding? We will discuss some approaches to this problem in the following chapter.

CHAPTER 4

INVENTION: CREATING SOMETHING NEW

If inquiry is the solid foundation of grounded innovation, *invention* is what makes it fly. The risk of relying too much on inquiry is always that by staying too close to what we already know—whether it is technical details or user studies—we will produce only incremental improvements to existing technology or obvious solutions to well-known problems. Without new ideas, there can be no radical innovation.

But where do new ideas come from? The—perhaps surprising—truth is that ideas are usually the easiest thing to produce in an innovation process. For example, a group manager at Apple Research Labs was quoted as saying that as he walked from his office to the cafeteria he could "easily come up with 20 new ideas for products." What really matters is the quality of these ideas, and this is a much more difficult call. Of course, most or all of these ideas will be unrealistic, impossible to implement, have no real market, or be just plain stupid. In the process of coming up with new products, this kind of blue-sky thinking is necessary, but it has to be handled with care so that a company can avoid spending years of effort or millions of dollars developing something that seemed like a great idea at the time but simply will not work.

Coming up with new ideas is sometimes considered a "black-box process," hidden from view and thus impossible to understand and affect. There is actually some truth in this. Ultimately, it is not possible to predict exactly when and where a good idea will strike—it may just as well come at the desk after a long hard day of research as in the morning shower. Although there are many methods—several of which we will describe in this chapter—that can help anyone come up with new ideas, ultimately there are too many factors to control the outcome completely. There is no simple way to consistently create new ideas with any guarantee as to their quality or quantity. Great ideas often come from random sources, and the talent for picking up such impulses is probably partly a function of personal qualities, such as creativity, perseverance, and intelligence. But a large part of the process can also be learned and improved. Although we do not know exactly how ideas work, most great ideas do not strike at random but are the result of a conscious and laborious process that can take months or years to produce results.

There has been much written about idea generation in design-related areas, including human-computer interaction. However, design and innovation are *not* the same thing. A designer is typically trained to come up with a solution to a problem given by a client, whether it be the layout of a magazine, the shape of the steering wheel in a new car, or the size and colors of the buttons on a smartphone interface. There is room to be innovative within such boundaries, but there will be limits. The smartphone interface designer might be free to invent a new layout for the buttons, but the functions that these buttons trigger will most likely already have been decided by the engineering department that produced the phone's operating system. The software engineering department in turn is bound by a set of specifications from other parties, such as the hardware manufacturer that produces the device and the network provider that is the ultimate customer.

Innovation, on the other hand, is the process of giving solutions to problems that do not yet exist (or that we did not know existed). The innovator works with the materials at hand, but instead of being bound by them, a true innovator will transcend the material and create something unexpected—an invention. If we continue the case of the smartphone, there can be inventions at many different levels, from hardware features such as sensors and buttons, to software functions such as music players and cameras, to systemic inventions such as different data plans or methods for distributing applications. Such new ideas cannot originate in a design process with a preset specification. It is not a coincidence that the most innovative phone of recent years, Apple's iPhone, was created by a company that had no previous experience in designing phones and no existing ties to the other actors such as network operators. This allowed Apple to introduce new ideas in every area of the phone, including hardware (such as multitouch screens), software distribution (the App Store), and relationships with operators (for instance, fixed-rate data plans). These innovations go far beyond the design of the user interface (impressive as that is), and a company with more established ties and practices in the area would have had a hard time carrying them through. Similarly, another disruptive phone paradigm, the Android operating system, was developed by Google, a company that did not previously produce any consumer hardware (although this has now changed with the company's acquisition of Motorola's mobile phone division). This allowed Google to abstract the software layer and create a platform that is now manufactured by many different vendors to a common specification, resulting in savings in development cost and improved software interoperability.

We can thus think of the traditional design process as being bounded by a specification (such as the brief from a client) and the material (such as the screen of a smartphone or a study of user needs). An innovation, on the other hand, has no predefined specification and strives to transcend the limitations of the material. This bounding by specification and material is reflected in most commonly used design methods, which explicitly or implicitly assume there is a specification or an "ideal state" that will be reached through the design process. However, if we consider most of the methods developed for user-oriented research in academia, there is usually no specification with which to begin. Instead, the researcher employs various methods to make an inquiry into the user setting, such as observational studies, questionnaires, interviews, and so on. The researcher then uses the results from this inquiry, alongside his or her knowledge of technology, to produce a new artifact that solves the problems that have become apparent during the process. In essence, although there is no original design specification, the results of the user-oriented inquiry here replace the design brief that a client would give to a professional designer.

These methods were designed to ensure that new artifacts fit with the needs of the users. But there is another way of looking at the results of an inquiry. Rather than considering it as a specification that has to be followed, we can choose to see it as *inspiration* for the innovation process. This represents a departure for human-computer interaction, a field that has always stressed the needs of users as the foundation for new technologies (participatory design being one obvious example, among many others). What if we acknowledge the fact that most users are not designers, have no particular technical skills, and do not have the time or inclination to come up with new product ideas? Then, instead of being a specification, a user study becomes one of many inputs into the process of inventing new artifacts. This is closer to an artistic process, where the goal is to create something that is unique and has a certain effect, rather than something that fulfills specific set criteria. On the surface, this seems very different from the scientific process, where every outcome has to be the result of an a priori articulated hypothesis. Yet despite the demands on formal rigor, successful scientists also sometimes take inspiration from unexpected sources and come up with solutions based on impulses that may seemingly have nothing to do with the work at hand.

I find it useful to think of all possible input collectively as potential *generators* of inventions. A generator is simply a jumping-off point for new ideas. It can be anything—results from a deep multi-man-month ethnographic study; a new technology that has just become available; or inspiration from other sources, such as everyday life or popular culture. After all, as long as an idea is good, does it really matter if it comes from spending two years studying the work practices at a London Underground station or a night of watching science fiction movies? Thinking of any kind of input as a generator of ideas—rather than a specification to be bound by—frees up the process of coming up with new inventions. It lets the innovator look at every input equally and mix and match as appropriate. This can take some determination—it is easy to become wedded to the results of an inquiry that has taken months or years to achieve or to a technology that a company has spent millions of dollars to develop. But ultimately, for innovation, it is the result that matters. The process of maximizing invention thus becomes the process of using generators that allows us to come up with the best possible ideas and then carefully select the ones that are worth taking further.

Case Study: Cultural Probes

One way of using inquiry into users as inspiration rather than specification in an innovation process is the *cultural probes* method, devised by Bill Gaver, Tony Dunne, and Elena Pacenti. It has become popular in the human-computer interaction community and has also been used in some commercial settings—one reason is probably that it is clearly delimited and produces a rich set of materials from users. This method is sometimes confused with traditional user-oriented approaches. It is important to be aware that although some of the data collection techniques used in cultural probes are similar to those used in participatory design and other methods, the end goal is very different. For user-oriented methods, the data are collected and analyzed with the intention to use them as direct input to the design of a new system. Although designers may take many ideas along the way, and the same data can result in many different outcomes, the line from users to results will usually still be quite transparent in such a user-oriented process. For cultural probes, on the other hand, the results of the data collection are used as *inspiration* in a process that can also include many other factors. The data from the probes should thus act as a way to generate new ideas, rather than as a specification, and there is not necessarily any clear connection between user input and the resulting designs. At the same time, since the original introduction of the concept, there has been much debate in the human-computer interaction field on probelike methods, as well numerous creative crossover methods, making the distinctions sometimes unclear. The following is an account of how the method was originally introduced and used.

In their first instance of using cultural probes, Gaver and his team were working with elderly people in a diverse set of communities. They faced the problem of designing for a user group that they really did not know much about, even though they had many preconceived (and possibly erroneous) notions of what their lives were like. The team came up with a way of soliciting user input that deeply involved the prospective end users yet allowed for a much more open interpretation than traditional user-oriented methods. The central mechanism was to give out a package of instruments that would let the users collect material about their daily life—they called these *probes*. In the first instance, this included postcards, maps, a disposable camera, and various other material, all collected in an attractive package. Already at first glance, the probes were designed to be as far away from dry, formal questionnaires as possible and were instead intended to be informal, intriguing, and inviting. With the materials came different tasks that the respondents were invited to perform, such as writing answers to specific questions, taking pictures in particular situations, and so on.

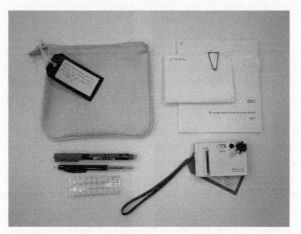

Figure 4-1

Example of a "probe" pack, including a camera, maps, pens, stickers, and various other items for soliciting user input. (Image courtesy of Lalya Gaye/Viktoria Institute)

In the probes packages that the team gave out to their subjects were both obvious and less straightforward tasks and items. One important part of the contents was about 8 to 10 addressed, pre-paid postcards, each with an image on the front and a question on the back. Because of their informal, friendly connotations, the idea was that the postcards would encourage a more casual attitude than, for instance, a questionnaire. The images were evocative rather than informative, and the questions were designed along the same lines, with wording such as "What do you dislike about [the city where you live]?" or "What place does art have in your life?" or "Tell us about your favorite device." Another instrument in the probes were a collection of maps with accompanying inquiries. For instance, the elderly were asked to answer the question "Where have you been in the world?" by putting stickers on a world map. On a local map, they were asked to mark different zones for different activities, such as where they would go "to meet people," "to be alone," or "to daydream." A more challenging task was to imagine "If my hometown was New York" by placing stickers depicting the Statue of Liberty, drug addicts, and other Big Apple phenomena over a map of their own local area. Because of their ease of use, postcards became common elements in later probe packages.

Another component of the probes that has often reappeared in subsequent uses of the probes concept was a disposable camera.

In this case, it was repackaged to be integrated with the visual style of the other probe materials. On the back was a list of requests for pictures, such as the respondent's home, what clothes they were planning to wear, the first person they would see in a day, or more open-ended assignments such as "something desirable" or "something boring." The use of a camera is particularly evocative, with the right wording of the tasks it leaves a lot of creative leeway for the respondents and has the potential to generate material that is both informative and stimulating. The final two items the respondents received were a photo album that they were asked to fill with pictures that were meaningful to them, and a media diary where they would record their television and radio use (including not just what they consumed but also who they did it with).

Although some of the probes techniques are similar to (or have since been adopted by) other user-oriented data-gathering processes, the difference is, in fact, quite profound. Rather than hard data on what kind of problems the users encountered or what kind of technology they might be interested in, the cultural probes brought back a much more open-ended material. This was intentionally reflected in the overall design. The probe packages and content were designed to be aesthetically pleasing, while not appearing too finished, in an attempt to reduce the distance between the researchers and the respondents. The concept and tasks of the original probes incorporated techniques from art, such as collage, juxtaposition, and ambiguity. Even the presentation of the probes was carefully designed; rather than being mailed out, the researchers presented them in person in order to engage in a direct dialogue with the elderly.

For over a month after handing them out, postcards, cameras, maps, and other items would appear regularly in the researchers' mail. In pure numbers, the rate of return on this first probes experiment compared favorably to other methods. Some postcards were intentionally left blank, when the task at hand proved too difficult, but a large number of photos, maps, and texts were collected.

Rather than being analyzed or summarized, the materials from the probes were used to get a feeling for the overall characteristics of the different sites. This in turn was taken as inspiration for designing potential technological interventions in the different sites. For instance, one of the sites was a strong community in a dangerous area. For this, they suggested a network of computer displays to communicate the values of the inhabitants and attitudes about the culture. Another group was affluent and well educated; here the researchers proposed a community-wide conversation system based around the local library and electronic displays in trams, cafés, and public places. At an Italian village, the suggestion was instead to complement the relaxed social life in a beautiful setting with social and pastoral audioscapes that included the sounds of the surrounding countryside. The probes were successful in generating novel yet grounded ideas, and the team went on to use the technique in several later projects. The method has since been picked up by many other researchers.

Since they were originally presented, the subversive cultural probes technique, with roots in avant-garde art movements such as dadaism and surrealism, has been widely adopted into mainstream HCI—but its original purpose is often lost or misunderstood. Used in the way it was originally intended, the probes method has some clear advantages: it provides a set framework for collecting inspirational input into a design process, yet it is open enough to be adapted to many different contexts. The results of the probes are often interesting in themselves and reflect the users' creativity and everyday lives. However, when the probes method became popular, it also started to be used in ways other than that originally intended. In the human-computer interaction research community, probelike techniques have sometimes been employed to gather user requirements in a way more in line with user-oriented techniques, such as interviews and participatory design. In these cases, researchers typically hand out probelike packs with post-cards, cameras, and other material. The difference is that the tasks are usually more rigid, and in particular that the results are treated to a more rigid analysis sometimes to get a more objective view of the users' environment and their needs.

The use of probes in this way can still be fruitful, as it is a light-weight way of gaining insight into users' attitudes and environments, but it has also been criticized for its lack of depth and it has even been called "shortcut ethnography." Although this approach can also be valuable, it is important to acknowledge that this way of using probes techniques is far removed from the original intention with its empha-sis on uncertainty and ambiguity. Instead of being used as open-ended inspiration and idea generators, the results of these probes are seen as direct user input or specifications in a user-oriented design process. The original probes method is thus a method for generating ideas and *inventions*, whereas some other probe-inspired methods should more correctly be grouped with the *inquiry* methods we mentioned in the previous chapter.

BRAINSTORMING AND OTHER IDEA-GENERATION TECHNIQUES

The probes technique provides a good case study of grounded innovation; it is based on deep insight into users' experiences, as expressed in their own words and pictures, yet it encourages open-ended designs. The results from the probes can thus be used as powerful idea generators in an innovation process. At the same time, the results of the probes may be too open-ended. The method is not a shortcut to good ideas—it is essential to work creatively with the material and tease out the relevant inspiration. However, the cultural probes literature often gives little guidance on the crucial step from user input to design. In fact, the researchers often seem to jump from probes to finished ideas without much explanation. Partly, this comes back to the difficulty of formalizing creative processes that we touched on earlier, and the probes in particular seem to lend themselves to this drawback with their emphasis on ambiguity and lack of exact specifications.

But there are a number of practical and easy-to-use methods for creating new ideas given a specific material or theme. The most well-known technique for generating ideas is *brainstorming*. It was first documented in 1953 by A.F. Osborn, who outlined a detailed process for how to perform a successful brainstorming session. Since then, many have adopted the general idea, and it has developed and mutated in a multitude of different ways. Thus, there are now several different ways to brainstorm, some with little resemblance to the original concept. Usually, however, a brainstorm follows these overall stages:

- *Idea generation.* This is the actual "brainstorm," when a whole group tries to come up with as many ideas as possible with no limitations. At this point, no criticism of the ideas is permitted.
- *Sorting.* Here the participants organize the ideas—for instance, by collecting them into clusters of similar ideas.
- *Selection.* The best ideas are selected for further action.
- *Elaboration.* Finally, the selected ideas are fleshed out and documented into proposals that can be acted on.

Brainstorming works best in fairly small groups (15 to 20 people) in a limited amount of time (a couple of hours up to a day for the whole process is typical). A brainstorm usually has a facilitator who makes sure that the process moves along and that data are generated and collected, such as on Post-it Notes and PowerPoint presentations. It is usually a good idea to document the results of a brainstorm as soon as possible; otherwise they tend to be forgotten. Although completely open brainstorms are a possibility, the normal procedure is to focus on a specific problem. For instance, it would be a natural follow-up to a cultural probes session to organize a brainstorm to come up with design ideas based on the probes.

Even though brainstorming is an idea-generation method, in my experience most brainstorms do not actually result in any useful ideas! Very often, brainstorming sessions end up with the participants either going off on tangents that are too blue sky and unrealistic to have any real use or becoming too limited by preconceptions to think of anything truly new. This does not mean that the session has been useless; brainstorms can be exciting and fun, they can make a diverse group of people interact about a common theme, they can sow the seeds to creative processes that may bear fruit much later, and so on. But to run a brainstorm that really generates useful, actionable ideas within a limited time takes a lot of care and preparation. For successful brainstorming, it is necessary both for the facilitator to provide the group with a motivating and stimulating structure and for the participants to work hard to come up with results within the given limitations.

It may seem like the steps are simple to carry out, but a successful brainstorm process is difficult to facilitate successfully. It requires a fingertip feel for the group dynamics among the participants, and the facilitator has to be prepared to step in and move the process along if participants get stuck on a particular theme or if some people come to dominate the process too much. In particular, the idea-generation phase is crucial—upon it rests all the other results. But it requires some hard work to unleash the creativity of a diverse group of people, some who may never have met before. On the one hand, it is important to get ideas that are creative and out of the box—not an easy task in itself. The idea-generation phase should have a "no holds barred" feel so that participants are not afraid to contribute even the most outlandish ideas. On the other hand, it is easy to drift into a territory where all ideas are a little too outlandish. This may be fun for the participants, but it leaves the session with little workable material for the following phases.

A few modifications of the brainstorming method have been developed to increase the likelihood of creative, out-of-the-box thinking. For the idea-generation phase, one possibility is *random words,* which tries to introduce an element of chance to inspire the process. Here, two random words are drawn and combined. This can be done in several ways: for instance, by opening a dictionary in two random places, by drawing words on paper slips from a hat, or by using dedicated software (there are also websites that provide random word pairings). The resulting pair is supposed to inspire new ideas and help participants brainstorm outside the box. For instance, if the two random words are "policeman" and "food processor," combining them might lead to ideas about food preparation in specific circumstances or about novel ways of performing crime prevention. However, a weakness of this process is that the random words are just that—random. Although the resulting pairings may sometimes be inspiring, they might also often be completely irrelevant and lead to a long struggle where the participants try to come up with anything of value.

It can also be useful to think around unusual scenarios or users when brainstorming. The *extreme characters* method, devised by Djajadiningrat, Gaver and Frens, can be a way to do this. Here, the participants first come up with an unusual character with extreme yet easily identifiable traits. This can be either a real or a fictional character, as long as the character evokes a clear image of different situations and traits, such as "secret agent 007," "a fireman," or "a Hells Angel." The participants can then use this character as a jump-off point to inspire ideas. For instance, the originators used the extreme characters method to come up with ideas for different calendars. They designed calendars for specific personas, such as "a drug dealer" or "the Pope," based on their respective needs and character traits. The drug dealer, for instance, was given calendars in the form of gaudy rings for his fingers, which he could rearrange to manage his different complex criminal relationships and deals. Of course, the idea is not that the extreme character is the actual end customer, but that the character helps the creative team to think outside the box. The original ideas that come out of the method can then be adapted and generalized so that they can be applied to products for actual users. In this case, the idea of a modular, tangible calendar that sprung out of using the drug dealer example could actually be adopted into a consumer product based on multiple smart components that allow users to compose their own personalized agenda.

Another extension of the traditional brainstorm is *bodystorming*. Here, participants are encouraged to physically act out their ideas, using various props if needed. The intention is that it can be easier to spot potential problems as well as opportunities in a full-body interaction than if it is simply described verbally. For instance, if the task is to come up with new ways of utilizing a limited space, such as an airport cabin, a bodystorm session might use available props such as tables or chairs to simulate this space. Participants would sit, stand, lie down, and rearrange the props in different ways to come up with new ideas. Similarly, if the task at hand has to do with the functionality of a music player, it might help to physically act out different activities such as jogging, meeting friends, or relaxing while listening to music and then to utilize a representation of the player and its controls—a simple cardboard box might do. Bodystorming is also a great way to elaborate on and present the ideas generated in a brainstorm, as it is both visual and fun.

Case Study: Bootlegging

Many idea-generation techniques rely on the juxtaposition of different elements to inspire creativity. By putting two unrelated concepts or artifacts together, something new might emerge that is more than the sum of the parts. This is a common technique in visual art, for instance, in the form of collage. But juxtaposition can work outside of traditional collage works too. The surrealist art movement of the 1920s used the juxtaposition of elements not normally found together to provide illogical and startling effects. In a typical quote, movement founder André Breton talked about this as "the chance meeting on an operating table of an umbrella and a sewing machine." Several artworks of the movement explored unusual combinations of form and material, such as a fur-covered coffee cup created by Salvador Dali.

A few decades later, Beat era writer William S. Burroughs wished to transport the qualities of visual collage to the literary world. His new method was called "cut-up." He describes it like this:

> The method is simple. Here is one way to do it. Take a page. Like this page. Now cut down the middle and cross the middle. You have four sections: 1 2 3 4… one two three four. Now rearrange the sections placing section four with section one and section two with section three. And you have a new page. Sometimes it says much the same thing. Sometimes something quite different.

Burroughs applied the technique both to his own work and to that of other authors, arguing that cut-ups could reveal hidden layers or create unexpected meanings in just about any text, for instance, any famous poet: "Now take [a] poem and type out selected passages. Fill a page with excerpts. Now cut the page. You have a new poem. As many poems as you like. As many Shakespeare Rimbaud poems as you like." Burroughs and his collaborator Bryon Gysin also applied the technique to other media, such as film and audio.

More recently, especially now that digital mixing technology has allowed the easy combination of different audio elements, juxtaposition has become a common technique in popular music. The practice of remixing adds new sounds and beats to familiar songs, often using the technique of sampling. Taking this one step further, so called *bootleg* or *mash-up* mixes typically take the vocals from one song and marry them to the instrumental part of another, often from a completely different genre and artist. The results can be surprisingly successful, such as when bootleg pioneers Soulwax in "Smells Like Booty" took the smooth vocals of R&B singers Destiny's Child and layered them on top of Nirvana's grunge epic "Smells Like Teen Spirit"—the resulting mix sounded like nothing before, yet had easily identifiable components of both. Remix artist Danger Mouse took the bootleg trend to its ultimate conclusion when he released *The Grey Album*, where he juxtaposed an a cappella version of rapper Jay Z's *The Black Album* with instrumental samples from The Beatles' *The White Album*.

Inspired by these different approaches to juxtaposition, I have developed a brainstorm process called *bootlegging* (the name is inspired by the musical "bootleg" mixes mentioned earlier). Instead of using completely random juxtapositions to inspire out-of-the-box thinking, bootlegging tries to leverage the knowledge and experience of the brainstorm's participants. This is accomplished by letting the participants first generate the raw material of the brainstorm themselves, based on their own often significant expertise with a specific topic. It then applies a measure of randomness to the original ideas to spark creativity, much like Burroughs's cut-up version of familiar texts. Thus, when successfully carried out the results of a bootlegging session should be ideas that are outside of what the participants would normally come up with in a regular brainstorm, yet grounded in the things that they know best. The process is quite strict in order to make sure that participants do not get stuck, but experienced facilitators might find it useful to open it up and allow for more free-form generation and combination of concepts.

Over the years, I have run a number of bootlegging sessions, and while the basic format stays the same, the method has been refined and adapted for different purposes. The main goal of the method, which it seems to accomplish very well, is to create novel yet grounded ideas, which can be outlandish or practical depending on the framing of the session. It has also proved to be a good way to establish a common ground among a diverse set of participants. One major advantage is that it is straightforward enough for others to pick it up and apply it independently, which has happened several times, even by participants who only attended a single session. Despite the simple framework, my experience is that bootlegging can be much more effective in coming up with useful results than simpler or less structured brainstorming techniques. I have led many bootlegging sessions where the results have been significantly enhanced insights into specific problem domains, or practically useful but at the same time novel application ideas, results that the participants tell me were a direct consequence of applying the technique.

A bootlegging session typically follows the following steps (with suggested time limits):

1. Preparation (done beforehand by facilitator)
   - Decide the overall theme of the session—for instance, applications for intelligent buildings or entertainment applications on the road.
   - Define four categories. Typically, two of them should constrain the user side (e.g., user group and activity), one should be directly related to the theme (e.g., type of vehicle), and one should constrain the technical aspect (e.g., infrastructure)
   - Decide on a presentation format (physical mockup, video prototype, an improvised performance, etc.)
2. Generation (whole group)
   - Brainstorm in the whole group on a category to create individual instances. Write down each instance on a single Post-it Note, with one color for each category (5 minutes per category)
3. Mixing (whole group)
   - Pick one item at random from each category to create a combination
   - Repeat until you have generated several combinations for each group (at least four to five each)
4. Brainstorming (smaller groups)
   - Pick one of the combinations and brainstorm about potential applications (15 minutes for each)
   - Repeat several times depending on the available time
5. Final ideas (smaller groups)
   - Select one or more of the ideas for final presentation

- Prepare a presentation of the idea in the chosen format (45 minutes)
- Allow each group to present its idea to all participants in the chosen format (10 minutes each)

The process is best illustrated with a few examples. In one bootlegging workshop we wanted to explore the use of robot technology, beyond the images of popular culture and the narrow topics explored in most research labs. This workshop gathered about 20 participants from a wide variety of backgrounds, both industry and academia. The group first brainstormed ideas within each of the following categories:

- Place or situation (in the kitchen, running, commuting to work, etc.)
- User or user group (grandmothers, musicians, a secret agent, etc.)
- Type of robot (humanoid, wheeled robot, etc.)
- Property of robot (autonomous behavior, collaboration with others, etc.)

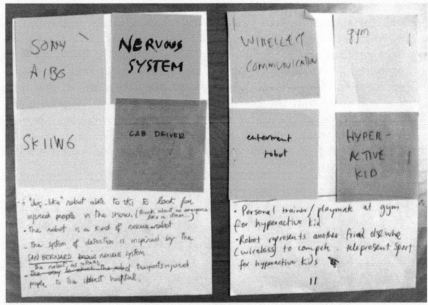

Figure 4-2

Examples of combinations generated in a bootlegging workshop on robot technology. (Image courtesy of Viktoria Institute)

There were colored notepapers for each category, and the participants generated several hundred notes in total. Next, we generated combinations by randomly pulling one note from each category and stapling them to a paper. The participants now split up into smaller groups and brainstormed for 10 minutes about the potential application suggested by each combination; they wrote the results directly on the paper. Many combinations seemed surprisingly logical even though they had been generated completely at random. In most cases, participants found it easy to turn the combinations into application sketches. However, a few combinations were obviously unworkable because they contained combinations that failed to generate any useful application ideas. Here is a typical example of what came out:

- Type: Entertainment robot
- Property: Wireless communication
- Place/situation: Gym
- User: Hyperactive kid
- Application idea: A personal trainer or playmate for hyperactive children; the robot represents another friend somewhere else through wireless communication and lets the kids compete remotely

The participants then went through several guided steps to refine the application ideas, again within strict time limits. The final results were presented as physical mock-ups built with available material such as clay, paper, straw, and glue.

The overall impression of bootlegging from this workshop was very positive. Because participants came from many different backgrounds, the technique allowed them to explore novel ideas on a level playing field without any particular discipline or viewpoint being allowed to dominate. Although many of the application ideas that were generated were far-fetched and not likely to become products any time soon, it was clear that the bootlegging technique also inspired many unusual and potentially useful application areas for robots. Overall, we felt the discussion, as well as the final results, were much more stimulating than they would have been if we had conducted a more traditional brainstorm.

Figure 4-3

Participants in a workshop on mobile music are acting out the results of a bootlegging brainstorm session—in this case, a bicycle taxi driver becomes a social hub for digital music distribution! (Image courtesy of Viktoria Institute)

Another workshop explored the emerging field of *mobile music technology*. It attracted about 20 participants from industry and academia, including participants from the fields of sociology, technology, and art. This bootlegging session took about four hours. The whole group first brainstormed collectively for five minutes each in the following categories:

- Situation or place (driving, swimming, etc.)
- Users (school kids, artists, etc.)
- Type of music use (share, listen, organize, etc.)
- Technology (mobile phone, global positioning systems, etc.)

The categories were slightly different from those used in the robot workshop in order to represent the domain of mobile music. Instead of robot-related key words, we had a generic technology category (not necessarily music related) in order to create unexpected combinations. To delimit the ideas to those relevant for music use, we had a category for "type of music use." As participants called out ideas, they were written down simultaneously on a whiteboard and on paper notes. Combinations were created by randomly selecting one note from each category. The participants then split into smaller groups. Each group was assigned three of the combinations to brainstorm on. An example outcome was the following:

- Situation: Riding a bicycle
- User: Taxi driver
- Technology: 10-second flash memory
- Type of music use: Discovering new music
- Application idea: The driver of a bicycle taxi plays short music fragments through a horn on the roof to attract customers. Because a bicycle taxi is about leisure rather than efficiency, the driver becomes a "social hub" for music. He helps passengers find new music and even sells songs to them, getting a cut of the profit.

Each group then selected its favorite idea and acted it out using bodystorming to explore the interaction in the application. Finally, the results were presented as a performance before the whole group.

Others and I have been running similar bootlegging sessions around many topics, such as domestic technology, smart furniture, and mobile services. Although these sessions are always inspiring, many of the ideas that come out of them are too unrealistic to ever be real-world products. This is not unique to bootlegging—as already mentioned, brainstorms are often better at creating a common ground and exploring a domain than actually coming up with original and grounded ideas that can be carried out into the real world.

However, it is possible to use brainstorming techniques for coming up with ideas that are more practical. To achieve this, it is important to work with the mindset of the participants in order to reign in the most far-out ideas. By clearly stating the expected outcome, and by requiring the participants to keep within well-defined limitations (such as a specific technology or a timeframe for implementation), brainstorms can be used to come up with ideas that are both well grounded and novel.

For example, in one project we were exploring new applications for mobile phones. There was a diverse set of stakeholders, including a major handset manufacturer, a mobile network provider, and an infrastructure builder. I organized a workshop with representatives of all these organizations, which, together with members of my research lab, formed a group of about 12 people. This time, the goal was much more strictly defined than in the earlier bootlegging sessions: we wanted to come up with projects that could be realistically carried out by a skilled programmer during a three-month internship. In my introduction I made this limitation very clear to all participants so that they would have it in mind when brainstorming.

The categories were modified slightly, also in an effort to make the results more realistic and relevant to existing mobile phone technologies. Instead of the usual four, there were five categories for the initial brainstorm:

- *Relationships.* Human relationships that can be of interest to support, such as friend, neighbor, spouse, or colleague.
- *Activities.* Things we could be doing while using a service, or that could be supported by the service, like walking, chatting, or dreaming.
- *Context/sensors.* Things that can be sensed on current (or near-future) phones, such as location (GPS), activity (accelerometer), ambient sound (microphone), or light (camera).
- *Content.* Things that are (or could be) available on a phone in digital form (address book, text messages, photos, etc.).
- *Output.* How a phone can express itself to the user, through icons, beeps, or vibration.

In this case, we wanted to emphasize the social and collaborative nature of mobile services, which is why instead of having "users" the participants were asked to come up with "relationships." Similarly, instead of a "situation," we brainstormed "activities." The final three categories were designed to pinpoint the technical possibilities of mobile phones that are available right now, rather than in some distant future. As usual, the whole group first brainstormed ideas for five minutes in each category, which were documented on Post-it Notes. After this, the participants were split into three groups, with one representative from each stakeholder in each group in order to make sure that there was a good variety of competencies in each.

For the smaller group brainstorms, the participants were encouraged to associate freely about the combinations. Rather than try to come up with ideas that fit all limitations, if a set of combinations did not make sense, the group could take inspiration from just one or two, or simply take them as a starting point for free association. Although this kind of free association might sometimes lead to blue-sky ideas, in this case it worked well because each group had representatives with deep competence in different fields, and they were constantly reminded that the results had to be possible to implement on standard phones within a short period of time.

The results of this bootlegging brainstorm turned out to be highly useful. In total, about a dozen ideas were generated, and just about all of them were potential new mobile services that were both unique and realistic—an extraordinary result for a brainstorm! Some of the ideas included a time-killer application that would use content already on your phone, a visualization of the phone owner's travel history, as well as more speculative ideas such as an evocative "dreaming" application where the phone would start recombining and showing content as a sort of idle mode.

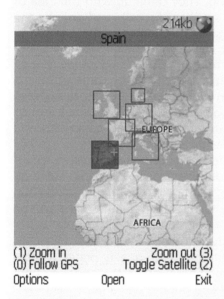

Figure 4-4

The GeoChat application lets users create virtual chat rooms tied to specific locations and was a result of a bootlegging brainstorm session. (Image courtesy of Mobile Life Centre)

After the workshop, two of the ideas were selected to go on to the implementation phase. One came out of a combination that included "asking questions" and "positioning technology." The initial idea was that the user could send out a question or a poll to a specific geographic area. The question could be, for instance, "What is the weather like?" directed to a tourist resort. People who were physically at the place could respond, but also other people who for some reason had an interest in this particular location might join in. The group generalized the idea in a position-based chat application, *GeoChat*, where users can create geographically delimited chat rooms at different positions. For instance, one might create a chat room for a particular bar or workplace, to be accessed both when at the place or when somewhere else. GeoChat was first implemented as a Java Mobile and iPhone application, and one of our industry partners found it so interesting they decided to independently implement it for Android phones.

When we have presented the GeoChat service externally, it has generated a lot of interest. For instance, the city of Stockholm became interested in using it for several purposes, including for home health care workers, as well as for volunteers who walk the city at night. Thus, while the original idea had no particular use case in mind, it turned out the concept had a lot of potential applications.

The other service resulted from a combination that included the activity of "sharing" and the content "photos." One participants brought up the practice of distributing school photos in Swedish primary schools, where each child not only gets a catalog with group photos of all classes but also gets a set of personal photos of him or herself. These photos become valued possessions that are given away to the pupil's friends. The group started thinking of ways of reproducing this experience in a mobile setting. They came up with the idea of a service where a photo could only be shared locally and only by the original owner. This would create a situation similar to the one stimulated by the photos in school, and it could potentially make the act of sharing and receiving photos much more important and personal than simply viewing photos on the Internet. The resulting application, the *Portrait Catalog*, was implemented in Java and used Bluetooth technology to limit the sharing to people nearby. Bluetooth has the advantage of being free and not requiring an Internet connection, something that can be important for users without fixed-rate data plans.

Again, when presenting the results externally, there were a lot of ideas for how to apply the service to different user groups. We ended up working with the local Department of Culture at a large summer festival for teenagers. Together with the city, we created a whole event around the Portrait Catalog. The teenagers first got their photo taken by a professional photographer. They were given the option to share the photo on Facebook and also to have it printed on high-quality paper. A team of researchers helped them install the application on their phones; here we noted that implementing for low-end phones was a good idea—less than 1% of the users we encountered owned smartphones, such as an iPhone or an Android. When the application was installed, the teenagers could send the pictures of themselves to others who had the application, and they could receive pictures from their friends. To encourage use, we had a competition for "best networker"—the user who shared the most pictures during the festival. About 400 kids had their picture taken and 350 installed the app on their phone, a large penetration for a mobile service in this user group with access to only low-end phones.

Thus, as we continued working with our partners, the original idea from the bootlegging brainstorm grew to a much larger event with many actors. Furthermore, one of the original limitations with the workshop—to focus on ideas that were possible to implement with existing technology—contributed greatly to the success of the results, as the teenagers in the event used mostly low-end phones and did not have general access to data services. If we had not had these limitations and the representation of so many different actors at the

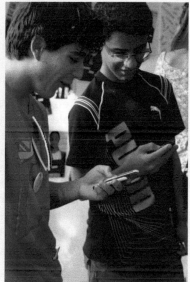

Figures 4-5–4-8

The concept of the Portrait Catalog, which lets you collect the portraits of nearby people, came out of a bootlegging brainstorm session. It was developed into a big event, Most Wanted, at the Stockholm youth festival Ung 08, which was attended by several thousand visitors. (Images courtesy of Mobile Life Centre)

original workshop, we might have come up with more advanced and far-fetched ideas—but then it would not have been possible to actually implement them, like we did here.

Brainstorming can also deepen the participants' understanding of a particular topic, even if the application ideas are not usable. A major telecom company asked us to help its team understand the topic of indoor positioning techniques. The company was in the process of exploring hardware infrastructure and software solutions for high-precision positioning that would complement GPS, which does not work indoors. The problem was to figure out exactly what kind of services it would need in order to use this infrastructure, something that would put direct demands on the capabilities of the company's systems—and since there are no services utilizing indoor positioning, it was hard to see what these demands might be! During a half-day workshop, we brainstormed indoor positioning applications using the bootlegging technique. Because the technology in this case was given, the categories all had to do with the use case. They were as follows:

- User
- Task
- Indoor location

As usual, the participants brainstormed examples in each category and then split into smaller groups to come up with applications. When discussing in the groups, I asked the participants to specifically consider the following questions:

- *Precision.* How precise must the positioning be in order to make the idea work? Meters, centimeters, millimeters?
- *Infrastructure.* What kind of infrastructure will be necessary? A device in every room, access to a mobile base station, something else?

The overall picture that emerged was surprising. It turned out the simple positioning of people that the company had anticipated as the core value was rarely enough for the applications that emerged. Most of them also required the positioning of things or features in the environment, a different problem that they were not really addressing. Also, it turned out that the relative position between people (or between people and things) is often very important. This requires access to the position of others, again something that was not easily achievable. Thus, though the results here were not "killer applications," the brainstorm provided a valuable expansion of the problem space.

Inventions can come from many different places, and there are many methods that can stimulate thinking and novel ideas. It can be useful to bring in some form of grounding in the invention process and to use process limitations to reign in the most outlandish ideas. However, no matter how great an idea seems on paper, one thing is certain: when you implement it and bring it to actual users, you will be surprised! The process of taking ideas for digital products from concept to prototype to users is extremely valuable and may often lead to a reevaluation of the original starting point, something we will explore in the next chapter.

CHAPTER 5

PROTOTYPING: FINDING OUT IF (AND HOW) IT WORKS

According to Peter Denning's definition that we used in Chapter 2, innovation means "the adoption of a new practice in a community." In other words, be it ever so well founded on careful inquiry, an invention does not become an innovation until people actually start to use it. Of course, we cannot really know if an invention will be popular and used until we actually give it to real users to try it out. But this is not easy—it often requires a lot of work just to get a working product into the hands of people who will actually use it. Therefore, there are a number of techniques to test potential product ideas, from questionnaires and interviews to focus groups and laboratory studies. This can let us try ideas at any stage of development against a subset of potential customers and provide invaluable input for further development. For digital products this is particularly important, because some of those that are the most groundbreaking rely on a complex combination of emerging technologies that may be expensive, difficult to maintain, or barely working at all by the time of testing.

Another factor to take into account is that whatever great ideas we have in the product design department or research lab, when you put real people in the equation, the results will always be surprising. Often, users will figure out a way to take advantage of a service that the creators never anticipated. In technology, most startups will discover this at some point during the lifetime of their products, and they will align their offering accordingly so that in the end the most successful product may be something quite different from what they originally put to market. One example is Bump, the sharing service that we talked about in Chapter 3. It was originally conceived as a way to share business cards and contact information. This means that the scenario the company built the service for was to share information between people who just met. But when looking at the user data, the company started seeing that in fact the opposite was happening; most users were sharing with the same small set of people and not with new acquaintances. Furthermore, the company discovered that sharing activity was spiking during weekends and evenings, rather than during business hours. What was going on? It turns out that instead of being used mostly in professional situations, Bump had found its main users in social situations, where users would be sharing photos and other media. And that was another thing the founders had not really anticipated—photo sharing had been built in just as an afterthought, not as a main feature, but it turned out to be a major form of usage. People were even using Bump to send photos from one to another of their own devices—for instance, from an Android phone to an Apple iPad. Armed with this unexpected but highly useful information, the company could put more effort into the social sharing situations (adding music, apps, and other media) and improve the experience for these users.

But when developing a digital product, we don't usually have the luxury of access to millions of existing users. So how can we determine if our ideas are in fact potential innovations? A useful technique is to use a limited and incomplete representation of the intended final product, so-called *prototypes*, to test out an idea or technology in the early stages, whether with potential end users or internally among the developers. We can distinguish between two forms of prototypes: *mockups* and *demonstrators*. Both of these have their advantages, but they also come with side effects and risks that are important to be aware of. In reality, we will see that for successful innovation, our prototypes will have to incorporate elements of both. But first, let's discuss what the distinction is between different kinds of prototypes.

Mockups are objects that have the appearance but not the function of a certain artifact. They have a long history in traditional design and more recently in the development of digital products. By constructing a simple representation from readily available materials, the designer can often identify potential problems and explore alternative avenues early in the process, without investing the work involved in creating a fully functional artifact. For an industrial or product designer, this is a natural way of working, because the functionality of the object is usually already specified or known to be confined within certain parameters. In fact, sometimes the mockup has qualities that are so close to the finished article that certain aspects can be tested for real; for instance, a chair might be produced in a material strong enough to sit in once or twice but not suitable for eventual production.

Demonstrators, on the other hand, can be defined as having the functionality but not the appearance of a finished artifact (at least, not necessarily). Constructing demonstrators is a common activity in engineering and computer science, where they can be used to prove or disprove a certain theory. If a researcher believes that technology can be used to solve a problem, the best way to prove it is by constructing a functional instance, in the form of a piece of software, a circuit board, or something else. This demonstrator will most often not have the appearance or properties of the envisioned end product—for instance, it might be larger and heavier, or have a much shorter operating time, or only partially implement the desired functionality. But by its very existence, the demonstrator constitutes an existence proof that a technology works.

Mockups have a natural role in many development processes. It is common for designers of all disciplines to make use of sketches and models that will help others to envision a product before it is actually constructed. For instance, it is common for designers to not only make drawings of a house before it is built, but to also construct three-dimensional models, either in computer software or using tangible materials like paper and wood. This can show a prospective client how the house will look and fit into its surroundings in a format that is easier for a layperson to understand than a blueprint would be. A furniture designer might make a full-sized cardboard model of a chair to be able to see it in different locations and find out how it works with different body types, even if it is not strong enough to sit in. Similarly, product designers will make many different physical models of the same product before it is actually produced. This allows the designers as well as executives, marketers, and others to get a feel for what the product would be like. It also makes it possible to catch design errors and make sure that the product is ergonomic and usable. For instance, when producing the controller for Sony's original PlayStation video game system, the product designers went through literally dozens of models in various sizes before arriving at the final design.

Although such methods for producing early sketches and models are well known, they do not always fit well with digital products. As we said in the definition in Chapter 1, a digital product relies on computation to perform its primary function. This means that somewhere there is a piece of software running on a microprocessor that controls how the product behaves. This function is essential for how the product will be used, but it is not always easy to represent in paper or plastic! Therefore, representations of digital products generally have to include some form of dynamic behavior to come closer to the intended end product. In other words, they need to be interactive. For screen-based interactions, this can sometimes be done simply—for instance, with paper sketches that are shifted around or exchanged according to the "user's" input. Various software tools are available that make it easy to quickly create interactive sketches of graphical user interfaces and even implement parts of the intended functions, such as Adobe's Director scripting language and various web-based tools. For physical products, there are several toolkits that make it possible to construct fully functioning tangible artifacts, such as the Arduino platform that is often used in educational settings, and .NET Gadgeteer, produced by Microsoft Research. The electronics can then be combined with various tools that generate complete physical designs, such as laser cutters and 3D printers, to create fully functioning artifacts.

But the problems with mockups and demonstrators go deeper than just including a few button presses and flashing lights that simulate a function. If a product relies on purely mechanical functions, the function is usually closely related to the form. Humans have a good understanding of the physical world, and we can identify obvious impossibilities—we can see and feel if an elegant chair is too flimsy to support anyone's weight or if a great-looking bag is too small to hold anything of value. But the algorithms that govern the function of digital products are not always so easy to understand. There are many seemingly simple problems that are hard or even impossible to solve with software. The limitations of algorithmic problem solving are often not intuitive, at least not for people outside of computer science. For instance, it is now quite easy for software to isolate faces in digital pictures, and given a suitable database and modern face-recognition techniques, a system can actually automatically identify most of the people in your holiday snaps. At the same time, there is no computer program that can reliable identify the objects in a random picture, even if they are easy for any human to discern. This is because the problem of recognizing faces is limited to a certain domain, and it works on a specific set of visual features that can be isolated and computed; the general image recognition problem will not be solved until we have computers with a formalized knowledge of every object in the world (we will get back to this issue in a later chapter). Yet these problems *seem* similar—does it not stand to reason that recognizing hundreds of faces in a matter of seconds is a harder problem than seeing if a blurry picture depicts a bowl of oranges or a basket of golf balls?

It is true that image recognition and other computational algorithms have come a long way and can now do things that were only recently thought impossible. We had long accepted that computers could beat grandmasters in chess—a limited and abstract domain—but winning a televised *Jeopardy* competition, as IBM's Watson system recently did, certainly brings computers one step closer to "real" intelligence. Strides in machine learning and statistic techniques have also led to impressive progress in areas such as automatic language translation, shopping recommendations, medical diagnostics, and so on. These great strides, coupled with the fact that computational power increases according to Moore's law, make it easy to believe that computers can do just about anything. Yet there are limitations, not only in processing power and algorithms but also and perhaps more importantly in factors operating outside of Moore's law—such as battery power, networking bandwidth, sensor capabilities, mechanical feedback systems, and so on—that means this assumption can be very wrong.

The reliance on algorithms is one reason that a mockup of a computer-based artifact may be much farther from the "real" object than a chair made out of painted cardboard. Developing and testing demonstrators is a way to get closer to solving such problems. But demonstrators can also give the wrong impression, because while they may well work on a technical plane, the proposed artifact may be completely useless when considered from a social, commercial, or user-experience perspective. The crux is not the type of proto-types that are used—it does not matter if they are empty cardboard boxes or fully functioning circuit boards. Instead innovators must be aware of the fundamental issues involved in creating digital products, and that not every-thing can be solved simply by introducing a faster, smaller computer.

I like to tell a story that I think illustrates this point, as it relates to the capa-bilities of digital products as well as the power—and danger—of relying too much on prototypes. I once spoke with a representative with the research arm of a large company in the telecommunications business. He told me that his group had just developed an "intelligent mobile phone" and would soon exhibit it at a big industry fair. This phone, he explained, could automatically detect the state of the user and by itself adapt the ringtone and other behavior to what was suitable. For instance, it could detect if the user was in a meeting, turn the signal off to keep from disturbing the other attendees, and then turn it on again when the meeting was over. The phone could also detect other situations, such as when the user was on her off time or working toward an important deadline, and adjust itself accordingly. Because I work in the field, I was very impressed that this group had apparently solved the many difficult problems associated with detecting what the user is doing. But because this large company was now exhibiting this product on the occasion of the big fair, I assumed the company had made some progress I was previously unaware of. So I asked how the phone worked.

"Oh, it doesn't work at all at the moment," was the reply. "We are just exhibit-ing a mockup." It turned out that what the company was showing was not, as I had been led to believe, in any way a functioning prototype of the intelligent phone. Instead, it was a plastic casing, produced by an industrial designer, which represented how the company thought such a phone *might look*—if they were ever to perform all the necessary research and development to construct it!

But how bad was this really? Can't we assume that technology will catch up soon enough and that the detection of what the user is doing will be a mere formality, far subordinate to the attractive shape of the phone? First of all, to do this requires a lot of advanced computation of various sensor values, such as the location, the surrounding ambient noise, the movement of the phone, and so on. Even if these calculations were solved in theory, the fact remains that most of the sensors on a standard phone are imprecise, so that it may, for instance, be very difficult to determine if the user is really in the meeting room or in the office on the floor below. Furthermore, all this computation and sensing takes a lot of energy; therefore, most phones performing all these calculations could probably not function for more than a few hours before needing a recharge. Finally, even if all these components did come together, it is hard to predict how well they would work in the real world—do we really want our phones to automatically sort between work and private life, between business and leisure, at the risk of missing important personal messages as well as crucial business information?

Still, all of these factors have been solved to some degree in the research community. There is even a downloadable experimental app called *Nokia Situations*, which seemingly does some of the things this intelligent mobile phone was supposed to do, including changing ringtones for different locations and showing different wallpaper during someone's office hours than that shown during one's free time. (Nokia, I hasten to add, is not the company depicted in the previous story!) But so far these phones are all limited to specific conditions that can easily be identified and are a long way off from the "intelligence" promised by the phone in our story—in fact, they are much like a computer program that can recognize the faces of all your friends but cannot distinguish a bowl of oranges from a golf ball in a random picture. However, for someone not deeply into this research like I am, the distinction can be hard to grasp. Because this phone can tell when I'm at work or at home, shouldn't it also be capable of working out if I am in a meeting or taking care of the kids? No, simply because the algorithms and sensors we have today are not good enough, and even if they were, you would probably be highly annoyed as soon as the phone made an error, and it would be running out of batteries in no time anyway! Maybe someday soon a phone will perform all of these functions, but right now there is no app that can detect these kinds of complex situations reliably, and to promise anything of the sort is highly deceptive.

This, in a nutshell, is the reason that care should be taken when using prototypes, be they demonstrators or mockups. If the intention is to show the function of a complex digital product, it is not enough to produce a plastic casing that has all the necessary buttons but does not actually perform any function. At the same time it is not enough to demonstrate a limited set of functions and promise the rest will appear later, even though many highly complex problems remain to be solved. By doing so you risk fooling other people—and yourself.

THE LURE OF THE CARGO CULT

A surprising but helpful parallel can be found in the fascinating story of the *cargo cults*, a religious movement in the Melanesian islands in the South Pacific. At the beginning of the 20th century, as a result of an influx of Western technology, variations of the cargo cult started to spring up in areas that were until then untouched by the industrialized world. These religions thought that the goods—the *cargo*—that started to arrive on ships and planes had a divine origin. More specifically, the indigenous population started to believe that the guns, canned food, walkie-talkies, and other seemingly magical artifacts had been sent to them by dead ancestors. But the intruders had found a way to lure the ancestors' planes away from the intended target, and when the planes landed the intruders would steal all the cargo! To ensure that the white man did not continue to steal the riches arriving on the planes, the Melanesians developed rituals through which they tried to imitate the behavior that seemed so successful in attracting cargo. They built imitation landing strips, control towers, and even full-scale airplanes out of straw and bamboo in the hope that their ancestors' cargo planes would be attracted and land. The Melanesians reasoned that if they could build exact replicas of the white man's things, they would also receive the same benefits. What they failed to realize

MONDO CANE
Produced by GUALTIERO JACOPETTI · TECHNICOLOR
A Times Film Release

Figure 5-1

In the cargo cults of Melanesia, natives built imitations of Western technology, such as airplanes and landing strips, in order to attract "cargo" that they believed was sent from their dead ancestors. (Image courtesy of Blue Underground)

was, of course, that their replicas, while superficially similar to the real thing, did not capture the essence of the original artifacts. The story of the cargo cults in itself is much more complex than this short summary illustrates (and it is outside the scope of this book), but it makes for an excellent metaphor. (For a good primer on the cargo cults, I recommend the segment in the Italian "shockumentary" *Mondo Cane*, released in 1960, which is available on YouTube. Though much of this film is sensationalistic, it contains unique footage of this now vanished culture.)

The most well-known use of the cargo cult as a metaphor is probably by Richard Feynman, physicist and Nobel Prize winner. In a Caltech commencement address in 1974, Feynman talked about *cargo cult science* and used it to describe a certain type of scientific dishonesty—fooling other scientists or the general public by presenting research results as "facts" even though they have not been proved correctly. One example of this is "pseudo-science," like mind reading or astrology, which has no basis in fact. But cargo cult science could also be a scientific experiment where the researcher fails to include previous work that invalidates the outcome. For example, Feynman mentioned an experiment involving rats, where the researcher wanted to perform a variation of an earlier experiment, but without first trying to repeat the conditions of the original study. Feynman explained that this would mean that the outcome—whether it was the expected one or not—might easily be due to a factor that was not controlled in either experiment, and the results would be misleading. In such a case, the results have little or no value even though they appear superficially correct. An expert in the field might spot this, but the media or the general public would take the scientist for his or her word. Therefore, Feynman stressed the importance of "a principle of scientific thought that corresponds to a kind of utter honesty." He advised scientists to follow two principles: do not fool yourself, and do not fool the layman.

These rules apply to the development of digital products as well—not the least because when it comes to understanding what is possible to do algorithmically, most of us sometimes feel as lost as the Melanesian native looking at a landing plane. If not experts in the field, we are quite likely to be fooled by a persuasive presentation. This is what happened in the story of the intelligent mobile phone; even though the person who presented it very well knew that it did not actually work, he talked about it as if it did. This impression was made even more persuasive by the fact that the company had actually produced a physical representation of the product that to all intents and purposes looked like it would work as intended. The only way to find out that it didn't would be to take it out of the exhibition display and try it out. And even then, as we saw in the Nokia example, it would have been possible to produce a demonstrator that worked in some situations—just not enough to be in any way useful!

But who did they really fool in this case? There are two parts of this kind of cargo cult behavior: producing a representation of a digital product without having enough of a knowledge base to understand how it would actually work, or presenting such a representation without acknowledging this knowledge. The first is a lack of inquiry. It means that you have not sufficiently researched how your proposed product would work in real life, whether regarding technology, usefulness, social acceptance, or something else. In that case you are most likely fooling yourself. The second is lack of honesty. Here, you know that you do not have the technology to build whatever has been presented, yet you talk about it as if you did. In that case, you will be fooling others, be they investors, the media, or potential customers. In both cases, as an analog to Feynman's cargo cult science, it is a case of pretending that the apparent functionality of a proposed product is based in fact, when it actually is not.

It must be stressed that there is nothing in itself wrong with the use of demonstrators and mockups—on the contrary, they may often be the best way to find out if something works! For instance, in architecture, physical mockups have a long history of being used as tools for thinking and presentation. They can be used for exploring the physical constraints of a proposed building, something that was particularly valuable before the availability of mathematical tools that could verify the structural integrity of a design. Physical mockups are also much better than 2D images or drawings for showing the body and volume of buildings and presenting how they fit in with existing structure, especially when presenting a project for laymen. Thus, in such cases, mockups play a very important role—and anyway, nobody will mistake a scale model for a real building!

But care must be taken in the presentation. In the case of mockups, they are often used to explore potential avenues for design in more or less realistic situations. In this type of design process, representations are used as a "prop" for designers to explore potential digital products, sometimes involving the intended users. If this is done as a sort of playacting and all concerned are aware that the representation is not real, this can be a useful exercise. For instance, in video prototyping, a form of participatory design, participants use various props to act out a scenario in a specific situation. It is also possible to add some functionality by having humans control the output, the so-called "Wizard of Oz" technique, which can make a product do things that are not yet possible for a computer to calculate. But it is important to note that participants in such an exercise are either working on developing the technology or people who have sufficient insight into the process to not mistake the representation for the real thing. This is a legitimate way of using prototypes, and it is one that has recently been gaining a lot of interest in interaction design research, as it is a way of "prototyping the future."

But when an artifact has a surface appearance that closely resembles that of a finished product, it is easy to start treating it as if it was just that, especially if the audience does not have insight into the development process or the particular problems involved. Newspapers and magazines often carry stories about concept designs produced by design schools and corporate design labs that are described as if they were real products. Here, the responsibility is both on the people presenting the concept and on the media, who may get carried away and simplify their reporting to make a story more readable. The skilled observer can probably tell which concepts are realistic and which ones are basically wishful thinking, but because of the way they are presented, most of us are likely to occasionally be fooled by these seemingly functional representations.

Finally, though mockups have their particular perils, even a functioning demonstrator is prone for misuse. A particular technical solution may work very well in isolation, but it may have a completely different result when other environmental factors are taken into account. The world is full of failed products that were demonstrated to be completely functional on a technical level but that were designed in a way that did not take into account the many other factors that are required for a successful innovation. For instance, there have been a large number of Internet-enhanced kitchen appliances—so-called "Internet fridges"—none of which have found a meaningful use, much less a market, even though they were fully realized technically. Yet the various demonstrators produced in-house have apparently been convincing enough to have several companies sink large development and marketing resources into this product category; there are over half a dozen examples from 1998 onward, none of which have been commercially successful.

A key insight here is that prototypes are always *representations* rather than the real thing. To work efficiently with demonstrators and mockups, it is important to understand what they actually *represent* and what role they can have in an innovation process. Both of them are tangible instances of something that otherwise would only exist as an abstraction. Without getting into epistemology, we can say that they are representations of *knowledge*. As such, they can be useful for sketching and testing ideas for a digital product, whether it has to do with a new form factor or a novel form of digital communication. But they represent knowledge in different ways.

A demonstrator represents the knowledge of *function*; it is an artifact in which the necessary technology to achieve a particular functionality has been implemented. However, the demonstrator says next to nothing about whether the end result will be a successful product or not. For an engineer, function is the primal problem, and the demonstrator is an existence proof that it has actually been solved; the engineer would then leave it to the product designer to actually give the demonstrator a usable and attractive form. A mockup, on the other hand, represents *form*; this is how a digital product could look and feel in the world, as a physical device or as interactions on a screen. For product designers, finding this form is the primary goal, and they assume that the engineers will implement the actual function. Thus, both engineers and designers somehow rely on the other to do part of the work. It is often when there is too little communication between these parties that we end up in the cargo cult.

To produce successful digital products (or any product for that matter), we must live in both these worlds at the same time and create artifacts that merge form and function! As we know, digital products rely on various degrees of computation, interaction, sensing, networking, and proactivity to perform their functions. At the same time, we are looking for innovations that actually are taken up and used. Thus, to be useful, a prototype of a digital product, no matter how basic, will have to be good enough to be taken up and used in something that at least is similar to a real-world situation. This is not easy, and neither demonstrators nor mockups are usually enough to do this. But if we get to the stage where there is a prototype that is good enough, it can give a lot of valuable insight into the viability of a product idea.

Case Study: The Context Camera

The context camera project is an example of how prototyping can be used in several steps along the development path of a potential digital product, all the way from early mockups to something that is basically a fully functioning product. It also shows how different stages of prototypes let us work with different user groups and incorporate their input into the final product. The original idea stemmed from our thoughts about what it would be possible to do with digital cameras, beyond what an analog camera already does. A modern digital camera has an amazing amount of processing power, yet all it really does with this power is to, as close as possible, reproduce the experience of using a regular, film-based camera. What if the computing power of the digital camera would be used to do something that would have been impossible to do with an analog camera? One possibility would be to use sensors to make the camera aware of the context in which a picture was taken—for instance, the temperature, location, and ambient noise—and change the visual appearance of the picture accordingly. The project ran approximately from 2002 to 2005, and the researchers who worked on this project were my students Lalya Gaye, Maria Håkansson, and Sara Ljungblad, with additional input and software development by Panajotis Mihalatos and Mattias Rost.

Since this was a new concept and there were no similar products to compare with (remember, this was in 2002, well before any hip iPhone camera "apps"!), we wanted to start out with something that could at least give a feel for what such a camera was like. After some initial design workshops, we produced a simple mockup: a piece of software for a handheld computer that simulated some possible effects of a context-aware camera. Actually, it did not do anything functional, because the handheld computer did not have any of the sensors we were planning to use. But it allowed you to take a picture and adjust different parameters such as color and saturation, to give the impression that sensors were affecting the image in real time. By deciding what sensor would affect which parameter and then adjusting the values manually, it was possible to perform a Wizard-of-Oz simulation of the camera's function. With this first prototype in hand, the researchers could go out and experience a realistic scenario of using a context camera. The result was a series of images where they photographed different environments outside our lab and adjusted the parameters to produce different effects. One example is the "Lady in the hat" series of pictures (Figure 5-2), where they followed an elderly woman from a distance and took pictures with different characteristics.

Thanks to this first mockup, we now had the possibility of demonstrating the basic concept of the context camera, rather than just talking about it in the abstract. We organized a number of workshops with different types of potential users to find out what they might be interested in should such a camera actually exist. For instance, one workshop was with students studying photography through a university program. It turned out that the photography students were not particularly interested in our ideas. They had a specific idea of what

Figure 5-2

To explore the potential of a context camera, we first produced a mockup, which could take pictures with various effects without actually having access to any real sensor data, such as this series of pictures following a lady with a hat. (Image courtesy of Viktoria Institute)

makes a "good" photograph and did not want to give any of the control away to a computer. On the other hand, another group was more receptive: *Lomographers*. This is a community of amateur photographers who make use of a Russian camera model that has certain defects, which makes the pictures unpredictable. They also like to shoot many pictures, often spontaneously or "from the hip," in the hope of catching unexpected results. With these and other potential user groups we discussed what kind of sensors might be considered, what kind of situations the camera could be used in, and what the end results could look like. Having the mockup available made it easier to discuss this on a concrete level, even though we were aware of that the end results might be completely different.

Figure 5-3

The first context camera demonstrator was constructed by attaching a web camera and a small mouse (which acted as shutter button) to a tablet computer.

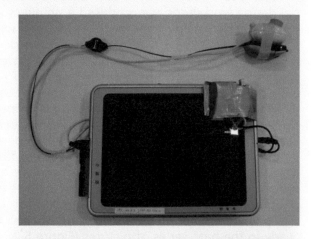

Figure 5-4

The original tablet-based demonstrator was not as portable as a "real" camera but sufficed for studies, such as here with a group of Lomographers at a train station. (Images courtesy of Viktoria Institute)

Armed with this input, we constructed a first functioning prototype of a context-aware camera. We did this by attaching a web camera to a tablet computer. A mouse was attached to the camera to act as a trigger. The tablet ran a piece of software that would take the incoming video stream from the web camera, analyze it, apply effects, and capture the results whenever someone pressed the mouse button. The context that the camera sensed was the movement in the picture, and the surrounding sound, using an analysis of the image and a microphone on the web camera. Based on this, the camera produced a number of visual effects:

1. *Color shadows.* Traces of colored shadows follow movement in the image; the color of the shadows is affected by the frequency of the surrounding sounds.
2. *Zoom.* The part of the picture with the most movement zoomed in, and rendered as a transparent layer on top of the rest of the image; the amount of transparency is determined by the surrounding sound level.
3. *Pixel.* Small white pixel dots appear in the image as a decaying trace; the size of the pixels in the picture is proportional to the surrounding sound level.
4. *Wave.* Movement creates waves in the image, which makes it look like a dense liquid; the size of the pixels in the picture is proportional to the surrounding sound level.

The user could switch between these different effects and also set the parameters—for instance, how much sound would trigger the pixelation effect. This prototype was much larger and more unwieldy than a regular camera, but it was a fully functional instance of a context camera.

We then set out to test the camera with a number of users. We could not give the whole system away for extended time periods, and it was too bulky to carry around effortlessly, so the tests were somewhat limited. However, the results gave a lot of information on what using this kind of product could be like. The tests were documented by video for further analysis. One of the tests was with a group of Lomographers at the local train station. These users would seek different things to photograph in situations where they thought there might be a lot of sensor input, such as when a noisy train was departing. Another test was with two teenage schoolgirls. They did not seek any existing context but instead created it themselves, generating noise and movement by screaming at the camera, jumping up and down, and so on.

Several important lessons came out of these tests, some of which were carried on into the next prototype. One interesting question that arose involved determining what kind of context was worth photographing—should the camera document the world as it is, or do users want to be able to actively affect the pictures? The Lomographers and schoolgirls seemed to have very different takes on this. Another concern involved the predictability of the results. Active lomographers can take a large number of pictures in the hope of getting a single good one, and they thrive on the unpredictable nature of these pictures. Our first prototype showed the video stream with the effects already in place. This meant that it was easier to create the picture

Figures 5-5–5-8

A series of pictures taken with the first context camera prototype. They demonstrate a number of different effects, caused by input from sound and motion sensors. (Images courtesy of Test participants/Viktoria Institute)

one wanted, but on other hand, there was no "surprise" when the picture was taken. Finally, there was the question of skill and user control over the end results. In one way this prototype gave users too much control, because they could tweak the settings of the sensors. On the other hand, the wild image effects made it almost too effortless to create cool-looking pictures. In fact, many of the context camera pictures

Figure 5-9

Thanks to advances in hardware, the context camera could be implemented on a regular camera phone, giving a much more camera-like form factor while retaining the same effects and sensors. (Image courtesy of Viktoria Institute)

Figures 5-10–5-17

Pictures showcasing the different effects possible with the context camera, where sound and motion affects the image in real time. (Images courtesy of Test participants/Viktoria Institute)

looked almost exactly like some of the photographs found on actual Lomography websites. One of the Lomographers in our study said that he would have been very proud of some of the context camera pictures if they had been taken with a Lomo camera—but with our system, it had been "too easy" to take such good pictures!

Based on these new insights, we now made a third prototype, this time for use on camera phones. This time the software was developed for a Nokia phone that was the most advanced camera model available at the time (around 2004). It basically performed the same function as the earlier tablet-based version but with some tweaks based on the studies. The most important one was that we removed the effects from the visible video stream so that the resulting photos would be a surprise, hoping to catch the unpredictability of the Lomo camera experience.

Because this prototype could be installed on any phone of the right model, the user tests could go much wider and were no longer limited to Lomographers, photography students, or any other specific group. Mobile software "app stores" had not yet been introduced, but we recruited a number of users by advertising on various blogs, as well as inviting some of the original test subjects. In total there were seven users from four different countries who took a total of 303 pictures. We set up a system for sharing the images and interviewed the subjects after the test, either via e-mail or in person.

In this final test, the context camera prototype was very close to an actual product. A lot of the pictures that we got from the different users made creative use of the camera's capabilities. During the interviews, the users explained their motivations for taking some of them and their thoughts on the results. For instance, one user pointed out a picture where it looked like "sound" was coming out of a person's mouth (Figure 5-18), and another captured a diver jumping into a pool with a trail of movement behind him (Figure 5-19). Other examples were pictures that users felt reflected the feeling of speed on a bicycle (Figure 5-20) or the thunderous sound of an approaching train (Figure 5-21).

From the interviews, it became clear that the context camera had created a new way of taking pictures. When asked what made a "good" example of a context picture, one user said that it had to look different from a traditional picture. For instance, she pointed out a picture of a town square that looked quite normal and said that this was a "boring" context picture. Users also took pictures in situations where they would not normally have done so, just to try to capture interesting effects, such as the speeding bicycle mentioned earlier. The camera had made them think differently about taking pictures and made them seek out situations and subjects that they would not normally have taken pictures of. At the same time, there had to be something "special" in the environment, like sounds or movements, for a context picture to be worth taking—a tranquil environment was not suitable.

Figures 5-18–5-21

Some examples of images taken by test users, including a stream of noise from somebody's mouth, a trail of movement from a pool dive, a speed-filled bike ride, and an approaching train. (Images courtesy of Test participants/Viktoria Institute)

Although the pictures the users took look cool and interesting, it is worth noting that the same effects could easily have been created with a photo-editing program, such as Photoshop. So what made the context camera different? Several of the users stressed that these pictures were better reflections of the actual conditions that existed when the picture was taken—they were more "real." As one user put it, even though the effects created in Photoshop might have looked the same, "this [the context picture] is how it *really was*." Thus, for these users, the context camera represented a way to capture more of the moment and the surrounding context than would be possible with an ordinary camera.

This iterative process showed that the context camera was a viable digital product that allowed for a new way of taking digital pictures. When the project ended, there was still no easy way to distribute mobile phone applications to users. Had the work been carried out a few years later, we would probably have implemented the prototype for a popular smartphone platform, such as iPhone or Android, and made it available on an app store. However, this would not really have changed the end results; for research purposes the final user study was large enough. Today, there are a large number of mobile phone applications that apply different filters when taking pictures, such as Instragram and Hipstamatic, although to my knowledge there is yet nothing that uses sensors to affect the picture.

A couple of things are worth noting on how we used prototypes during this process. In the early stages, the simple mockup made it much easier to discuss the concept with potential users—even if they did not like it, they could give input and suggest changes. The first functional prototype made it possible to actually test the concept in the real world, even if the situation had limitations because of the size and other factors. Here, we found out important details of the experience in using the camera, which could be used to improve the next version. Finally, for the camera phone prototype, we could let users live with the system for an extended period of time and use it as they would a normal camera. This gave us insight into the qualities of actually taking pictures with the system and what kind of situations it was suitable (or unsuitable) for.

It is also worth pointing out how the different user groups gave different types of input. The Lomographers were particularly useful, because even though they were happy with their own technology and thus not particularly interested in the context camera itself, they could provide input that had a different viewpoint from regular photographers. However, the intention was never to produce a camera for Lomographers—the system was always intended for a much wider user group. The trick then becomes to generalize the input from "extreme" users like the Lomographers to a product that appeals to the general population. One example of where this was successful was the Lomo photographers' insistence on the element of surprise, which prompted us to remove the visible effects from the video stream—this delight in the unexpected was reflected in several of the (non-Lomography) test subjects' photographs and discussions. Taking the input from one specialized user group and having it affect products for a more general audience makes this process similar to that of the transfer scenarios method, which we discussed in Chapter 2.

This example shows how prototypes can be used in an innovation process, to support both invention and inquiry at different stages. Early on, the mockup of the context camera functioned as a *generator* of ideas, much like some of the methods we discussed in Chapter 4. Having this kind of tantalizing vision of future technology—even if it did not actually function yet—allowed us to spin new ideas and develop the concept of the camera. Similarly, the first tablet-based demonstrator inspired further inventions, but it also allowed us to inquire into how the technology really worked and to figure out what the best interaction and implementation strategies would be. Finally, having confirmed the technology's viability, the phone-based prototype allowed us to set the camera into realistic situations to see how it actually was used, and it allowed for a new and creative approach to photo taking. Thus, inquiry and invention can go hand in hand with the development of prototypes, the process becoming enriched every time they are put in contact with users.

Ultimately, when used right, prototypes can be invaluable in the development of digital products, as they provide a peek into what using a product might be like, even before it exists. At the same time, care must be taken to not promise too much—like an intelligent mobile phone—because then disappointment is sure to ensue. With the context camera project, we were always working close with both the technology and potential users, picking up input and adjusting the system as we saw the results of the different tests. Without this kind of careful dialogue among technology, users, and developers, there is always the risk of promising too much and delivering too little, thus fooling both yourself and others. And if you make a mockup of something without the proper inquiry, in the hope that the technology or user needs will catch up to your ideas, you may find yourself waiting a very long time—much like the Melanesian natives on their bamboo landing strip.

In the previous chapters, we explored the dimensions of grounded innovation—*inquiry* and *invention*—and looked at methods for achieving them. We also saw the value of putting ideas into practice in the form of prototypes. Many of these insights are not restricted to innovation in computation-based artifacts but apply more generally to product development. But what is unique for the field of digital products, apart from the presence of computation itself? In the following chapters, we will go back to the properties introduced in the first chapter and look at how they can be used to create digital products.

PART II

MATERIALS

CHAPTER 6

INTERACTION: SURFACES FOR INPUT AND OUTPUT

In the previous chapters we looked at methods for innovation in the two dimensions of *inquiry* and *invention*. We have also learned the importance of *prototyping* our ideas, to take them one step closer to the real world, and find out if they actually work or not! Although most of our examples have come from the digital world, the methods we have learned about so far are in fact quite general. You can use bootlegging, cultural probes, transfer scenarios, or any of the other methods in just about any innovation process, not just for digital products.

But digital products have some specific properties, and this is something we can use for grounded innovation. In the first chapter we learned about five properties of digital products:

- Information processing
- Interaction
- Networking
- Sensing
- Proactivity

The first, *information processing*, is so fundamental we will take it as given— today, any digital product will rely on computation. An understanding of the limits of computation is of course essential for inventing digital products, but it is outside the scope of this book. The fundamentals of computation are taught in many education programs and books, and the bibliography includes works by design theorists, including Jonas Löwgren, Erik Stolterman, Johan Redström, and others, which serve as good starting points for learning about how to think about computation as a material in its own right.

In the following chapters we will explore how we can leverage the other qualities of digital products as *raw materials for innovation*. We have already learned how innovations often come from the unlikeliest of sources—think of the Post-it Note example, which arose out of an effort to make glue that was *more* sticky, not less! By creatively using the results of that error, a new and very successful product was born. Of course, most errors are not so fortuitous. But to invent digital products, a good strategy is to make careful inquiry into emerging technologies and then to subject them to the kind of creative collisions that we have seen examples of in the previous chapters. By taking a technology that was meant for one thing and making it do something else, or finding one that does not yet have a clear use and putting it in real-world contexts, it is possible to come up with innovations beyond the obvious. Furthermore, an innovation can often come out of the combination of two or more technologies. Therefore, in the following examples, you will often see how two or more qualities are combined, even though we will attempt to focus on one at a time.

The first quality we will look at is *interaction*—that is, real-time input and output to a digital product. Interaction has been taken for granted since the first personal computers and video games in the late 1970s, and it has mostly taken the form of one or more input devices (keyboard, joystick, mouse) combined with visual and aural output (screen and speakers). This has been a powerful combination and has defined the personal computing device until today. Even recent devices, such as touch-screen mobile phones and tablets, use the same paradigm, the only difference being that the input device and output device now occupy the same space.

In the early days of human-computer interaction, a lot of effort was spent bringing real-world metaphors into screen-based computer interfaces. For instance, remember the terminology and images used in the original Xerox PARC workstations, which were directly inspired by office environments—desktops, folders, trashcans, and so on. In the 1980s and 1990s, thanks to increasingly powerful computer graphics displays, many researchers tried to improve the ways that information was shown on the limited area provided by a screen. For instance, in 1980 Bob Spence and Robert Apperley envisioned a future *office environment for the professional*, where a distortion-based view would make it possible to show more information on screen at the same time, by displaying both the most important items (the focus) and the surrounding (the context) at the same time. When I first started in the field in 1996, I was very influenced by this type of presentation, often referred to as *focus+context visualizations*. I imagined how people normally work with documents—for instance, by placing the most important in the middle of the desk, and surrounding it with other scraps of paper. I tried to find a way to replicate this way of working on a computer screen. The result was the *flip zooming* focus+context visualization technique, which split up web pages and other text documents into small chunks (Figure 6-1). The most important – the *focus* – would be seen in the middle (and would be fully readable), whereas the others would appear around the screen in left-to-right, top-to-bottom reading order. Flip zooming was implemented as a regular web browser, and in 1999 it also served as a browser for small screens, to be used on emerging mobile devices. There have been many other examples of this kind of visualization, and in fact the "dock" in Apple's OS X interface has an option for "magnification" that is very reminiscent of Spence and Apperley's technique.

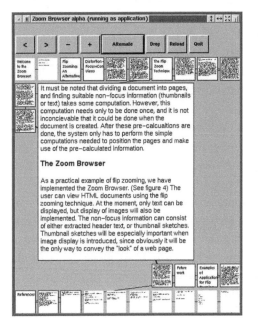

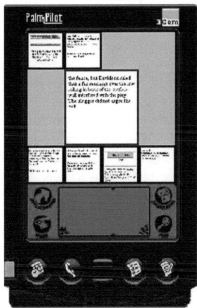

Figures 6-1–6-2

Inspired by how people work with documents in real life, the Flip Zooming focus+ context visualization technique breaks up a document to offer both detail and overview of a large text at the same time. It was implemented in a variety of applications, including a regular web browser and a browser for small screens. (Figure 6-1 courtesy of the author | Figure 6-2 courtesy of Viktoria Institute)

But trying to compress the whole world onto a small screen can only take us so far. What if we instead would start playing around with the physical circumstances of screen-based interaction, placing screens in different contexts and different configurations—effectively *bringing the screens into the world* instead? This is something that is directly facilitated by new technology. Screens used to be bulky and heavy—you may remember the deep cathode ray screen that until a few years ago was the staple of computer monitors and living room televisions—but in the past few years screens have become smaller as well as bigger, while at the same time becoming more colorful, more responsive, and much, much thinner. This is due to the replacement of cathode ray technology (the one used in old monitors, where a ray of light sweeps over to literally "paint" the picture dozens of times per second) with modern LCD, LED, and OLED technology. Today, there is a whole ecosystem of display sizes based on these technologies, from the 50-inch television in the living room to computer and laptop screens, down to smaller tablets and pads, and finally down to the smallest screens found on phones, cameras, and media players.

But these displays are merely the beginning of a display revolution that is happening right now. On the horizon are displays that are as thin and light as paper and draw almost no energy. We have already seen how electronic ink displays have made it possible to make e-book readers (such as the Amazon Kindle) that are light and small as a regular book and draw literally no power except when changing the page or updating the library. These displays are still black-and-white or grayscale only, but soon similar technologies will be available for full-color paper-like displays. But it does not stop there; many companies, such as Philips and Sony, are working on displays that are integrated directly with other materials, such as textiles. Electroluminescent textiles (i.e., cloth made of fibers that emit light when subjected to electric current) may make it possible to weave a display right into your next T-shirt. New display technologies such as these will make many new digital products possible in contexts where we might never have thought of placing a computer before. It will become possible to integrate displays into environments and activities in ways that create new opportunities for interaction—in many cases way beyond what is actually shown on the screen!

So assuming that we can put a dynamic display just about everywhere, what new opportunities will open up? One idea would be to replace the static pictures that we already see around us. On the walls of my workspace right now I can see a movie poster, a calendar, and a cross stitch art piece given to me by a friend. What if the poster would display advertisements, not for just one movie but for whatever is playing at the nearest cinema? Or what if the calendar would update itself to show my schedule for the day? And what if the artwork would reflect the state of mind of my friend who made it—not just in the moment she created it, but what she is feeling right now? The possibilities are literally endless, and with the various electronic and textile-based display technologies we just mentioned, each of these displays could still look just like a movie poster, a wall calendar, and a cross-stitch picture.

At the same time, this approach creates obvious problems. I put the movie poster on my wall because I like the design and the movie it represents, but not because I am interested in watching the movie right now—not to mention that the movie is more than 30 years old. Modern movie posters might not have the same aesthetic qualities and might advertise movies I have no interest in. For the calendar, its main function is to display artworks by one of my favorite artists, a new one every month—the calendar function is almost incidental. It is likely that if my work schedule started to show up there, it would stress me out and significantly diminish my appreciation of the calendar. Finally, the cross stitch is the expression of an idea that my friend had several years ago, and having it on my wall reminds me not just of that time but also of the other apartment where it used to hang—if it would change, those feelings might be lost. So just from these examples it is clear that introducing information into decorative images is not without complications.

There is also the issue of how much information we really want pushed on us in our everyday life—a situation hinted at by the calendar example and made ever more pressing by the proliferation of mobile devices, with their constantly updated tweets, status updates, and alerts we see today. Already in 1995, Mark Weiser at Xerox PARC talked about the need for "calm technology." He made the argument that most information technology is "the enemy of calm," while at the same time other technology—"a comfortable pair of shoes, [a] fine writing pen, or [the] *New York Times* on a Sunday morning"— gave a sense of calm and comfort. In particular, he argued that technology should engage both the center and the periphery of our attention, and allow users to move freely between the two. The artist Natalie Jeremijenko designed an illustrative example called "The Dangling String." It consisted of a piece of Ethernet cable hanging from the ceiling and attached to a motor. The motor was directly influenced by the amount of traffic in the local network. When the traffic was normal, the string would sway gently, like it was being moved by some invisible wind. But when the network was overloaded, it would shake violently, whereas if the network for some reason stopped working, it would hang dead still. The idea was that this kind of display would be available in the periphery of the user's attention. Rather than constantly monitoring a string of digits, a network technician could get on with other work and have the string in the periphery of her attention, only focusing on it when there was an anomaly.

A related idea is that of *ambient media*, introduced by Hiroshi Ishii and his group at the Massachusetts Institute of Technology (MIT) Media Lab. The idea was to integrate information as fixtures in the interior architecture. The group showed a number of examples, such as pinwheels that would spin at different speeds depending on the network traffic; background sounds of traffic and weather that grew or faded in intensity depending on the user's e-mail inbox; and even a block of wood that would vibrate at different speeds depending on the activity of a hamster running in a wheel.

These ideas were influential enough to lead to a number of additional *ambient displays*, which were both physical and screen based. For instance, Beth Mynatt and other researchers at Georgia Tech introduced the *digital family portrait*, a screen-based ambient display designed to increase awareness between younger and older family members living in different places. It took the form of a screen that could be placed anywhere in the home, like a photograph. In the center of the screen was a portrait of the family member in question. Around the edges, however, was a display of continuously updated information related to the person in the photograph. Based on sensor input, the system would calculate the overall activity level of the person (e.g., eating and sleeping habits, movements in the home, whether she was in or out, and so on) and abstract that to a border of icons around the portrait. In one study, the portrait of an elderly woman was placed in her son's home, and the border consisted of butterflies, the number and appearance of which would indicate on a rough level how busy his mother was. He could then touch an icon on the screen to find more detailed information—for instance, the local weather, the indoor temperature, the specific movements of the person in the room (detected by motion sensors), and historical data.

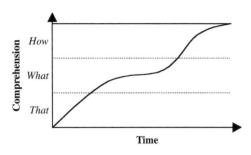

Figure 6-3

An example of how the understanding of an ambient display might change over time. First users learn that it is an information display; then what it is showing; and finally, how to interpret this information. Of course, it is possible that some of this knowledge is forgotten over time! (Image courtesy of Viktoria Institute)

Of course, the fact that an ambient display may look nothing like the information displays we are used to might complicate matters. What if people do not even understand that the dangling piece of wire in the ceiling is supposed to convey information? Part of this has to do with the setting of the display; for instance, it is different to select and install a display in your own home, like the Digital Family Portrait than it is to see one featured in a public space where you spend much less time and have little control over the environment, like the Dangling String. I find it helpful to think of this as a *that/what/how* progression. First, potential users have to realize *that* something in their environment is an information display rather than, for instance, a work of art with only aesthetic value. Second, they may find out *what* information is being displayed—whether it is public transport departure times, Facebook updates, or something else. Finally, they need to learn *how* to read the information on the display—like for instance how the amount of movement in the dangling string corresponded to network traffic. This learning is affected both by the way an ambient display is designed and by how it is situated in an environment. The understanding can also change over time; for instance, it is unlikely that after first learning about the digital family portrait people would forget that it is an information display, but perhaps after some time they would forget which kind of data it was associated with.

Case Study: Ambient Information Visualization and Informative Art

Figure 6-4

A living room environment with several pieces of informative art—*information displays that are reminiscent of visual art. (Image courtesy of Viktoria Institute)*

Inspired by these emerging technologies and concepts, a group at my lab, including Johan Redström, Tobias Skog, Lars Hallnäs and myself started thinking of how to turn existing fixtures into information displays. The visual sensory channel is the one easiest to ignore, as long as there is not too much movement; thus, any displays would have to change fairly slowly in order not to require too much attention. At the same time, they should be attractive enough to hang on the wall without detracting from other aesthetic qualities. We toyed with the idea of a digital painting, say, of a house, where the sky would reflect the weather forecast, the surrounding vegetation, the time of year, and so on, but we could never quite make it gel. We experimented with other more abstract displays, such as one where words and phrases generated from local e-mails would slowly appear and disappear to reflect ongoing conversations.

A breakthrough came when Ph.D. student Tobias Skog came up with a simple but highly effective idea—that of using the manner of modern, abstract art to represent information. He constructed a display that looked very much like a painting by the Dutch artist Piet Mondrian. Mondrian presented a distinct and recognizable series of works, where he used abstract blocks of colors—red, blue, and yellow—carefully composed together with black lines. These compositions were precise and probably impossible to accurately reproduce, but for the untrained observer, Tobias's mock Mondrian looked very much like the real thing. However, it was in fact a dynamic display! Each of the color blocks represented a member of our research group, and the size of the blocks changed depending on the content of the member's e-mail queue. Thus, the "painting" directly reflected the state of work in the group. Whereas some members kept their e-mail inboxes nice and empty, others let the mail pile up. Changes could be easily seen, so that when the workload was high, all the color blocks on the painting would grow; other times they might almost all disappear. Thus, we had a piece of decoration that could be put on the wall—in the form of a thin LCD display—and pass for art (or at least imitation), yet would to the initiated show at a glance important information. We called this approach *informative art*.

Based on the strength of the Mondrian piece, in 2001 we were invited to a prestigious exhibition in computer graphics. To get inspiration for new pieces, we went on to raid the local library of art books! The idea was simple: find artworks that had a style that was easy to replicate, and tie them to some kind of information. We first did a new version of the Mondrian, this time showing the weather in different cities across the world. We got the real-time information from a free Internet weather service. Each of the colored blocks now represented a world city, and they were organized as if they would be on a world map with Europe in the center, so for instance Los Angeles would fall in the top left quadrant, Tokyo in the upper right, and Cape Town somewhere in the middle. The size of each block represented the temperature in the city, and the color represented the type of weather—blue for rain, yellow for sun, and red for clouds. Thus,

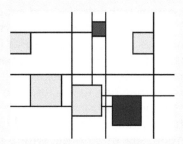

Figure 6-5

The "Weather Mondrian" shows the weather in six cities, as blocks laid out on an imaginary world map with Europe in the middle—from west to east Los Angeles, Rio de Janeiro, Cape Town, Gothenburg, Sydney, and Tokyo. The size of the blocks represents temperature, and the color represents rain (blue), sun (yellow), or clouds (red). On this picture, it is cold and cloudy in Gothenburg, hot and raining in Sydney, and temperate and sunny in Tokyo! (Image courtesy of Viktoria Institute)

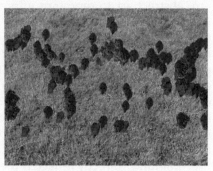

Figures 6-6–6-7

Other pieces of ambient information visualization included a timer inspired by Andy Warhol's paintings of Campbell Soup cans and an earthquake indicator inspired by landscape art. The timer would gradually turn from being all yellow (asparagus soup) cans to all red (tomato soup), and the lawn would be covered by stones indicating real-world earthquakes, the size reflecting the magnitude and the position based on a world map. (Images courtesy of Viktoria Institute)

by simply glancing at the display, it was possible to get a feel for the weather across the world; for instance: "It is raining and cold in Tokyo, but it's hot and sunny in Los Angeles."

This weather display thus gives another type of information than what is gained from a traditional weather service, which is more precise but also much less glanceable—and presumable less decorative. We also constructed other art-inspired pieces. There was a kind of egg timer based on pictures of soup cans, inspired by Andy Warhol's famous paintings like "100 Campbell Soup Cans." It would start out being all asparagus soup (yellow cans), and gradually flip over to tomato soup until the time ran out, when it would all be red cans. There was a piece of "landscape art"—images of stones in grass, similar to works by Richard Long—that reflected real-time earthquake data around the world, again based on the map metaphor; every time an earthquake happened, a new virtual "stone" would be placed on the grass. Several other ideas, inspired by other art styles, were implemented as well. Of course, some art experts cringed noticeably when we presented what clearly could be seen as bastardizations and shallow simplifications of the underlying artistic ideas. However, the idea got across nicely: it is possible to hang something attractive, perhaps even artistic, on the wall of your living room or office that will change appearance according to some information stream. To get away from the connotations of art, we subsequently changed the term to *ambient information visualization*.

For showing the pieces, we projected on large screens in a sort of "living room" environment, complete with a nice sofa, chairs, a coffee table, and a shag carpet. Visitors to the exhibition would stand or sit, trying to figure out what was going on—which was made even more difficult because the changes in the displays were slow and bordered on being nonexistent. Initially, viewers would be puzzled about what the displays meant; it was in no way possible to figure out that the "Mondrian" was showing the global weather or that the "Warhol" was counting down the time until the exhibition closed for the day. However, when we explained how to read the works, most visitors would immediately get the idea. What was even better, we observed many times how one visitor, after being briefed by us, would literally turn to the next and explain how to read the works, independent of our involvement. This to us proved that we were onto something; by putting display surfaces into a new context and giving them a new purpose, we were on the way to creating a useful digital product.

But as we discussed earlier, showing something off in an exhibition context is very different from actually putting it to use. We decided to try to make an ambient information visualization that would actually be useful in everyday environments. To get ideas, we handed out some simple questionnaires at the local university about what kind of information people would like to see. Weather and local transport schedules both came up high on the list. The weather Mondrian had been a hit at exhibitions, being both a recognizable style and showing easy-to-understand information, so we started with that concept. One way to imagine how this could work in a home would be to allow users to choose the different cities themselves, to reflect places in the world where they had friends, were planning to visit, or had some other connection. However, we wanted to try our technology in a public space and decided to go for the local weather. However, the current weather situation is often not all that interesting—for that, it is better to look out the window!— so we modified the display to show both today's weather and a five-day forecast, again taken from an online service. We installed the new work in a public place at the university, which most students and teachers would pass every day and where there were also some opportunities for lounging. To make it easier to pick up the information, we printed an instruction sheet and put it up next to the display.

After a few weeks, we did a feedback session with some of the students. The results were mixed. It did seem that some of them were able to use the display and accurately read the weather prediction. However, not many of them actually did it, and for most of them it was not very useful information. In any case, they only really bothered with the weather report about once per day, and for this they could just as well look in the newspaper or go to a web page. It seemed that although the technology did work, the information we provided was not suited for this kind of constant, ambient visualization.

We decided to keep the Mondrian-inspired looks but to find a new source of information that would be more timely and more frequently updated, in the hope that this would encourage people to use the display more often. Local transport information was another area that the students had shown interest in, but we did not find that displaying static time tables would be much help, as they were often unreliable because of delays. But luckily, that local transport authority had just made real-time information about bus departure times available as a web service. The presentation on the web left a lot to be desired, and there was no mobile service yet, which made this a perfect source for our experiment. We designed a new "Mondrian" that would show the actual time to departure for the most popular bus line from the university to the city center.

Our first attempt was only partly successful. It showed the time remaining as the size of colored fields in the Mondrian-inspired layout. However, it was difficult to tell which direction the buses were heading or exactly how much time remained until a bus left—crucial information to catch a bus! Tobias Skog and Sara Ljungblad organized another feedback session with students and got a lot of useful input. It turned out they reasoned about the display based on the geographical features of the actual bus stop, much like the map-based layout of the original weather map. They speculated if some of the lines, which were in fact random, actually carried information or represented roads or rivers. They also expected the colors in the blocks to carry information. Finally, they wanted to know where the buses ended up—some would stop at the central station, whereas others continued beyond. Based on this response, we made a new design.

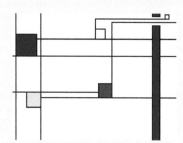

Figure 6-8

A "Bus Mondrian" that visualizes real-time departing times of a local bus stop. The time to departure is reflected in both the size and the color of the blocks. The layout is logical to how the students visualized the bus stop's geography, with extra cues for buses crossing the river and stopping at the central station. (Image courtesy of Viktoria Institute)

In this final visualization, colored blocks again represented the buses to and from the city, and the size of the blocks represented the time until the bus would leave. But we also color-coded the blocks based on the time it would take to walk to the station. Blue would mean you had plenty of time; yellow that it was time to leave; red that you would have to hurry to catch the bus; and finally, a white block meant that it was just pulling out and you had missed it. This overloaded the display with two indications of the same information (size and color), which made it easier to read. Furthermore, we modeled the position of the blocks after the actual layout of the bus stop so that the students could visualize a "line" of buses to and from the city. We also added a mnemonic in the form of a thick blue line (not something Mondrian would have approved of)—this represented the river by which the university was located and helped further orient the display of the buses. Finally, we added a line from each bus to the city that would either stop in a small loop, in case the bus terminated at the central station, or continue off screen if the bus continued past it.

Figure 6-9

The "Bus Mondrian" was installed in a public space at the local university, where it became a modest hit. (Image courtesy of Viktoria Institute)

We installed this display in the same public space, where it turned out to be a modest hit. In a follow-up questionnaire, we found that most students knew what it represented, many could read it, and a few had actually used it to catch the bus—thus representing a clear progression on the that/what/how continuum! Although we could not continue running it at the university for practical reasons, we did install it in our local office nearby and had it up for over two years. The half-dozen researchers in the office used it every day to catch the bus.

Figure 6-10

We adapted the bus display to our local office, where it was in use continuously for several years. (Image courtesy of Viktoria Institute)

It turned out that after learning to read the display, it was the perfect way to gauge how much time would be needed to gather one's things and move to catch the bus—or if there was another one coming that was more suitable. We also installed it in another local office, with similarly good results.

The lessons from this experiment with display surfaces were as follows: that it matters a lot where you put a display, and in what context. The same information might be meaningful in one place, but useless in another. For instance, we found that in the university, since the students would not lounge in the area of the display, they often could not make use of it since, when they passed it, they had already made the decision to take the bus. It is also important that the information *changes* frequently enough to make it worth checking the display. The weather forecast was relevant for the local users, but it did not change more than once per day, thus providing little incentive to check it. Finally, it is important to *encode* the information well. It should be done in such a way that it is easy to remember and explain to others— for instance, by basing them on geographical mnemonics—and also so that once the user has learned how to read the display, it can be done instantly, for instantly by overloading using colors and size.

Although our experiments in putting display surfaces in unexpected places were successful, there is still some time until this kind of display becomes a commercial product. A setup like our bus Mondrian, which required an LCD screen, a laptop, and an Internet connection, is still too costly to motivate most people, not to mention that it consumes a lot of electricity. While there have been noticeable advances in low-cost, low-energy displays, we have not yet reached the sweetspot where you can replace the posters on your wall with dynamic information displays. Several companies have this ambition, however, such as Boston-based Ambient Devices, which produces various information displays that provide "information at a glance," such as weather forecasts or baseball scores. My guess is that it won't be long until we reach the point where ambient information visualization and other informative or artistic everyday display technologies take the step from a good invention to an innovation used by many people.

Putting display surfaces in unexpected places is one way of extending the notion of interaction in digital products. But most of the ambient information displays we talked about earlier were not very interactive; they were mostly reacting to information flowing in from the Internet or other sources, taking minutes or even hours between updates. What are some other ways to construct interactive surfaces?

One way is to combine display surfaces of different kinds, with different advantages and disadvantages. For instance, large projection displays have the advantage that they are big and thus could facilitate collaborative work—say, when working on a large plan or map. But the drawbacks are that they have a fairly low resolution and providing input on large surfaces can be difficult (although there are some good examples of large multitouch-enabled screens, including Jeff Han's multitouch sensing displays and Microsoft's Surface tabletop display). On the other hand, tablet devices such as Apple's iPad have very good resolution and excellent interactive input, but they are too small for more than one person to access at a time. What if we could combine the best of both worlds and have an information display that covered multiple devices, drawing on the strengths of each?

Case Study: Ubiquitous Graphics—Combining Different Interactive Surfaces

This is what we did in the *Ubiquitous Graphics* project, which Johan Sanneblad and I devised in 2005. There had already been examples of static displays that combined low and high resolution, such as Patrick Baudisch's *Focus Plus Context Screens* at Xerox PARC. However, we wanted to go one step further and combine untethered interactive displays with a large display surface. The system consisted of a projection display and several tablet computers that were connected via a network to a separate laptop that acted as a server. In this way, all the displays could show an entire image or just a part of it. For instance, if the main projected image showed a map of Los Angeles, each table could show a section of that city, such as the area around the LA Convention Center.

Figures 6-11–6-13

The Ubiquitous Graphics *system integrates displays of different sizes with different resolutions. Users can see a detailed version of a large image, make annotations that are reflected on all displays, and "tear off" a piece of the larger image to work with separately. (Images courtesy of Viktoria Institute)*

But what really made the system unique was how the small displays were tied directly into what was showing on the large display. Once you took your own screen and put it up on the large screen, the tablet view would snap to exactly the same spot as what was showing on the wall-size image—but in much higher resolution. Because the tablet had a much higher resolution per inch, it would show many more details, such as small roads and names of places that were too small to show up on the larger, coarser display. By using a positioning system based on ultrasonic transmitters (originally used for interactive whiteboard pens), we could position the tablets very precisely on the large screen. When the user moved his or her display over the main image, it would seamlessly update and give a feeling that the two views were perfectly in sync. Furthermore, users could take advantage of the fine input sensitivity of the tablet screen and, for instance, draw diagrams and write text directly in the place where they wanted it—the results would automatically appear on the main image and stay there when the tablet was removed.

But showing the same information in higher resolution—like a sort of magnifying glass—was just one way to use the system. It also gave us the opportunity to show a *different* view of the same data! For instance, on the map image, the main picture might be the regular map view, but the tablet image could show a satellite view of the same area. When the user moved the small screen over the large one, it looked like a lens was transforming the underlying map data into realistic photographic images. Another example might be to show "before" and "after" versions of the same image. For instance, in one demonstration, we showed the painting "The Last Supper" by Leonardo Da Vinci as it looked before and after a major restoration took place. Users could sweep their portable screens over the main image, which was showing the "before" version, and by examining the "after" image on their screen they could identify the many areas where the painting had changed significantly. Finally, by using the touch screen they could mark interesting areas and make annotations directly on the image, which the next visitor could view.

The system facilitated a unique combination of working: there would be both a public screen that everyone in the room could see and several personal screens where users could do work privately or in smaller groups. Although we used the tablet PCs available at the time, today it would be easy to replicate the system using more recent devices such as Apple's iPad or the various Android-based tablets that have recently come to market. It would also be interesting to combine it with even smaller screens, such as phones. There are already some phone applications that try to merge the real world with an onscreen display, so-called augmented reality. However, the tight integration of different displays of different sizes seen in Ubiquitous Graphics has so far not been seen in any commercial apps, partly because standard positioning and networking technologies do not yet support the kind of precision and speed that would be needed.

When showing this system at exhibitions, we got many creative suggestions from potential users. One would have liked to apply it to the planning of emergency services, such as the fire department's route during a rescue operation. Another idea was to show off real estate under development for potential buyers. The seller could have one satellite image on the big screen—perhaps the area before development, with only sketches of new houses put in—and then sweep the smaller screen over to show off different possibilities for new estates. A commercial version was not developed at the time, but with recent tablet and display technology it would be possible to make a setup tailored for a specific use case.

Combining small and large displays with different properties in this way can create a whole that is more capable than its parts. But there is a lot more that can be done by tightly integrating displays of all kinds into activities. In that case, the shape and form of the displays themselves can become part of the user experience—especially if they are small enough to carry with you at all times.

Even without the advances in electronic ink, textiles, and other emerging technologies, interactive surfaces have become portable and flexible to an unprecedented degree. The display on a standard smartphone has virtually the same resolution and responsiveness as a 20-inch computer screen—but fits in your pocket. New tablet computers have the same form factor as a magazine. This means that interactive displays can appear in just about every location where people spend their time, not just in tightly controlled work situations. Displays are used on the living room couch, on the subway, in the line to nightclubs, and on playgrounds. But there is still little that makes a mobile phone feel part of the situation that it is in; my iPhone or Android does not take advantage of where I am.

One way of doing this is by using sensors, such as position awareness sensors or cameras, to adapt the software to the current context, which we will discuss in a later chapter. Another involves the so-called *augmented reality* approach, used in commercial applications such as *Layar* and *Sekai Camera*, that lets you use the mobile phone as a "virtual window" that overlays information on the world (we'll mention this option in a later chapter). But it is also possible to integrate displays with the environment with no advanced sensing at all. We already saw how the usefulness of ambient information displays is directly related to where they are placed. We also saw how the Ubiquitous Graphics system leveraged the strengths of different types of displays into one experience. But there are also intriguing possibilities for integrating the environment using standard mobile displays, such as phones.

Case Study: Collaborative Games—Making the World Part of the Display

One application area is games. Starting in 2002, my student Johan Sanneblad created two software frameworks for the rapid development of mobile phone games with interactive graphics and networking, *GapiDraw* and *OpenTrek*. His systems made it easy to develop for many different phone platforms simultaneously. This was necessary for the fragmented mobile phone market that existed before the iPhone and Android operating systems became widespread standards, and where the requirements for software development would literally change from phone to phone, even those produced by the same manufacturer. So successful was Johan's efforts that GapiDraw was the de facto development platform for advanced game development on mobile phones and handheld computers for several years.

But we were interested in pushing the potential of mobile phone games further, beyond simply translations of hit games made popular on stationary computers and game consoles. When teaching a course in mobile programming, Johan posed the students a challenge: make games that have to be played on two or more screens, simultaneously, and where the players have to communicate with each other *in the real world*! This unlocked a well of creativity. We saw examples such as a rally racing game where the play was divided over two handheld screens: one showed the view through the car's windshield in 3D, as in a normal racing game; the other screens showed an overhead map view of the track, with the car's current position marked, as well as obstacles, curves, and other vehicles. Players had to be seated next to each other, just like a driver and map reader in a real rally. One driver would control the car, and the other would read the map, shouting out instructions in advance as to when to turn, and when to avoid tricky obstacles, step on the gas, chase other cars, and so on. This made for a game experience where the physical configuration of the players, as well as the communication between them, expanded the game beyond the limits of the tiny screens.

Another example was called *Pac-Man Must Die!*, developed by students Alexander Jaako, Annelie Lundén, and Staffan Lönn. Disregarding potential copyright infringements, it leveraged the famous Japanese arcade game Pac-Man, but with a twist. First of all, rather than playing the eponymous yellow disc with a big appetite, the players took on the roles of the little ghosts chasing Pac-Man in the game. Each ghost (there could be up to eight players) had a different color. Just like in the original game, their mission was to negotiate the maze and pick up the game's "energy dots." Each player could only benefit from the dots that matched the color of its own ghost. When you started the game, each device would show a part of the whole maze, filled with dots of different colors.

But here comes the twist: not all of the dots necessary to win the game would be visible on your own device! Because the game area was spread over all the screens, at some point you would have to enter the other players' arenas. This was in principle quite easy; there were "doors" in all the mazes of different colors, which led to the screens belonging to the player using that color. However, in practice, this simple addition changed the mechanics of the game completely, from being something played on separate screens to where just about everything in the outside world literally became a part of the game.

To see this in real life, we performed a study where teenagers at a local high school played the game. For two weeks they had access to handheld computers with the game installed. We deliberately left very few instructions but let the users pick up the details themselves—not hard for this demographic! The results were extraordinary, as some of the pictures show.

First of all, the game mechanics made it necessary for the teenagers to start negotiating space in a very unusual way. Because the action could move from one screen to another, there were various strategies for players to do this. In Figure 6-14, we see how four people are playing simultaneously. The one to the far left has his eyes fixed on his own screen and thus is still working on picking up the dots on the portion of the map visible on his own device. But some of the other players have moved their game characters over to one of the other devices. Of the three girls standing together, the middle one seems to have her eyes focused on her own screen. But the ones standing on either side are also looking at her screen! Apparently both of these players have moved their characters to the middle girl's screen and are busy picking up points there.

Figure 6-14

A complex configuration of players playing Pac-man Must Die*! The playing field is spread out over several devices. The left-hand player is focusing on his own screen; the next is viewing the screen in the middle while controlling the action from her own, as is the right-most player; and one is literally caught in the middle! (Image courtesy of Viktoria Institute)*

This complex cross-cutting of vision is in itself almost mind boggling, but the way the game would flow over different devices added a whole other dimension, as illustrated in our next series of pictures (Figure 6-15 to 6-17). First, two girls are playing and have arranged themselves so that they are looking at the same screen. It is easy to pick up and join the game at any time, which is what happened in the next picture. Because a new area of the game has just opened up with the new player, we see how the two original players have moved over to the screen of the boy who just joined. After a while, this new player decided to leave the game. But the two girls were not happy about this—they wanted to clear the new area of all possible points! So they kept the device with the game still open and continued to play on the new screen after the temporary player left.

As the kids got the hang of the game, it got even more elaborate! When everyone is playing nicely, as in the previous examples, it is possible to set up arrangements where all screens are visible to all players. But what if somebody does not want to be "fair"? If one player moves over to another player's device, the player holding that screen has unprecedented control over the game—if the other player cannot see the screen on which he or she is playing, the game becomes almost impossible! This gave entirely new options for game play, which were not built into the original design but became possible simply by the integration with the environment. A player can start to obscure a screen to make the game difficult for the other players, getting into all sorts of sticky situations as the other players try to keep visual contact with their on-screen representations. In Figure 6-18, we see a group of five players in a hugely complicated arrangement. From this picture it

Figures 6-15-6-17

In this series, two girls are playing the game; a boy picks up a new device and joins them, immediately expanding the playing field to his new screen. However, when he decides to leave, there is still some action left and the girls continue to play with the device he leaves behind! (Images courtesy of Viktoria Institute)

Figure 6-18

As the game heats up, it becomes increasingly important to keep the other players' devices in view—even if it requires physically restraining them! (Image courtesy of Viktoria Institute)

Figure 6-19

The one that got away! After several of the other players' characters ended up on her screen, this girl broke away and ran off, making it impossible for the other players to finish their game. (Image courtesy of Viktoria Institute)

is hard to tell exactly what is going on, as everyone is trying to crowd in and get a peek on the screen they are playing on right now. Some of the players even discovered that their most effective strategy was to run away with the screen, as illustrated in our final picture (Figure 6-19).

Although this is a highly complex, multi-screen setup, it is clear from this picture as well as the data from the study that this was a fun experience for the participants. Perhaps older players would have found it somewhat awkward to be tangled up like this with strangers, but these kids clearly did not mind. Some of these examples do look quite extreme, and, of course, it might be chaotic if this kind of game were being played on your local bus ride in the morning.

However, the lessons from the game are important. By tweaking some simple variables—extending the game field beyond the device under the player's own control—a completely new style of game was discovered. The action on the screen became complemented and enriched by the action outside it. Even more so than in the rally game example, the physical space became a vital part of the game play. The players did not need any instructions to make this cross-over happen; they figured it out themselves by working with the natural resources at hand. Thus, without any complex sensors or artificial intelligence, this game incorporated the real and the virtual worlds in a way that was often more effective than many so-called augmented reality games.

The main lesson of these three examples is that the *setting* for screen-based interaction can be just as important as the technology. Although many digital products still use screens in a way that does not really reflect the context of use, there is a big difference between putting a screen on a desktop and putting one on a running shoe. In this chapter we used screens as an example of interaction, as it is the most well-known and flexible platform we have access to for creating digital products. But using screens is just one way to interact, and it is not always the most appropriate one. It is important to remember that we can wring completely new forms of interaction from the simplest input or output devices—a button or a light diode can often be enough to communicate with a user, as long as the purpose is clear. Finally, though interaction is fundamental to almost all digital products and we have only covered a few examples here, it will be intrinsic to all the following chapters. Whichever of the other qualities of digital products we use, interaction will almost always be a part—sometimes directly and actively, like in the games; sometimes passively, like in the ambient information visualizations.

But interaction can be shaped in many different ways, and screens are only one way to create a means for input and output. In the following chapter, we will look at what happens when even everyday objects start to become connected to a digital *network*—even if sometimes the objects themselves do not do any computing on their own.

CHAPTER 7

NETWORKING: WHEN THINGS GET CONNECTED

For most digital products, *networking* is a property that is almost as fundamental as computation. In fact, all the examples of interaction in the previous chapter relied on networking in some sense, whether it was between local handheld terminals or to an information server, such as the real-time weather or bus departure times. With large parts of our lives now lived on the Internet, today it is hard to imagine a computer or any other kind of digital product that does *not* include networking in some form.

But let us take a step back and examine this property of digital products on a more fundamental level. The fact is that networking is so powerful that a connection to a network might be enough to turn an object into a digital product—even if it is not in itself in any way capable of computation! By adding an electronically readable tag, we can turn just about everything into a digital product. There are many examples of such tags, such as Quick Response (QR) codes, which look like small checkered squares, and radio frequency identification (RFID) codes, which can be read remotely and be completely hidden. Some systems can even do away with the need for tagging altogether and recognize an object simply on sight! These technologies have enormous potential for connecting just about every physical object to a digital counterpart of some sort. When this happens, we may have a world where everything is searchable and available for information processing—literally, a search engine for the world. But although this is already a reality in some industrial settings, the technology and applications for everyday use are still some way off.

ONE-DIMENSIONAL BARCODES

Starting at the beginning, the most well known example of a tag is the ordinary printed barcode, which you are familiar with as a set of black-and-white stripes on everyday products. This *one-dimensional* barcode (so called because the information is encoded in one direction only) has been used to identify products for almost four decades, mainly through the Universal Product Code (UPC) system. The first object with a UPC barcode to be scanned was a packet of chewing gum in 1974. Today, most shops and supermarkets use barcodes to identify and charge for items at checkout, as well as to keep track of their inventory. However, it is important to not confuse the barcode itself and the UPC system. The barcode is simply a sequence of numbers or characters encoded with the spacing and thickness of the lines, which makes it possible to scan it. UPC is the specific type of barcode that has been agreed upon to identify products internationally so as to standardize inventory keeping and charging. A barcode is not limited to the UPC numbers but can encode anything, such as the International Standard Book Number (ISBN) code for books—in fact, any arbitrary sequence of characters. There are many ways to scan a standard barcode, from the laser-based scanning pens that require you to swipe the code, to the stationary scanning tables used at many supermarkets, to specialized mobile scanning devices. Recently, many mobile phone cameras are able to provide enough quality to scan a one-dimensional barcode.

On a fundamental level, what the barcode offered was a way to *connect everyday objects to a digital representation.* The barcode has an additional advantage in that it already exists on many everyday products. Thus, barcodes could offer a way to augment any object with virtual information or make the object into a "pointer" to some other online information. In the late 1990s, there were a number of experiments with tying the preexisting barcode on products to online information. For instance, in 1999, researchers at Andersen Consulting presented the *Pocket Bargainfinder,* which combined a mobile computer with a wireless connection to a barcode scanner. By scanning an arbitrary product in a supermarket, users could bring up a web page on the handheld terminal that showed the best online prices of the same item—quite possibly severely disrupting the business of the traditional "brick and mortar" shop! Today, this functionality is available in a number of mobile phone apps, such as *Shop Savvy* for Android and iOS.

Case Study: WebStickers—Turn Everything into a Connected Object

Intrigued by these new possibilities, Peter Ljungstrand and I started to play around with the possibilities of encoding information into ordinary barcodes. This was around 1998, so mobile phone-based scanners were not readily available. Instead we hooked up a standard pen scanner to a PC. When a barcode was scanned, it would be sent directly to the computer as a character string. We reasoned that whereas tying products to inventory and price databases is one thing, what if we could allow users to connect *arbitrary* physical things to sources of information on the Internet?

The system, called *WebStickers,* allowed users to print a barcode sticker that could then be associated with any web address. The system would be running in the background on your computer, and whenever

Figure 7-1

The mug has been augmented with a WebSticker barcode and is associated with the home page of the conference it is promoting. On the screen are also a number of Post-its enhanced with WebStickers, turning them into tangible pointers to online resources. (Image courtesy of Viktoria Institute)

a barcode was scanned, it would open up a web browser to the page that had been assigned to this particular code. If you needed more stickers, you could simply print out more (the numbers were assigned using an algorithm, ensuring that no number was printed twice). When you first scanned a new barcode, the system would ask you what web address you wanted to assign it to and let you do that manually. There was also an interface to let you change the assignments should you care to do that. Finally, in a clever twist, the assignments were stored in an online database available from any computer, so that even if you assigned a sticker on your own computer and then gave it to a colleague to use, it would still produce the same address.

The advantage of this system was that it allowed an Internet address to be assigned to literally any physical object, at very low cost—thus allowing us to make anything into a physical bookmark to the web. This in turn moved the digital world out into the physical world and made it possible to build on natural activities and properties of the things around us. For instance, say that you wanted to remind yourself of an annual conference event. If you had a mug purchased at last year's conference, with a promotional logo, you could assign that to be the representative of the conference home page by attaching a WebSticker. Any time you wanted to check on the upcoming conference, you would simply scan the mug, and the website would pop up automatically. Similarly, if you wanted an easy way to access the online telephone directory, you could assign the link for the directory web page to the physical object most related to that action—your office phone. By scanning the code on the phone before making a call, the directory would immediately become accessible. For future usage scenarios, we imagined that various types of merchandise—for instance, posters and T-shirts for bands—could be tied to pages showing upcoming events and shows with the artist.

Another powerful way of using the stickers was to make augmented Post-it Notes. A Post-it has some very attractive physical qualities; it is easy to customize by writing on it, it is easy to share with others, and it can be disposed of when it is not needed anymore. Imagine that you want to alert a colleague about a new website. This was in the days before easy social sharing sites, like Delicious, Facebook, and Twitter, so an e-mail was the only available mechanism, outside of actually writing down the entire URL on paper. However, with WebStickers, you could pick a preprinted Post-it, scan the barcode, write a note giving your colleague the reason for checking it out, and affix it to her door. When she comes in the next day, she sees the note, takes it the computer, reads your comments, scans the barcode, and is immediately shown the related website. When this is done, she can choose to keep the note as a reminder for further action (maybe placing it on the computer screen or some other readily available surface), or she can pass it on to somebody else who might be interested, or she can discard it altogether. Although in no way ideal, this kind of sharing gives a tangible form to what might otherwise just have been an e-mail lost in an overflowing inbox.

The WebStickers system was thus unique in that it provided a user-controlled way to make physical objects into bookmarks, but it was in no way the only system at that time that tried to facilitate a connection between barcodes and the web. For instance, in 1999, Ericsson spun off a company called *Connect Things*, which proposed to connect complex products such as a box of medicine or a television set to the correct online instructions. The most famous was the *CueCat*, a cute USB barcode scanner shaped like a cat. In 1999 and 2000, the company behind this product gave away many thousands of barcode scanners, through outlets such as Radio Shack, and even mailed them out for free to all subscribers of popular magazines such as *Wired* and *Forbes*. The idea was that magazines and catalogs would print barcodes alongside product advertisements, and the users could go to the relevant web page by scanning them. In principle it sounded like a good idea, but despite the free scanners and big investments in marketing, the product flopped. It was such a failure it was named the number one "worst gadget" of the first decade of the 2000s by the influential Gizmodo blog.

So why did CueCat fail, and why have we not seen web bookmarks embedded into just about everything? It is not that the technology is too complicated or expensive—today, a barcode reader only costs a few dollars. But in this case, the benefit was simply not enough to create a new practice. When we are sitting at a computer, we already have quite good navigation capabilities, including a full keyboard. In addition to entering web addresses manually, we can also easily type in questions into a search engine, such as Google or Yahoo!. Although scanning a barcode might in some cases mean saving a little time, for the most part, the effort of finding and scanning the code, not to mention having an extra device connected to the computer, is not worth the effort. But even more than this, the problem with these earlier experiments was that computers were still, for the most part, *stationary*. Although we might sometimes encounter barcode-tagged objects in the real world, for the most part, they would not be located at the place where we have a computer. After all, how often do you read a magazine at the computer desk? CueCat didn't take into consideration the fact that the natural setting for interacting with the target audience was not, for the most part, where the consumers could actually use the product, but rather on the couch, on the bus, or somewhere else entirely. Thus, not only was there all the effort in making the computer capable of reading barcodes in the first place—you also had to bring all the objects to the computer! Therefore, although the invention had a lot of promise, the time was not right.

TWO-DIMENSIONAL BARCODES

Today, we have access to better technology for barcode reading—the camera on a standard smartphone, which also has the advantage of always being connected to a network. However, the original one-dimensional barcode requires a lot of precision, and most early phone cameras were not good enough to read them. Therefore, a number of other barcode encoding schemes have been developed to be easier to read with a lower-quality camera. These are called *two-dimensional* barcodes, because they encode information in both the vertical and horizontal dimension. The most popular example is the Quick Response (QR) code, developed by a Toyota subsidiary in Japan in 1994. These codes can be found in many Japanese magazines and products, and are even used in the immigration sticker routinely put in foreign visitors' passports. The QR code appears as a black and white matrix pattern and has significantly higher information density than the standard one-dimensional code—it can easily encode a whole web URL. Other tags with similar properties include the Data Matrix, which is often used for labeling small electronic components, and the colorful *high-capacity color barcode* developed by Microsoft as an even more high-density way to store information.

Figure 7-2

2-dimensional barcodes can be attached to everyday objects and when scanned lead to sources of information - for instance, accessing the website for this book by photographing its QR code. (Image courtesy of Mobile Life Centre)

Furthermore, some barcodes are designed specifically to be visually attractive and suitable for the brand they are associated with—for instance, those provided by the Silicon Valley startup *Paperlink*, which are based on standard QR codes but allow the logo of the brand to be included in the code. You can decode all of these tags using a standard camera phone, simply by taking a photo and running the right decoder application.

Having the tag reader literally in your pocket makes it much more likely that it will be on hand when you are in a situation where there might actually be some benefit from scanning a tag from an object or a magazine. QR codes have already had some success, especially in Japan and South Korea, where they are often used to encode web addresses in advertising posters and flyers, as well as on magazines and products. We are also increasingly seeing them appearing in the West—for instance, on business cards and promotional materials. Several magazines have run experiments where a variation of two-dimensional barcodes have been used to link to online content, such as movies. For instance, the Swedish newspaper *Aftonbladet* used the *Beetag* barcode system to include tags in its paper version. By downloading a tag reader to their phone, readers could take a photograph of tags that accompanied certain articles and would be shown additional graphics or animations; they could also enter into competitions, vote, and participate in other online activities.

With the improved performance of mobile phone cameras, some startup companies have also tried to leverage the standard one-dimensional barcodes that can be found on most products. For instance, *Stickybits* is a mobile app for barcode scanning that works on UPC barcodes as well as custom-printed codes, much like WebStickers did, but with the advantage of using mobile technology. Just like with WebStickers, scanning a code leads to digital online content. For instance, if you scan a code of an existing product, you will see its "wall," a kind of virtual chat room to discuss the product in question. The application allows users to add text and photos as well as video and audio files. For purposes that are not tied to a specific product, it is also possible to generate and print out new codes and attach information to them, as long as they are unique. For instance, if you are selling your car, you might include a barcode with "For sale" posted on the windscreen. When a Stickybits user scans the code, she might see more information about the car, such as a detailed history, or additional photographs or videos. The company's idea was to form partnerships to promote brands by giving rewards to users who scan barcodes, much like Foursquare is offering rewards to users who check in at various locations—using Stickybits would be somewhat like "checking in" to products. So far this particular company has not been commercially successful, but the concept is powerful and could eventually gain traction.

But in general, the uptake of mobile barcodes has so far not been as large as expected. Some figures in marketing studies indicate that about 30% of smartphone users have at some point scanned an optical tag, but this gives little indication of the awareness of the "man on the street." In late 2010, Zeynep Ahmet and Sebastian Büttner at my lab performed a study to gauge exactly that. They showed a QR code to 108 random people on a street corner in Stockholm. Of these, 77% had no idea what it was and claimed to have never seen one before. Of the remaining, 8% had seen an optical barcode before but did not know what it was for. This leaves only 15% of this sample who even *knew* what the code was (i.e., that it could be scanned with a mobile phone to get access to information). Although the study did not ask about usage, it can be presumed only a small portion of these people had actually used one! Thus, it seems that despite all the resources poured into QR codes and other optical tags, the general awareness is not nearly as high as it should be.

One reason for this failure could have to do with the same argument that was part of the failure of the CueCat—that there simply is not enough benefit in scanning a barcode versus entering an address manually. This is borne out by how most barcode readers so far have been integrated into regular phone use: very poorly. The act of finding and opening a special application, snapping a picture, and then waiting for a result to come up is simply too cumbersome. This tends to break whatever activity the user was originally engaged in, such as reading a magazine, and if the content is not served up swiftly and easily, it makes the user unlikely to repeat the process. Until barcodes are better integrated with everyday activities, they might not see as much traction as they could, although there are currently several startup businesses investing heavily in a variety of mobile barcode schemes for consumers, rather than specialized business tasks. Two-dimensional QR codes are now appearing more frequently—I have recently seen them on magazine covers, advertisements, posters, billboards, and so on—and sooner or later somebody might discover an application that offers the right combination of value and ease of use. Then, printed barcodes will represent an inexpensive way of turning everyday objects into digital products.

RFID: THE INVISIBLE TAG

An alternative that potentially allows for a more effortless interaction is the radio frequency identification (RFID) tag. This consists of a small electronic chip that contains a unique identification number, much like a barcode. But unlike the barcode, it can be read by simply bringing the tag close to an RFID reader. It works by having the reader emit a radio signal at a certain frequency, which resonates with the tag's own frequency. The energy contained in this radio pulse is strong enough to allow the chip to respond with its identity number, and thus it does not need to have a battery to function. Some chips also have a space in their memory that is rewritable, so that part of the content can be changed. One advantage of the RFID method is that depending on the strength of the signal from the reader, the range of response can be anything from a few centimeters to several meters or more. RFID tags can be found in retail stores for theft protection, in casinos to identify markers, as automatic key cards, in library books, and in many other situations. The required readers have come down in size and cost and are now becoming small enough to be integrated into mobile devices. The tags themselves can be made very small, and the downward limiting factor for size is not so much the identity chip itself but the antenna that is required for it to pick up a radio pulse.

In a 1998 demonstration similar to the WebStickers concept, researchers at the Xerox Palo Alto Research Center (PARC), including Roy Want, Kenneth Fishkin, Anuj Gujar, and Beverly Harrison, showed how RFID tags could be integrated into an everyday environment, forming a bridge between the digital and the physical. They employed hidden tags in objects such as books, posters, and papers, as well as both mobile and computer-connected tag readers. For instance, one part of the system showed how a printout of a document in progress could be tied to the electronic version. By swiping the paper to the user's computer (equipped with a tag reader), the current editable version would come up in the word processor. Actions could also be represented by tag-instrumented objects. For instance, by touching a French-English dictionary to the computer, the text currently on the screen would be translated from French to English (or vice versa). With the mobile reader, a user could be passing by a poster announcing an event; by touching the reader to the poster's embedded tag, he could add it to his calendar or bring up more information. This vision showed how it would be possible to create a hidden network, where any physical thing could have a digital counterpart, which could be brought up by a simple touch to a reader.

With RFID technology, it is thus possible to do everything that can be done with barcodes, and much more. The tags can be read and identified (even surreptitiously) when tagged objects are simply within the vicinity of the reader, they can be completely hidden in an object, and the content can be amended to reflect changes in the system. In fact, RFID tags would probably have replaced barcodes by now if it were not for one reason—cost. Even though a typical tag can now be manufactured for around 50 cents, this is still far too much for mass-market products. Compare this to an optical barcode, which can be included in the packaging of any product virtually for free, because it is printed along with other text and graphics. The price of electronic tags has been coming down and continues to do so, but it is unlikely they will ever match the cost of printed tags.

However, for many applications, RFID does make a lot of sense. If the tag can be used multiple times, the cost can easily be justified. One example is the mobile payment card systems that originated in several countries in Southeast Asia and are now being used in public transport systems around the world.

For instance, the so-called Octopus card was introduced by Hong Kong's public transport system in 1997, and in Japan, the Suica card (for "Super Urban Intelligent Card"—also a Japanese homonym for watermelon!) was introduced in 2001. These cards contain an RFID chip that can be read at the entrance to subways, as well as payment stations in small shops. The user preloads the card with money, which can then be used to pay for trips as well as goods in all participating stores. The card is very convenient to use because the signal from the reader is strong enough to pick it up at some distance and even go through other materials. Thus, there is no need to remove the card from your wallet— you can just touch the wallet to a reader, and some people even leave the card in their handbag. The Suica is particularly popular because it provides a solution to the problem of the many competing subway and train lines in Tokyo, all of which use different fare systems. With Suica, one payment card functions through all transfers, and it also does away with the need to fumble with coins to pay for small goods at the city's many convenience stores.

Because the active component of the Suica is a small RFID chip, it can also be integrated in other devices, and it is quite common to have Suica chips in the user's mobile phone instead of as a stand-alone card. By swiping the phone at a pay station, it is possible to pay for a trip or an item "with the phone"—but in fact, in this case the Suica is not in any way integrated in the functions of the phone. Furthermore, a Suica chip in your phone can only work in one direction—the chip in the phone will provide a unique identification, but it does not actually allow you to read other cards. A standard that provides both reading and writing of RFID in mobile phones is *NFC*, for near-field communication. This is designed for very short-range communication (around four centimeters). An NFC unit in a phone can work in several different ways, including reading tags from the environment, generating and providing unique tags to be read by other readers (such as an RFID pay station, thus allowing the phone to emulate a payment card like the Suica, a key card, etc.), and passing data between two devices (so-called peer-to-peer transfers). At the time of writing, there are very few fully featured NFC phones on the market, but they are coming. The standard is being implemented in new versions of Google's Android operating system, and Apple is also known to be working on an NFC payment system, potentially to be included in a future version of the iPhone. Should it become widespread, NFC technology would facilitate many of the RFID scenarios imagined in the Xerox PARC demonstration, with standard smartphones acting as readers in different situations.

IMAGE RECOGNITION: CONNECTING WITHOUT TAGGING

There is a snag with every tag-based technology. To go beyond payment and industrial applications and achieve the connected world envisioned by many researchers, it seems we would have to put a tag on almost everything. In some cases, some of these functions can be achieved by using optical tags, such as by having a QR code on a printed poster link to an event's website. But the reality is that most of the objects in our world are not tagged yet, and many may never be. So how can we connect objects together, even if they do not have tags?

One way to do this is to identify them visually. As long as the set of objects we are trying to recognize is limited, and we have a set of representative images of each one, the problem of identifying an object is quite manageable. A number of computer graphics algorithms have been optimized to compare two images, identify specific visual features, and detect if they appear in both places, thus confirming that they depict the same object. These algorithms are now good enough to be fairly reliable even across different camera resolutions, light conditions, and angles of view. This means that as long as we have the right database, we might not have to attach a barcode to an object and photograph the barcode—it might be enough to photograph the object itself. For instance, going back to some of the examples earlier, today it would be entirely possible to identify the logotype of the conference that was featured on the mug in the WebStickers example and bring up the correct web page—no sticker required. Similarly, you could take a photo of something like a movie poster for a current film and immediately be shown the trailer for the film or be directed to a page where you could buy tickets for tonight's screenings.

However, although this approach does away with the need for tagging an object to identify it, it still requires there to be an image of it in a database in the first place. For instance, the problem of identifying a picture of a movie poster by automatically comparing it to images of other poster images is relatively tractable, even if the number of other posters is large—it can be done by comparing a limited set of visual features using standard computer vision techniques. If the poster is *not* in the database, on the other hand, it might be almost impossible to identify it—in fact, it would probably be difficult to figure out if it was a movie poster in the first place!

There are some shortcuts that can be taken, a chief one being to use optical character recognition. If the title of the movie is visible in the picture, and the typeface is not too different from standard fonts, software can be used to extract the title and thus identify the movie. This method can be used on any product that has text, such as a book cover, a candy wrapper, a bottle, or a can, producing a more or less reliable identification depending on how unique the text in question is. Face recognition is another technology that is now well established. The reason is again that we can work with a limited data set and a set of computationally tractable features. Given that a person's face is more or less fully visible and the light conditions are good enough, the results can be so good that they border on creepy. For instance, Facebook recently introduced a feature whereby the site automatically identifies the faces of people in your photographs, based on your previous manual identification of them (so-called tagging, not to be confused with the other tags we have talked about). This technology is capable of trawling through all your online photos and identifying the same person over multiple photos. You are then offered the option of automatically tagging the person in all the photos he or she appears and to do so all at once, rather than through numerous passes.

Although this is convenient—you don't have to go through all your photos and tag the same person multiple times—it also raised serious privacy concerns among users, who understandably might not want the system to automatically identify them in every photo they might appear in on Facebook. But the ever-improving capabilities of face recognition software means that it is already technically possible to automatically identify a person from a photograph, something that is already used in security and antiterrorist applications, which is where much of this technology originated. Even more tantalizingly, we might soon be able to tie together other databases, such as with our contact list, to identify people on the fly. Don't remember the name of the business associate you just chatted with? Soon you might be able to snap a stealth photo and have a bio pop up on your Blackberry instantly!

Eventually, this kind of technology could lead to a world where literally everything is searchable. Imagine, if you will, a Google for the real world! But we have a long way to go before every object in the world has been tagged or added to an image database. However, there are efforts to create systems that automatically recognize and search for an object, and not surprisingly Google is behind one of the leading efforts, Google Goggles. This product complements the traditional text input that allows users to search the Internet for relevant websites. With Goggles, the idea is that instead of typing your question, you simply snap a picture of what you are interested in. The system will then translate the image into a text string that can then be input to the regular Google search engine. Of course, the crux lies in the translation! To accomplish this feat, Google taps into its vast image database, searchable through Google Images. By comparing the visual input to images in the database, the system tries to do what is essentially a reverse lookup of pictures. Additionally, the system will use other techniques, such as optical character recognition, to find text in the image—this then becomes the search query.

The Google Goggles vision is tantalizing, and for some objects it works very well—such as for popular logotypes, books, and visual landmarks. For objects that are actually in the database, the results can be very impressive. The system is capable of recognizing and giving information about the Eiffel Tower in Paris, famous artworks by historical painters, newly released books and magazines, and many other things. But just as often, it breaks down completely. For instance, I photographed a pair of open scissors—not a difficult object to recognize. But the results that came back were not of other scissors but, more surprisingly, of scantily clad women! It turned out that the system had matched the orange color and angle of the scissors' grip with the flesh color and posture of the legs of a human model. This is a mistake that a human observer would never make, but that is explainable enough for a system that bases its recognition algorithm on purely visual features, such as color and geometry, rather than an actual insight into what the picture is showing. But for things that have easily recognizable features, or some other identifiable feature such as text, systems like Google Goggles are already offering ways to connect things to the Internet that are very efficient.

However, the general image recognition problem—that of actually understanding the content of an arbitrary picture—is still outside the reach of computers. There are, however, some clever ways to work around it. One way is to tap into a network of people who do the job that computers cannot—what is sometimes called *crowdsourcing*. For instance, a team of researchers at the University of Rochester introduced an application called *VizWiz*, which lets blind people ask questions about their surroundings by taking a photo. Here, the user could use his phone to take a photo of three cans of food in his pantry and speak a question into the microphone such as "Which can is the corn?" And in a short time, on average about two minutes, an answer will come back: "The can to the right."

What is remarkable is that answering an open-ended question like this, in real-world conditions, is outside the scope of any current artificial intelligence software. It would require a computer program to understand the content of an arbitrary image, to understand the implications of a question formulated in natural language, and finally to provide an answer based on the interpretation of the question and the image. This is not yet possible. So how did they do it? It turns out that they turned the problem over to humans! Using a service provided by Amazon called Mechanical Turk, the system called upon an online workforce that is prepared to do simple tasks for a small monetary reward. To improve the accuracy and response time, the VizWiz software spread the work out to several potential online workers, or "Turkers," and synthesized the answers. The overall cost of using this online labor force came to about 7 U.S. cents per question.

There are some commercial attempts at using crowdsourcing for image recognition. For instance, a Berkeley-based startup called IQ Engines provides an application interface for image recognition that is available through a variety of mobile apps, including the company's own *oMoby* shopping tool. oMoby lets you bring up information about an object by snapping a picture—for instance, if you photograph a woman in a blouse, it would take you to other online shopping and price comparison resources for similar garments—much like the barcode-based Pocket Bargainfinder prototype or the Shop Savvy app. For some products, oMoby is using the same set of image recognition techniques as, for instance, Google Goggles, but even casual use shows that its capabilities go way beyond what is possible with automatic means. For instance, oMoby is capable of spelling out so-called *Captchas*, the wiggly pieces of text that you encounter on certain websites and which are designed specifically to be impossible to decode by computation. Thus, even though it is not explicitly stated on the website, a little experimentation confirms that the company is using human operators to determine the content of any picture that fails the automatic recognition—which is probably most of them. Although this approach may work in limited situations, it is doubtful if it is scalable to have real-time manual classification as the needs of this system grows. Finally, it is not clear what the conditions are for those people who sit and pick out blouses in images all day, although the company claims in its FAQs that it is using the human input to ultimately improve its own recognition algorithms.

Although taking still pictures of an object or location and seeing information pop up is impressive enough, the current frontier in this area is so-called *augmented reality*. Here, the idea is to overlay information over a live view of the world, as seen through the mobile phone's camera and screen. The vision is to have a kind of information overlay on everything you see, much like the "robot view" envisioned in movies like *The Terminator*. This technology has been under development for many years in the research world and is currently on the way to becoming commercially available. Although originally most systems were based on wearable screens that would be worn sort of like glasses, current commercial systems are based on mobile phones.

There are essentially two ways of achieving augmented reality: *marker-based* or *marker-less*. Marker-based augmented reality uses the kinds of codes that are similar to two-dimensional barcodes but have additional information to assist the software in detecting the angle of view and rotation of the code. An example is the Sony Cybercode, which was used in the PlayStation game *Eye of Judgment*. Using codes printed on cards and the attached Eyetoy camera, players could place virtual "monsters" on their desk and see them move and react on the screen. A general research platform for marker-based augmented reality is the *AR Toolkit*, developed by Hirokazu Kato of the Nara Institute of Science and Technology and later released by the HIT Lab at the University of Washington. This toolkit has made it possible to create many different types of augmented reality demonstrations, such as games, music making systems, and more utility-oriented applications such as interior planning. The AR Toolkit was originally developed for desktop computers with attached cameras but is now available for mobile devices, including Android phones and iPhones.

The more fascinating, but much more difficult, approach is to use no markers at all. This would give the robot view of an information overlay without any kind of visual tags in the world. One example is offered by the Dutch startup *Layar*, which produced "layers" that can be viewed as overlays on real-world locations.

When starting the app, the user can choose different "layers" to add to the view. This can be anything from the best restaurants and coffee shops to updated information on the latest criminal activity in the area. You hold up your phone at eye level and use it like something of an enhanced viewfinder. Rather than trying to interpret what is actually on the screen, like the previous systems we talked about, the system uses the phone's sensors for location and direction to calculate its position and where it is currently aimed. As the field of view moves, different labels pop up to mark points of interest. The result can be very impressive, giving the feeling of revealing hidden information in the world, much like the Terminator's enhanced vision. The Japanese company *Sekai Camera* also produces a similar technology, which lets users post so-called air tags, similar to the labels in Layar.

However, the sensing in these systems is often not accurate enough to give a truly tight integration between the virtual information and the actual position of the camera. It is quite possible for the information to be off by tens or even hundreds of meters, which limits the usefulness of these systems. A potential way to solve this would be to use the visual information scanned by the camera, to ensure that information stays attached to visual elements in the view. For instance, if the user is looking at the Eiffel Tower, it would be possible to use not just the location and orientation of the device, but to also to analyze the actual content of the image, to accurately position a label on the tower. However, this solution is still limited by factors such as the available bandwidth and the computational power of mobile devices, as well as the need to create accurate visual databases for the identification. As these systems continue to be refined, we will get closer and closer to the almost science fiction–like capabilities promised by augmented reality.

The methods we have talked about so far have all allowed us to tie objects into the network without adding more than a sticker or tag—and in some cases, like the computer vision-based methods, nothing at all. This is the starting point of an "Internet of Things," where literally billions of object are connected to a digital network. This tantalizing idea—where everything around us would be indexed and searchable, and information about people and places would pop up like bubbles in the air—is still a long way off. But with the techniques described here, it is certainly possible to create limited versions of this Internet of Things for specific situations. For instance, the inventory of most libraries is completely RFID tagged and updated live as books are taken out. The librarians can have an instant live view of the content of their storage and will know whether a book is in or out. Combine this with the various continued efforts to digitize books and thus make them searchable—such as Google Books, Amazon's Search Inside the Book, and Project Gutenberg—and in extension, this could provide a system where it would be possible to search every book in your local library. Just enter your query, and if the answer is in any of the books currently on the shelves, you would be pointed to the cor-rect place and go in and read it. And even though the availability of more and more books on electronic book readers may soon remove the need to go to a library all together, this example shows how a combination of different tech-nologies can make a part of the physical world electronically searchable.

But even though libraries do have an established organization system and occasionally still make concessions for humans to search their shelves, other large inventories do not. Already in industrial settings, there are examples of inventories that are entirely processed by robots, using RFID tags or other means to identify the objects. For instance, *Kiva Systems*, whose customers include Walgreens, Toys 'R' Us, Office Depot, the Gap, and many other large businesses, provides fully automated warehouse solutions, where the inventory is organized to be efficient for robots, not humans. For any outside observer, a Kiva-operated warehouse seems completely illogical—a mess. Boxes are stored with no apparent logic, with seemingly completely unrelated items sharing shelf space. To go in and find something would seem to be impossible. But the organization is not meant for humans, but for robots. The company uses arti-ficial intelligence to accurately predict the need for different inventory items and provide the most efficient ways for the robots to retrieve them at any given moment. When new items come in, the robot simply puts them down on the nearest empty space, and the location is recorded in the system's database. When an item is needed, the system can calculate not just where the items are, but which is the nearest unoccupied robot and how quickly the robot can pick up and deliver the item based on the positions. Thus, the whole inventory is optimized almost as if it existed inside computer memory, not in the real world. In a large inventory, this plan is so complex, it is not even possible for a human to comprehend—but it can be accessed by the computer system with lightning speed. What we have here is a fully searchable and retrievable net-work that literally runs itself, with human intervention only needed to send in orders and receive the items at the doors of the warehouse.

In all of these examples, the objects were passive and they did not even per-form any computation themselves—instead, that was performed in the net-work. But if we add a little computation to the object, we can have products that communicate with each other. This takes us to the next level of network-ing, when there is not just a digital shadow of an object through a passive tag or other means, but the object is actually active and aware of its surroundings. To do this, the object needs to have a *sense* of its environment, which is the subject of the next chapter.

CHAPTER 8

SENSING: BEING AWARE
OF THE CONTEXT

In the previous chapter, we saw how input and output surfaces can be integrated with the environment in various ways, and how tagging and other recognition techniques could connect things together. But whereas on a physical interaction level they were more a part of the world around them, these objects had little or no knowledge of what was actually going on in the world they were situated in—in other words, they were not aware of the *context* of the situation. This made sense for most digital products, up until quite recently. For instance, the operating conditions of a stationary personal computer in an office did not used to change very much. It would be situated in the same room, used by the same person in the same work situation, surrounded by the same coworkers, and subjected to more or less the same light, temperature, and other environmental factors all the time. For a mobile phone, on the other hand, these same conditions change a lot. The phone is used in different situations—taking an important work call one minute, making arrangements to pick up the kids from school the next—and finds itself in wildly varying social and physical contexts, from a night out with friends to the first meeting with a new boss. This is true for many other digital products as well, so it seems like it would be a good idea to let the product find out a little more about what is actually going on around it. By using a variety of *sensors*, it is possible to detect the conditions of the situations—and make use of them in different ways.

We have already seen one way of using sensors in a digital product in the context camera, introduced in Chapter 4. However, despite the name, this example did not really take into account the context in a meaningful sense. The sensors in the context camera were indeed used to create visual effects in the image, but they had little or no actual meaning related to the surrounding situation. For instance, whereas a loud high-pitched sound would produce a distinct visual effect, the camera application did not represent this in a way that made it obvious what the sound actually was. Instead, it affected the image in a more abstract way, such as increasing the coarseness of the pixels or the opacity of an overlaid image. This was intentional, because we wanted to keep the images aesthetically pleasing and open for interpretation. Thus, although the camera took advantage of the sensors to make the photo-taking experience more interesting and creative, it made no attempt to actually *understand and adapt* its functions to the situation in which the picture was taken, which is what we will talk about in this chapter.

A *context-aware* digital product is capable of detecting what is going on and acting on its surroundings in a more complex way than we saw with the context camera. As sensors become more advanced, this is becoming a more common feature in digital products. Even personal computers now have certain aspects of context awareness on account of being portable and thus used in different situations. On many laptops, for instance, the brightness of the screen can be set to adjust automatically according to ambient light. Although previous stationary computers rarely were exposed to changes in the light, laptops often are, and it is not necessary to have the screen brightness turned all the way up if the computer is moved from a bright office to a dim coffee shop. Thus, by using a built-in light sensor, the computer can detect and adapt to the situation, saving energy and offering a more ergonomic user experience in the process. This is a simple example of a context aware digital product.

But context is much more than the difference between dim and bright lights, and thanks to an array of new sensors, it is becoming easier for products to adapt to more and more complex situations. In 1994, Bill Schilit, then at the Fuji/Xerox Research Center in Palo Alto, defined context-aware applications as software that "adapts according to the location of use, the collection of nearby people, hosts, and accessible devices, as well as to changes to such things over time." He continued, "A system with these capabilities can examine the computing environment and react to changes to the environment." Thus, if we start thinking about digital products with context in mind, a large number of factors can be taken into account when coming up with new functions. Some, like social situations, are for the most part still too complex to fully act on yet, whereas others, like light and temperature, are easily sensed and interpreted.

Case Study: The Active Badge, the Hummingbird, and Location Awareness

One of the most fundamental as well as most interesting and useful pieces of context is *location.* As Mark Weiser wrote in the 1991 article that introduced ubiquitous computing, "Little is more basic to human perception than physical juxtaposition, and so ubiquitous computers must know where they are. ... If a computer merely knows what room it is in, it can adapt its behavior in significant ways without requiring even a hint of artificial intelligence." But the computers of 1991, Weiser pointed out, had no idea of their location. Today, there are many ways of determining the position of a digital product and, by extension, also the position of its user. As all owners of a modern smartphone know, today's technology can often pinpoint you down to a couple of meters or less on a map—more than enough precision to help you find your way from A to B or find information about interesting places around you. This does not mean that location is trivial; there are still unsolved issues both in determining somebody's position objectively and in understanding what that location actually means.

One early experiment in location awareness was the *Active Badge,* originally developed by Andy Hopper and colleagues at Olivetti's Research Lab in Cambridge between 1989 and 1992. Hopper had the notion of introducing *artificial sensing,* to amplify or complement the senses we are used to. For instance, if we had some way of determining the location of the people we care about, it would create a sort of superpower sensing—we could "see" through walls to find out if someone was in the next room, and even deduct the person's activity by the location.

The way they set about implementing these "superpowers" of perception was by creating a special device that was worn like a badge on the user's body. This was complemented with an infrastructure throughout the office building. The badge's function was simple; it would send out a continuous pulse of infrared light (not visible to human eyes) that encoded the identity of the wearer. This in turn was picked up by receivers placed in every room, which were wired up to a central information processing system. Because light has certain properties, like not propagating through walls, it was easy to determine the location of each badge by simply checking which receiver was currently picking it up. The location of each person could then be tracked in the system (provided the person was wearing the badge, of course) and various functions could be implemented on top of this.

One ingenious example of this function was created by hooking up the badge system with the local telephone network. Each researcher in the lab had a personal stationary phone in his or her office, but not everyone is in the office all the time; if somebody called a number and the intended recipient was not in the room, the call would, of course, be missed. One remedy would be to call the switchboard and ask for the person; if the operator knew where the person was, he or she could reroute the call to the nearest phone. But with the Active Badge it was possible to perform this function automatically. Because the system knew where the person was located, if someone called the office phone and the person was not there, the call could be automatically rerouted to the room the person was in, and the recipient would not miss the call. Of course, today this is a nonproblem for most offices, because everybody will be reachable by mobile phone! But it goes to show how knowing a person's location can provide benefits to a task that one might not have thought of.

The technology of the Active Badge system was subsequently adopted in the ubiquitous computing experiment run by Mark Weiser at the Xerox PARC. The researchers there, including Olivetti alumnus Roy Want, implemented a badge infrastructure, and they also used the same infrared light technology to give location awareness to the various portable devices they constructed. For instance, the PARCTab, developed between 1992 and 1994, was a small pen-operated computer that had access to constantly updated location information because it was connected to one of the infrared transceivers installed throughout the lab (initially there were 14 such transceivers; at the end of the experiment, some 50 had been installed throughout Xerox PARC). The PARCTab ran generic software such as a calendar, web browser, and weather information service, but interestingly, it also had the provision to integrate location directly into applications. For instance, a localized room booking system could automatically show up for the room the user was in. Another application was called Forget-me-not, which created a personalized history for the users, showing who they had met, which rooms they had been in, which documents they had accessed, and so on. This concept presages so-called life-logging applications later developed by Microsoft Research and others, as well as the histories created by location-based social applications such as Foursquare and Facebook—but because of the technology at hand, the PARCTab and Active Badge were always limited to the few locations where there were transceivers.

A few years later, around 1998, location was becoming an increasingly relevant research issue. Mobile phones had only recently become mainstream, and using them did away with some of the issues of finding people and coordinating meetings. But there were still a lot of things that could not be done with a standard phone and that would benefit from knowing somebody's location. The Active Badge system was capable of providing the absolute location of somebody within a

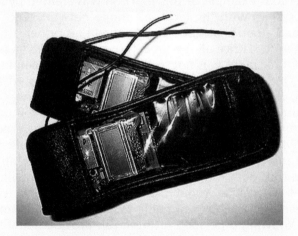

Figure 8-1

The Hummingbird *was an interpersonal awareness device that used radio to determine if other people were nearby. The presence of other people was indicated with a soft humming sound, and the identity of the people in the vicinity showed up on the device's display. (Image courtesy of Viktoria Institute)*

limited space. But what if you would venture outside that space and were still interested in knowing the location of other people? Or what if you just wanted to know what kind of people were around you, even if you did not know them?

The solution that I came up with, together with Jennica Falk and Joakim Wigström, was a device called the *Hummingbird*. It came out of an insight that the location of other people is not necessarily something absolute; sometimes it is more interesting to know if somebody is *near*, rather than *exactly* where the person is. This is the difference between relative and absolute positioning, and it still comes into play in location-aware applications today. What we did was to construct a set of simple radio transceivers (i.e., they were capable of sending and receiving at the same time), each of which had a unique identity. Radio waves have somewhat different properties than light; they can go through walls, although the range is fairly unpredictable. Our transceivers were set to operate at a distance of about 100 meters. By picking the unique identity transmitted by other Hummingbird users, it was possible to determine if the user was within a distance of 100 meters—even if the users were hidden behind a wall or on another floor in the building. The name came from the fact that whenever another user was in range, the devices would emit a low-level "hum." In addition to the audio indication, which was the same regardless of the identity or number of nearby users, the devices also had a display that would show the name of the specific users. Thus, it gave an ambient awareness (by giving indications like "somebody else just got to the office") as well as more detailed information on demand— answering questions such as "I wonder, is Jennica in yet?"

Thus, simply by indicating who else was nearby, the Hummingbirds enabled exactly the kind of "artificial sensing" that Hopper's Active Badges provided—but with the important difference that they worked anywhere, in any location, without the need to install any infrastructure. We tested the Hummingbirds with various users in a number of locations, everywhere from ski slopes to music festivals. In one example, we brought a few devices to a large conference, with tens of thousands of participants, and used them throughout the event. It turned out to be both useful as well as surprisingly comforting to know if other friends were nearby. In one instance, one of our test users arrived alone at a large party. Normally, this kind of situation can be stressful, because you want to find some familiar people to talk to rather than stand by yourself. Among thousands of people, it can be hard to locate somebody you know, especially if you don't know if the person has arrived or not. But in this case, she took a look at her Hummingbird and noticed that several other friends had already arrived; she thought, "Great, the others are here—I can relax," and she proceeded to enjoy the party. We got many similar responses in other tests, where people sometimes used the devices to find each other, but other times were simply happy to know that people were nearby.

These early experiments with the Hummingbirds showed that location is a powerful basis for creating digital products. Of course, the technology had a number of severe limitations. For instance, the battery life was quite short, the range of the radio was unpredictable and thus made it difficult to accurately tell the locations of others, and the devices frequently broke down. We also had to hand-build each unit, so initially we could only have a handful of users at a time (later we created a new version based on a popular handheld game console with an added radio, which enabled slightly larger user tests). The idea was even the basis for a startup company in the late 1990s, but the product, *Digibird,* never made it to the marketplace despite winning an entrepreneurship award. The main reason was that the hardware had to be manufactured from scratch and turned out to be prohibitively expensive—on the order of several hundred dollars per unit. Furthermore, with the radio solution, battery life would be very limited, even shorter than it is for a mobile phone, because the devices had to constantly transmit and receive radio signals. It was clear that despite the power of the concepts, there were too many pieces missing from the puzzle to turn the idea of location awareness into actual innovations.

Over a decade later, things are different and location technologies are available in many off-the-shelf devices. The most well known is the global positioning system (GPS). This was initially developed by the U.S. military, was subsequently opened up for external applications such as car navigation devices, and is now a standard feature of most smartphones. It uses a network of geo-stationary satellites to derive the position of the user with very high accuracy. The GPS receiver takes the precisely timed signal from several satellites and by using the fact that it takes a different amount of time for signals from different distances to reach the receiver, it can determine the position down to a few meters or even better. However, the GPS is limited in that it requires a free line of sight to accurately connect with the satellites. It is thus unreliable in areas with high buildings, ceases to function completely indoors, and can even have trouble in mountainous areas or jungles with high trees. Finally, because the system needs to pick up a signal from several satellites, it can take a long time (a minute or more) before it can start getting an accurate position.

In addition to GPS, mobile phones can use the fact that they are connected to a cellular network to derive their position. To place and receive calls and text messages, each phone constantly communicates with a base station in the vicinity; by knowing the location of this station, we can already get a rough idea of where the phone is. But modern phones use a more advanced method, cell triangulation, where they measure the signal strength from multiple base stations in the vicinity and use this information to calculate the position. This can be surprisingly accurate and has the advantage of being much faster in determining a position than GPS, as well as functioning well indoors. An issue with this system is that to function it needs an accurate database of cell towers correlated with real-world locations; this information can be costly and owned by different sources, and thus many companies, such as Google and Apple, have recently started to build their own databases. Finally, in a similar way, the signals from Wi-Fi networks can also be used to triangulate the position of a device, and companies such as Skyhook have built databases that allow any device with a Wi-Fi connection to be located. In practice, these databases are created by examining the phone and Wi-Fi signals picked up by a cell phone or other device and comparing them to the ground truth, such as that provided by GPS. To be able to build these databases, these companies will borrow your data every time you use an application where this information is available (such as looking at Google Maps), and over time, they can build an accurate map of the world's mobile phone and Wi-Fi network. This technology is what allows a phone that does not have a GPS receiver to find its position and can even locate your laptop based on Wi-Fi—although, of course, the accuracy is again entirely dependent on the accuracy of the database used.

Despite these advances, it is still difficult to pinpoint somebody's location precisely, especially inside a building, which limits the potential usefulness. The accuracy of even the best triangulation techniques is often not enough for an application to determine which room a person is in—and that is provided we even know enough about the inside of the building in the first place to know what the rooms are. After all, it can sometimes make a whole lot of difference if I am located in the local bookshop or in the pub next door, and current location technologies simply cannot determine that for the most part. Even if we have a fairly accurate geographical position, it might not be of much use if we do not know which *floor* the person is on, and current technologies have little to no accuracy in the vertical dimension. Technologies exist that solve these problems, including using ultrasonic transmitters and receivers, much like the infrared system used in the original Active Badge (and these systems were, in fact, pioneered by some of the same researchers). But so far, these systems require an infrastructure that does not yet exist on a large scale and is not standard in any mobile phones or other devices.

Until such systems come of age, other ways of determining location have been developed, mainly out of sheer necessity. The most popular and surprisingly effective is the *check-in* paradigm. Here, the user provides the final stretch of accuracy. When a user checks in using a service such as Gowalla, Foursquare, or Facebook Places, she is first provided with a list of *potential* locations. These are based on the system's best guess of the user's location, using GPS, cell triangulation, and so on. For instance, if I am at the neighborhood bookstore, the name of the store will be provided in the list, as well as other possible locations nearby, say the nearest pub, other stores, and so on. It is up to the user to select the correct one, thereby "checking in." Furthermore, if the right location is not in the list—perhaps the bookstore just opened and I am the first one to visit—the user can define it. In this way, these services build a database from the bottom up by semantically meaningful locations. The drawback is that to provide the correct location, users have to consciously tell the system where they are, unlike the Active Badge and Hummingbird, which constantly updated their location (we will discuss the advantages and disadvantages of the user-directed versus proactive approach in a later chapter). But provided the advantage is great enough, it turns out that people are happy to check in—for instance, to receive discount coupons for local businesses or to keep track of their friends.

It is still surprising to many users how low the accuracy of location systems still is, and selecting from a list of potential places is hardly high tech. What if we could use another sensor to improve the accuracy of location? There are a couple of standard sensors on every mobile phone that could be helpful for this. For instance, we might use the microphone to identify the ambient audio; the different audio signatures might tell us if we are in a crowded, noisy place (the typical pub) or in more relaxed and quiet environment (a bookstore). However, for the most part audio would probably not give us enough information, because one store would likely sound pretty much like another. Visuals, on the other hand, can be distinctive and can be picked up and processed by the camera of any smartphone.

Case Study: Better Locations with Cameras

In my lab we have tried to approach this problem in several ways. The first was the Φ^2, or *PhiSquare*, system, implemented in 2010 by Sebastian Büttner. This method applied a technology we talked about in the previous chapter: two-dimensional barcodes. The idea was that to check in, rather than selecting from a long list of potential locations, you could simply scan a barcode at the location. The Φ^2 system consists of two parts: a barcode generation website and a check-in app. On the web page you can turn an existing Foursquare venue into a unique barcode. Special software is available to print it out on stickers, so that you can easily affix the barcode to any location. With the app, you can then check in to the location simply by taking a photograph. The app connects to a database of all venues and resolves the identification number in the barcode to the correct one. There are several advantages with this method. First, it can make the process of checking in easier, because there is no need to manually select from a list of venues and, furthermore, there is no ambiguity of venues. Second, it makes the potential for check-in visible. Today, many people do not even know they can "check in" to a place, but a prominent sticker could draw attention to this fact and potentially increase the

Figure 8-2

The Φ^2 system allows users to share their location (i.e., check in) by photographing a two-dimensional barcode. It makes check-ins easier but requires every venue to have a barcode sticker. (Image courtesy of Mobile Life Centre)

number of people who use this feature. After we released the system publicly, several thousand people used it to print barcodes and check in all over the world. Although the current system is based on visual codes, it could equally well be used with radio frequency identification (RFID) tags when readers become more widespread.

But as we saw in the previous chapter, sometimes there is no need for visual tags at all. We applied this thinking to a setting where location is particularly tricky: underground. In the city of Stockholm, the local transport authority has invested in an extensive art program for the subway. A large number of stations have been decorated by artworks, of all shapes and sizes, from small sculptures and images all the way to installations taking over the entire environment. In fact, there is so much art that it is hard for visitors to be aware of it all! There are guided "art tours" through the system, and extensive information about all of the pieces is available on a website, but when it comes to identifying an artwork in the actual moment of seeing it, there is not much help. We wanted to give travelers an opportunity to spontaneously find out about an artwork as they were viewing it, not later on a website or on an organized tour.

This sounds like a natural application for a location-based system. After all, each piece of artwork has a distinct location and is not likely to move, so as long as we can find that location, it seems like we should be able to bring up the related information. This is true, except for the fact that location systems in the subway are very unreliable! As we already noted, GPS does not reach indoors, let alone to tunnels buried deep beneath the ground. But worse, the location systems based on cell information are also very unreliable. This is largely an artifact of how the underlying databases have been created. Because there is no "baseline" in the form of nearby GPS positions, it becomes hard to accurately build a database of cell locations. It turns out that it is often impossible to identify where in a station a user is, even with the best current smartphones, and thus identifying the location of a particular artwork is out of the question. In fact, the accuracy is so bad that sometimes it is not even possible to correctly determine which station the user is at, but there will be several possible stations to choose from.

Figure 8-3

The Subway Art Information *app combines input from the camera and location to identify works of art in the Stockholm subway system, providing much better location accuracy than is normally available underground. (Image courtesy of Mobile Life Centre)*

To solve this problem, we created a mobile application that used the camera as an additional sensor. The *Subway Art Information* application, implemented by Tengjao Ciao in 2011, uses the fact that each artwork has a distinct appearance. The app lets you simply photograph any artwork that strikes your fancy, and then shows you a summary of information about the work. If you like, you can then choose to be redirected to a web page with more information. To achieve this, we first took photos of each of the works and stored them in an online database. When the user opens the application on her phone, it first determines the location as far as possible. She can then take a photo of the artwork that interests her. This photo is uploaded to the database, where it is compared to the stored photographs using a standard image recognition algorithm, Speeded Up Robust Features (SURF). Image recognition has been the subject of much research in recent years, and many standard techniques are available, but it is still by no means trivial to identify an artwork in an image. However, we have the advantage that we already know the *approximate* location of the artwork, and in most cases the actual station where it is! Thus, we can limit our search to only those works that are present at this particular station. This greatly reduces both the search time and the risk of errors, as compared to searching a database of all images in the system. And although the current system is quite limited, if it would be expanded to all works in the entire subway, this advantage is significant. Even better, if the system would be expanded to include even more information—say, the art in other parts of the city or perhaps the art in another city—it would retain more or less the same speed and accuracy because it would only search through images that are relevant to the user's current location. An extension to the system might also cover other types of information—perhaps showing current train departure times when a user photographs the entrance to the subway station.

Figure 8-4

The Pic-In *system lets users check in on Foursquare by simply taking a photo of their current location! The system combines image recognition and location awareness with crowdsourcing to build up a database of venue images. (Image courtesy of Mobile Life Centre)*

However, as we already mentioned, this approach requires that an image of every piece of artwork—or other object—has already been entered into a database in order to identify it. A different and more scalable approach was taken in an application designed by my lab as an extension of the Φ^2 concept. As mentioned previously, we had already provided a way for users to check in to Foursquare venues using barcodes. But just like with any other tagging scheme, this would require that every location in the world was tagged. What if we instead used the camera to recognize the location? This would work fine, as long as we had a number of representative pictures in our database, much like in the subway art project. But for most venues, there would not be a picture. The system, called *Pic-In,* implemented by Sebastian Büttner in 2011, acknowledges that limitation by *crowdsourcing* the database. Every time a user attempts to check in by taking a picture, the rough location is found (just as with PhiSquare), and the newly taken picture is matched to the existing database. If it is recognized, everything is fine, and the user is checked in to the correct location. But if it is not, the user is asked to check in manually. The newly taken picture is then inserted into the database associated with this particular venue. If nobody has checked in at this venue before using Pic-In, it becomes the first picture in a new set. But it might also be that previous check-ins used pictures taken from a completely different angle or of another part of the location, and it was thus not possible to match them with the new picture. In this case, the database is amended with the new picture, and the chances for a correct check-in next time will increase.

The advantage of this approach is that it does not try to actually interpret the content of the picture but merely matches it to an existing visual database, much like, for instance, Facebook's face recognition. This is unlike the method use by Google Goggles, which tries to extract the content of the picture automatically based on previous data, or the approach used by VizWiz or IQ Engines' oMoby app, which use human help. This means that Pic-In can scale all over the world with the help of users doing the work, and that the actual image recognition is limited enough to be tractable. In the future, it could also be applied to other areas outside of check-in, becoming something like WebStickers, Stickybits, or other attempts at attaching digital information to the physical world, but without the need for any kind of tags.

In the last two examples, we combined the location information with the image given by the phone's camera to get a more accurate determination of the user's location. The combination of more than one sensor is sometimes called *sensor fusion.* It can be a powerful technique, because one sensor might not give nearly enough information to derive the current context, but two or more sensors combined could provide it with much larger accuracy. Sometimes we can derive a lot of information from different sensors on the same object. Other times, we need to put together readings from different types of sensors, situated on different objects, to get the full picture. But almost all the time, having access to more than one object raises the knowledge about the situation significantly. The following sections offer additional examples of how a set of sensors can give more information about the situation than any single sensor would be capable of giving.

Case Study: Context-Aware Cups

So far, we have talked about sensors with a single purpose—like the Active Badge—or provided by a general-purpose device—like on a mobile phone. But there are still many untapped possibilities for embedding sensors in everyday products that we don't normally think of as having any kind of digital function. Let us start with an example.

Figures 8-5–8-6

The electronic components hidden in the base of the MediaCup contained a number of different sensors as well as wireless communication facilities. (Image courtesy of TECO, www.teco.edu)

At the Tele-Cooperations lab (TeCo) at Karlsruhe University, researchers are developing platforms and applications for "smart objects"—everyday artifacts that are equipped with the ability to sense and act on context information. One way to go about this is to start with an object that has no current digital function, and add it simply to see what happens. What if, say, a seemingly ordinary coffee cup could sense information about its environment—for instance, if it was hot or cold, if it was moving, its location, and so on—and communicate this information through a network? The result was the *MediaCup,* conceived in 1999 by a group including Michael Beigl, Hans-Werner Gellersen, and Albrecht Schmidt.

The sensors on the MediaCup included a thermometer, which would let it sense the temperature of the liquid it contained, and a so-called accelerometer, which is a kind of motion sensor that can detect both how an object is moving, as well as determine its orientation when it is still (e.g., if it is upside down). There was an infrared light transceiver that could communicate with stations throughout the office building and thereby also determine each cup's position, just like the Active Badge. The light transceiver could also be used to encode data—for instance, to share the sensor reading in the cup over the network. A small microprocessor was included to control the sensors and network connection. There was a wireless charging system that allowed the cups to be recharged by simply placing them on a special surface. Finally, all this advanced technology was collected in a removable rubber enclosure, where it was isolated from the rest of the cup and could be taken off for dishwashing. Essentially, the MediaCups formed a context-aware ubiquitous computing network without a single "computer" in sight.

So what can a simple coffee cup tell us? If we assume that cups are personal, they are an indirect indication of the owner's activity. Through the infrared network, we can determine which room the cup is in and therefore, by extension, which room the owner is in. But what if I left my cup on a table and went somewhere else? Through sensor fusion, we can actually tell a little more. First, the thermometer tells us whether or not there is hot liquid in the cup—if there is, it is a safe bet that it has been filled with coffee or tea recently. Second, the accelerometer can be used to detect the cup's movements. If we can see that it is occasionally being lifted and tilted, it would be safe to assume that somebody is drinking from it. By putting these things together, we can thus determine where the owner of a cup is having coffee, if that happens to be the case—and this is without any additional devices, but just from the natural activity that is taking place with the cup.

Even if we cannot tie each cup to an individual owner, there is a surprising amount of information to be gleaned from ordinary activities. Suppose that the system indicates that a number of cups are gathered in the same room. They all contain hot liquid, and they are all being sipped from occasionally. This tells us that a meeting is most likely going on in the room. Waiting a few hours, if the same cups are still there but have now become cold and have not moved in some time, we can assume that the meeting is over and people have moved on—not to mention that it is time to go in, clean up, and collect the cups! This kind of information might not make a lot of impact in a small office building such as where the system was originally conceived and where it is limited to one type of object, but it can have an important impact in a more complex environment. Imagine being able to track the activitites of thousands of people in a large building, and using this information to adjust temperature, air conditioning, light, and other factors—this could conceivably lead to both great energy savings and a more pleasant work environment. And because the information collection is not done through personal badges but via everyday objects, it would be indirect and anonymous, preserving people's privacy.

With the MediaCups, we have seen how we can extract context from situations using sensors such as thermometers, accelerometers, and locators. When it comes to sensors, only the imagination limits what can be done. One unusual type of sensor, pioneered in 2002 by the Embedded Interaction group at Lancaster University, by Albrecht Schmidt and others was *weight measures*. It turns out that there is an unexpected amount of context information to be gained by measuring the load of objects on a surface, such as a table. The researchers first constructed a table where they placed one sensitive load sensor, capable of measuring changes in weight down to about 20 grams, in each leg of the table. The results are surprisingly powerful. Every time an object is placed or removed from the table, it changes the load of the four legs. The distribution of the load will be different depending on where on the table the object is. Thus, by taking into account the changes in load on the four sensors, the researchers found that they could calculate not just the weight of an object that is placed on the table, but also its position. By keeping track as objects are added and removed, the system can keep track of an arbitrary number of items on the table at the same time, as long as there is a minimal time between when each of them is put down or taken away from the surface.

Furthermore, because different objects have different weights, in many cases it is possible to determine the identity of an object—a particular book will have a different weight signature than a computer. In the test setup, it turned out to be possible to distinguish a notebook computer (about 2.2 kg), a book (about 500 g), a newspaper (about 200 g), and a water bottle (about 520 g) with greater than 95% accuracy. The interesting thing about this setup is that the objects are completely ordinary, with no added sensors, yet the table is able to detect their presence simply by registering changes in weight. It is possible to imagine many context-aware applications where the configuration of a workplace changes depending on the objects placed on it, for instance, turning on the reading lights when a book is placed on the table or bringing up a specific set of related electronic files on the laptop when it is set next to the book.

Case Study: Smart-Its—A Distributed Sensing Platform

Constructing smart objects like the MediaCup and the sensing table still requires a lot of hardware and software expertise. Therefore, in a follow-up project, researchers from my institute, Viktoria, as well as others including Karlsruhe, ETH Zürich, and Lancaster University, set forth to create a more general-purpose sensing unit: the *Smart-It.* The original inspiration came from Post-it Notes, which are easy to write on and can be stuck onto just about everything. What if you had a small sensing device that you could customize easily for different purposes and then stick on to just about any object, thus making it context aware and "smart"? The project which ran from 2001 to 2003 created a publicly accessible hardware and software platform for such stick-on sensors, as well as examples of what they could be used for. (This platform has since been continually refined and developed and was made available commercially under the name *Particle Computers.*)

The motivation was that although software prototyping is by now a well-understood process, with many resources in the form of software libraries and example applications, creating this kind of context-aware object is much more tricky. If I want to test an idea for an interactive web service or a mobile phone app, I can easily pull together components from earlier work and get a decent idea without investing too much work in the process. The Smart-Its were designed to provide the same ability for the physical world. Several other prototyping systems have been released that try to achieve similar things. The most well known is the *Arduino*, a software and hardware platform that makes it easy to construct and control input and output devices. The Arduino is popular in education and for creating interactive installations, such as museum exhibits; however, it is much more open ended

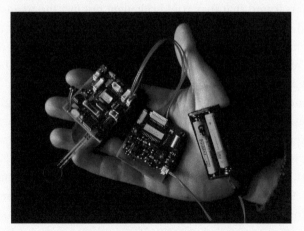

Figure 8-7

The Smart-It *node has sensors for temperature, movement, sound, light, and pressure, as well as radio networking capabilities and an onboard microprocessor. (Image courtesy of Smart-Its Project)*

than Smart-Its, as it relies on a central processing board onto which a variety of components can be attached. Closer to the spirit of Smart-Its were the *Motes*, small wireless sensor nodes, which were originally developed at Berkeley University and commercialized by the company Crossbow. Several operating systems have also been developed specifically to power small wireless sensor nodes, including *TinyOS* (Berkeley) and *Contiki* (Swedish Institute of Computer Science).

The original Smart-It contained a selection of sensors that together would be capable of giving information about the context. Like the MediaCup, it included a thermometer for sensing temperature and an accelerometer for movement and orientation. There was also a microphone to pick up ambient noise, a light sensor, and a pressure-sensitive switch. It also had a speaker for creating simple sounds. Rather than infrared communication, a Smart-It used radio communication to connect with other nearby devices as well as a local network—and by extension, potentially the entire Internet. Onboard it had a 20-MHz microprocessor and a couple of kilobytes of RAM to make it capable of running simple programs. The cost of components and assembly is in the region of a few hundred dollars for each unit, which means that they were not cost effective for using in actual products (a few of the current Particle Computer products are significantly cheaper but offer only a limited range of sensors). However, when a concept has been prototyped and tested using Smart-Its, it is usually possible to manufacture a specialized board that only uses the necessary sensors rather than everything the Smart-Its offers, and this would generally be a lot less expensive.

With the platform in place, it now became possible to develop a large variety of example applications for digital products with sensing capabilities. This resulted in prototypes of everything from a system for luxury restaurants, which monitored the quality and temperature of cheese, wine, and other sensitive goods, to a support system for avalanche rescue workers, which was capable of determining the critical condition of people lost under the snow and make a prioritized rescue list based on the gravity of each victim's situation. Although most of the ideas so far have not resulted in products, the goal for the project was to lower the bar for experimenting, and as technology continues to advance, we will be seeing sensing used in more and more digital products.

One of the advantages of Smart-Its was that they could be used to construct applications where a number of sensors communicated with each other through the onboard radio. As already mentioned, a combination of sensors can often produce more information than could be gained from a single type. If we look back at the weight-sensing table mentioned earlier, it had the advantage of being able to detect the identity and position of objects—but only if they were of different weights! What if we wanted to detect several objects of roughly the same weight, or what if we even had objects whose weight would *change*? In one example application produced by Martin Strohbach and other researchers at the University of Lancaster in 2003, a combination

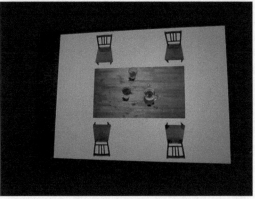

Figures 8-8–8-9

By combining a load-sensing table with objects augmented with Smart-Its, it was possible to accurately track the position of the objects on the table surface—and even determine how much water was left in the pitcher! (Image courtesy of the author/Lancaster University)

of Smart-Its and weight sensing was used to track a number of water-filled glasses and a pitcher on a table. Because the weights of the objects would change when the water was redistributed—for instance, by filling a glass from the pitcher or drinking from it—it was not possible to use weight for identification. So how do we find out the position of a glass or pitcher when it is placed on or removed from the table? By combining the information from two sensors.

Each glass and the pitcher had a Smart-It pressure sensor on the bottom, which would send an alert whenever the object was picked up or put down on the table. This gives us the *identity* of each object as it is moved. At the same time, the table would calculate the weight and position of each object that was picked up or put down—but it did not have its identity. But by combining the two sensor events—the weight and the pick up/put down switch—it was possible to tell which glass or pitcher had been moved, and where exactly on the table it currently resided. And not only that; because we had already measured the weight of the objects when they were empty or filled with water to

Figure 8-10

The components of a piece of flat-pack furniture were equipped with Smart-Its and LED lights, which made it possible to follow the progress of the assembly—and give feedback if something was going wrong! (Image courtesy of ETH Zürich)

various degrees, it was possible to figure out exactly how much water was in each of them. By combining all of this information, it was then possible to construct a visual representation of all actions on the table, consisting of a picture of the table surface and the various containers on it, which was updated in real time. The pictures of the glasses and pitcher would be changed depending on the amount of water they contained. In fact, this animation was so good that when it was demonstrated next to the actual table, people would often believe that it was simply showing a camera feed from above the table; those observers could not understand what the fuss was about!

Another example, which used several to support a real-world task, was when a group at ETH Zürich, including Stavros Antifakos, Florian Michehelles, and Bernt Schiele, embedded assembly instructions directly into a piece of flat-pack furniture. The problem when buying an unassembled product—whether a bookshelf, a bicycle, or something else—is that whereas the product lives in the physical world, the instructions are on paper and thus virtual. Making the connection between the abstract and the practical is not always easy, as unfortunately some pieces of misassembled IKEA furniture in my own apartment can bear witness to. What if we could integrate the instructions into the actual components of the product in question? To do this, we would need to be able to sense the state of the assembly and also give instructions on how achieve the next step. This is exactly what the group did with an ordinary unassembled wardrobe, straight from the furniture warehouse. In the demonstration, the individual pieces of furniture would have enough sensing capability for the system to determine the stage of assembly and give instructions on which step to take next—as well as indicate if something was going wrong.

This was achieved by using a combination of sensors, both the standard Smart-Its and some additional ones, which were embedded in pieces of the furniture as well as in some of the assembly tools. In the background, a piece of software was collecting the sensor readings through the radio network and interpreting how far the assembly had progressed and what the next step would be. The main sensors that determined the stages of the assembly were the Smart Its' accelerometers and pressure switches. An accelerometer can sense not only how an object is moving but also what orientation it has; it does this by using Earth's force of gravity—in itself a source of acceleration. Thus, by looking at the embedded accelerometers, the system could determine how they were positioned relative to each other—for instance, if a piece was standing up or lying down.

To complement this, the pressure switches of the Smart-Its were placed on the edges of pieces that were intended to fit together, which would trigger only when enough pressure had been applied by screwing them together. To detect the act of screwing, another sensor, a gyroscope, was attached to the screwdriver, where it could use the accelerometer to detect the rotating movement indicative of screwing. However, this was not enough, because the accelerometers can only detect orientation in the vertical dimension, and thus a standing piece of the puzzle could be facing in either direction. To detect if a piece was facing correctly, the standard Smart-Its sensors were complemented with an infrared light transceiver on one side of each board. Only when the infrared light transmitted from one side was picked up correctly by another sensor would the boards be aligned correctly—using the fact that light does not travel through wood. Through this assembly of sensors, it was now possible to detect every stage of the assembly process, from flat pack to finished wardrobe.

But how could the system give feedback to tell the user if she was on the right track? Initially, this was accomplished through audio instructions. The system would address the user through an artificial voice, indicating the next step. But this brings us back to the abstract versus practical form of the instructions—although errors could be caught more quickly, the instructions would still not be anchored in the reality of the actual furniture. Instead, the researcher embedded strips of light emitting diodes (LEDs) in strategic places of the components. These would light up green to indicate the next edges to be joined, giving a direct instruction on how to proceed. If the user was about to do something wrong, the LEDs would shine red, providing immediate feedback before the error was committed. Thus, all of the instructions for assembling the furniture had been moved from the printed page into the actual components.

So why don't all coffee cups, tables, and flat-pack furniture already come with embedded sensors? The most obvious answer is that the cost does not match the benefit in this case. For instance, even if we could bring down the cost of the Smart-Its to a couple of dollars per unit, flat-pack furniture is sold very much on the merit of its low cost, and margins are very low. If the trade-off is to pay $50 more for a shelf with embedded instructions, many people would probably rather hire an expert to assemble it! However, in other cases, the embedded instructions concept could have more utility. If we think of a factory assembling high-cost products, such as cars, maybe a few dollars extra per unit can be balanced by one less costly mistake. Similarly, if this idea were applied to a critical sequence of actions, such as putting on diving gear or preparing for a parachute jump, the investment might be well worth the reduced risk of accidents. Furthermore, if the sensors were reusable, it is likely that they could become more cost effective over time. The fact is that although embedded sensors like this are compelling, the sweet spot for turning them into digital products has not yet arrived.

But on the mobile phone, context awareness is already a fact, in particular through location sensing. Here we are talking about a general-purpose device that costs several hundred dollars or more and is often subsidized by carrier contracts. In this case, the sensors are a small part of the overall price, and manufacturers are now converging toward a set of sensors that will be standard on just about every phone. In addition to a camera and a microphone, an accelerometer is a de facto standard, as is location sensing, often through GPS, or at the very least using the less accurate cell positioning method. Some phones also use a light sensor to determine the ambient light and adjust the screen brightness accordingly, and Apple's iPhone has an infrared range sensor that detects when the phone is held to the ear. Furthermore, there are now many stand-alone sensors that can be connected to a phone computer, such as Nike+ and FitBit, both of which measure physical activity using an accelerometer. As these sensors continue to develop, we are sure to see many applications of context awareness in digital products.

As digital products become connected to networks and to each other, and as sensors let them start to know more and more about the world around them, the opportunities for computer software to make suggestions and even decisions based on real-world data are increasing. In addition to correcting a misspelled word or suggesting a search result, algorithms will soon be able to affect our actions in the physical world. This is what happens when digital products become *proactive*, as we will see in the next chapter.

CHAPTER 9

PROACTIVITY: PRODUCTS THAT DECIDE FOR THEMSELVES

As more and more objects become interactive and capable of networking and sensing, we are getting closer to a world where the difference between physical and virtual digital products will cease to exist. If the displays around us are plugged into real-time information about weather, traffic, and other data; if every book in a library is searchable; if every person around you has an updated location; and even the coffee cup on your table knows where it is and when it was last used—then not only do we have the potential to build individual applications from each of these components, but we can start applying information processing techniques—techniques that were previously limited to onscreen software— to just about everything around us. And as the algorithms that define these products become more efficient at understanding and acting on incoming data and as more portions of the world become available for processing, we will see an ever-increasing amount of self-directed action, or *proactivity*, in digital products.

Proactivity in digital products is far from a new idea. You experience it all the time. Whenever your word processor corrects a misspelling as you are typing or whenever your e-mail client files another message from "Prince Mike Okoye from Nigeria" as spam, you are letting software make decisions on its own. As the world around us becomes increasingly digitized, it will become more common to offload similar decisions regarding commuting, shopping, eating, even meeting people, to digital products. A common way to think about this kind of proactive software is as a *software agent*, which means software that acts on the user's behalf, with the authority to make its own decisions. Another common term is *intelligent* agent, although this can be somewhat misleading—most agents do not exhibit what we humans normally consider intelligence! For instance, take the simple case of a piece of software that controls the temperature in a building. It senses the surrounding temperature through a thermometer and acts on this information without user intervention. If the room gets too hot, it turns on the air conditioning; if it gets too cold, it turns on the heater. This software is an agent—it has a certain amount of agency—that is, the capability as well as authority to make decisions based on its (limited) knowledge of the world. Thus, it can act proactively on the user's behalf. But it does not exhibit intelligence in the intuitive sense of human intelligence. (Returning to our discussion about the properties of digital products, the thermostat has the properties of information processing, sensing, and proactivity.)

To successfully introduce proactivity in digital products requires a careful combination of technology and design. First, it is necessary for the software to have a good notion of what the conditions are on which it is acting. In digital products that are not limited to running on a computer screen, this often comes down to the available sensors. When it comes to a simple thermostat, this is comparatively easy; temperature is a well-understood property and can be sensed easily. However, to detect more complex context, such as the activities of a user, requires a lot more complex sensing. Second, the product has to act on this sensor data in a reasonable way. Here it comes down to the algorithms that are available to process the input. Often, as soon as it comes to more complex activities, this involves machine learning (i.e., letting the system build its own model of the world from available data and draw its conclusions from that). For instance, researchers have shown that given a history of a person's whereabouts and applying machine learning algorithms to these data, it is possible to predict one's future position with a very high accuracy.

Finally, the way that the system asserts its proactivity has to be carefully balanced. One of the most famous (or rather, infamous) examples of a proactive software product was Microsoft's *Office Assistant* introduced in 2003. It was embodied as a set of cartoon characters that would pop up when the system determined that the user was trying to perform a certain task in Microsoft's suite of productivity software. The thought was sensible—an online help system that would be offering suggestions proactively depending on the current context—but many found the presentation to be highly annoying and that it often disrupted the real work the user was doing. Many still remember how the animated office clip "Clippy" would pop up to offer its supposedly well-meant advice—"It looks like you are writing a letter. Would you like help?" Without going too deeply into the analysis of this feature's failures, the animated and cartoony presentation style and the general insistence of these assistants to engage in conversation would certainly feel out of place and disruptive for most users engaged in a serious office task. It probably also partly came down to a lack of ability to detect the greater context of use; even though I am writing a letter, the reason I am pausing may not be because I am confused about the system's functions but simply because I am thinking about what to write. The Office Assistant was removed completely in 2008 and replaced with a more conventional help system.

But proactivity has been successful in many other areas. One of the most successful examples is *recommendation systems*. Pioneered by researchers in artificial intelligence, these systems act on a simple basic principle: if I like something and it can be confirmed that another person likes the same thing, it is likely that we share opinions on other things too. A common application is in shopping, where recommendation systems are used to suggest new purchases based on the user's shopping history, as well as that of other customers. Although such software usually is not authorized to make the actual purchasing decision, it is constantly collecting clues about the user's preferences and providing suggestions for products to buy. One company that has turned this function into a major part of its business model is Amazon. When you look at a book, movie, recording, or other item on the Amazon.com website, the system will inform you that "Customers Who Bought This Item Also Bought...." It will even show you a few other items that are "Frequently Bought Together," in the hope that you will splurge on the set. These suggestions are based on exactly that—if a high number of users already bought both Book X and Book Y, buyers of Book X will quite likely also enjoy Book Y. This technique is sometimes referred to as *collaborative filtering*, because it uses information from other users to improve the recommendation for you.

But the system can also give you recommendations even before you have looked at a single book. It does this by looking at the items you have already purchased, comparing them to the purchases of other Amazon customers, and computing a list of items that you are likely to enjoy. Amazon also encourages you to tell the system what you thought about your previous purchases, giving even more information about what you like. As your purchase history expands—and the company's algorithms get more and more sophisticated— these recommendations become almost spookily accurate. The exact workings behind these systems are outside the scope of this book, but many of the underlying processes are well documented and used by companies such as Netflix (for renting movies) and Apple (for downloading music). However, although these systems learn about users and are capable of giving suggestions, for the most part they are not reliable enough for users to turn over the power of purchasing to them! Partly this is because the recommendations are not perfect; even though it is likely that I will enjoy the system's recommendations, it is by no means a certainty, because human taste is hard to quantify. Another reason is that purchasing decisions are quite important, and the system might not have the full information for us to put actual money in its hands. For instance, although Amazon knows what books I have bought from its site, the company has no knowledge of books I have acquired from other shops, and thus if I gave the system authority to make purchases I might end up with a book that I like—but already have on my shelves.

But there are also occasions when it makes sense to let the system act completely on the user's behalf, when the information is good enough and—most crucial—the margin for error is higher, and when a decision does not necessarily lead to a cost for the user. For instance, this method works well with streaming music services, where the user pays a monthly fee or the experience is subsidized by advertisement. Here the decision as to which song to play next does not cost the user any money, and it is easy for the user to skip over a track if it does not work. Companies such as Last.fm and Pandora have been very successful in creating personalized listening experiences based on their users' tastes, literally creating hundreds of thousands virtual radio stations with a target audience of one. Last.fm uses the collaborative filtering approach, letting users rate or "scrobble" music as they are listening to it, creating personal recommendations based on what other users have enjoyed.

Pandora, on the other hand, uses an advanced music recommendation engine developed by the Music Genome project, which was founded in 2000. Unlike methods based on user behaviors, like collaborative filtering, this system tries to understand the essence of music on a fundamental level. The developers first classified a large corpus of music according to a number of characteristics they called "genes." This includes factors such as instrumentation, tempo, vocalization, and lyrics. Based on this information, it becomes possible to create virtual radio stations that play music from many different artists that share specific musical characteristics.

One thing that the Music Genome approach fails to take into account, however, is the complex web of meaning that surrounds music and other cultural expression. Even though two artists may have the same characteristics based purely on how they sound, their cultural connotations and value for users might be completely different. Often, our social circles, friends, and aspirations will influence music choices as much or more as the parameters identified by the Music Genome project. Furthermore, music is often experienced in social situations with other people, such as at concerts and DJ parties, as well as when using portable players while moving from place to place, or when listening together at the office or with friends. New technology is creating completely new situations for enjoying, discussing, and sharing music, whether through peer-to-peer Internet services, commercial recommendation systems, or collaborative music playing such as Turntable.fm.

Case Study: Proactive Music Sharing with Push!Music

Inspired by this idea of music sharing, around 2005 my group started to think about how we could bring the idea of proactivity and recommendation in the context of music out into the real world. An obvious area to apply this concept would be portable music. The Apple iPod and other high-capacity music players had become available, which let people carry large parts of their music collections with them. But even though you could listen to your own music anywhere, in any situation, and among other people, there was no way to share the experience or to get inspiration from what other people were listening to. A few research systems had already approached the concept of getting music from nearby listeners by letting you listen to what other people were hearing, synchronously and in real time. For instance, *tunA* from Medialab Europe let you "tune in" to what nearby users were listening to on their portable devices, much like listening to a super-personalized and shared radio station. *SoundPryer* from the Interactive Institute performed the same function but in the context of car stereos. However, we wanted to make the experience more advanced and apply principles of recommendation systems to your entire music collection. To do this, we took inspiration from the concept of collaborative sharing, autonomous agents, and the idea of musical "genes" as popularized by Pandora.

First, let's imagine that rather than just being passive files, each song on your portable music player actually has some information about itself. It might, for instance, be aware of how often you have played it, what the other songs on the player are, and how often they get played. Then further imagine that the files can use the wireless network to peek into other portable music players around you. Each song could find out if there are other songs like it on other nearby players and then determine if it would have a higher or lower chance of being played and appreciated in the environment of other people's music collections. Finally, imagine that every song has the authority to proactively move between wirelessly connected players in order to find the environment that suits it best. Thus, every song on every music player would constantly look around to see if it could find an environment (i.e., another device) where its chances of being played are higher. The practical implications would be that both the content and the playlists of your own player would change depending on other music available nearby. Suddenly, as you are walking down the street, you might find that a song has literally jumped onto your player from a passerby and aligned itself in your listening queue! Similarly, after coming home from a party or concert, you might find your player loaded with dozens of new songs from people you had passed during the night. We called the idea of music files with a mind of their own *media agents*.

The system, which was developed by my Ph.D. students Mattias Jacobsson and Mattias Rost, was called *Push!Music*. Because this was before the iPod Touch and other Wi-Fi–capable portable music players, it was implemented on Pocket PC devices. As its primary function, Push!Music was intended to replace the user's regular music player, while incorporating the automatic recommendations outlined earlier. At first sight, the main difference from an ordinary music player was that the system listed the user names of other nearby people. But as users listened to music during their daily activities, the system would observe which songs were played most often and which were skipped over, and it would analyze clusters of the different types of

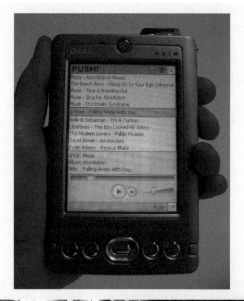

Figures 9-1–9-2

The Push!Music *system automatically shares music between portable music players when they are close by—even if the owners are not aware of what is being shared and who the music is coming from! (Images courtesy of Viktoria Institute)*

music in the collection. When other players came within radio range (determining user co-location much like the principle of the original Hummingbird), the systems would connect and start to compare notes. If there were songs that were likely to be appreciated and played on another player, they would copy themselves over and appear as upcoming titles in the current listening cue. (The original idea of songs actually *moving* from one player to another was considered too controversial—after all, even though it is an interesting thought, users probably did not want to find that some of their own music had abandoned them just because they did not play it often enough!)

Before producing a finished system and performing user studies, we had also performed some user interviews to find out what people enjoyed about playing music on the go and what they would value when it came to music recommendations. Apart from the expected results of wishing to find new music for themselves, it turned out that many people also enjoyed the act of giving out recommendations. In doing so, you can assert your own taste and have the pleasure of giving somebody else valuable information. To acknowledge this, the system included a function to send, or "push," songs to nearby users. These songs would copy over to the device and appear in the playlist just as automatically recommended songs did. This function could be used in two ways. You could collaboratively send somebody a song, typically someone you already knew and were sitting next to as you were sharing, similar to a sort of hyper-local file sharing or messaging system. Alternatively, you could send the song to any of the user names on your list of nearby people, even if you did not know their real-world identity, effectively recommending music by subterfuge. Thus, we now had a system where you would get music recommendations not from some abstract system handling masses of anonymous user data on the Internet, but from the people you passed on the street, sat next to at work, or shared a bus with. Some recommendations would be actively sent directly between users, whereas others were calculated and performed by the system automatically.

We then wanted to see how the system worked in practice. As mentioned, this was before capable networked music players and smartphones were available, and therefore we had to limit the user study to the number of devices that were available. Although this might mean that it would be difficult to create the kind of serendipity we hoped for—where songs would be shared between strangers in all kinds of situations—we hoped to design the studies in such a way that both friends and strangers would have the chance to exchange music. We also wanted the usage to be as realistic as possible, not in limited laboratory situations but in natural environments and over extended periods of time. However, because this software was experimental and under development, running on cutting-edge hardware with its own bugs in the operating systems, this also meant that researchers had to be on hand to help the test subjects with technical problems that would arise during the extended testing phase. Still, as we learned from other prototyping examples, putting the concept out into the real world generated a lot of insights that would otherwise not have been found.

My Ph.D. student Maria Håkansson performed several extended studies of the system during its various phases of development, with assistance from the developers. In the final and most extensive one,

10 students at our local university used the system for two weeks. The user groups were carefully composed so that some of them knew each other from before, whereas others were strangers. Furthermore, they were culled from a limited number of classes with fixed lecture hours, so that even the strangers would spend some time at the campus at the same time periods. We knew that all of the students used the same study areas, and thus they would be there working, even during off-lecture hours. To avoid questions of copyright, we let the users preload their devices with legally obtained music and took advantage of the fact that Swedish law allows for the sharing of digital music files in limited groups. Our hope with the study was to show that the Push!Music system provided recommendations that not only expanded the users' musical horizons but were qualitatively different from existing Internet-based systems. We were curious about how music would spread in the system, and how people would react to the self-directed media agents. Finally, as an indirect effect, we hypothesized that as users were sharing music with others in the surroundings, they would become more aware of the people around them, and we were keen to see if they took advantage of the possibility of initiating social contact outside of that mediated by the software.

The results of this study were both illuminating and surprising. First of all, the subjects all agreed that sharing with Push!Music was different from ordinary music listening. For the most part, it seemed they enjoyed getting new and unexpected music on their devices. They thought it was more "exciting" and felt "more alive" to know that the songs came from actual people around them, rather than some anonymous node in a distant network. This confirmed our notion that sharing with real, local people would provide a different experience than other methods. The users would also devise various strategies to play around with the system. For instance, they would try to listen to certain songs in order to force a particular recommendation, and they would send out-of-place and inappropriate songs as pranks to confuse or embarrass other users. Overall, despite some technical difficulties, we could see how the system placed users in the middle of a physically located discourse of music listening and recommendations that was unlike that provided by any online system at the time.

However, we also found that the social connections did not expand outside the system, as we had hypothesized. This was not for lack of interest; there was a lot of speculation going on as to exactly whom the other users in the study might be (apart from the ones the subjects knew personally). As mentioned, the other users would pop up as user names on the screen, but there was no way to connect this information with the actual people in the vicinity. There were even instances when users had observed somebody else with the signature handheld computers used in the study, listening to music, but still would not approach them to confirm whether this was a study participant. Cultural differences may have played a part in this behavior;

Swedes are less used to striking up conversations with strangers than are, for instance, North Americans. But these were socially active university students, and shyness can only have been part of the reason. Instead, what we had failed to do was to provide any obvious means for the connection provided by the system to jump over the border from virtual to real. It might have helped to include some kind of message-passing system, or even the simple "poke," now popularized by Facebook and other social networks.

This lack of feedback or back channels also contributed to a sense of awkwardness during sharing. Although there was the possibility of sending songs to other users, there was no way to indicate whether the recommendation was appreciated. This made users more reluctant to send songs, because they did not know if the new music would be considered an intrusion. It turned out that the songs were treated as a kind of "gift," much like SMS messages are considered among groups of teenagers, as was shown in studies by Microsoft researcher Alex Taylor. But it is difficult and socially awkward to give a gift to somebody you don't know! Even more pronounced is the fact that as you receive a gift, convention dictates that you reciprocate with another gift, or at least thank the giver. We had no such provision in the system, and thus we unnecessarily limited the amount of music that was passed between users.

Finally, the most surprising result came out of the proactivity of the media agents. Although it was socially awkward to manually send songs to a stranger, sharing through the automatic means presented no such qualms—it simply happened. Furthermore, it did not present the same problems or worries that the receiver would not appreciate the music, because after all as one respondent said, "the computer did it," not he. Thus, these automatically shared songs had all the advantages of getting new and varied music from real people around you, but at the same time they did not carry the social connotations of an actual "gift," and thus did not present the associated problems of reciprocations. When it came to contact between the users, it is possible that if we had included back channels, these automatic recommendations could have also generated social interactions but this was not something we had the opportunity to test.

With Push!Music, we thus found that we could use the property of proactivity in digital products in an unexpected way. Rather than just serving as a way to improve peoples' music listening experience, as it is used in most recommendation systems, the automatic features also turned out to be a successful social "alibi" for media sharing. Sometimes it can apparently help to turn over sensitive, and potentially even socially awkward, decisions to software, as long as the decisions are not critical and are taken in good spirit. For future media sharing systems, the lessons from Push!Music are that this kind of social sharing is not just a matter of getting the media you want; it can be enhanced by adding a social component to fine-tune the interactions, and possibly even open up the opportunity for deeper connections. After all, many people have gone on to real-world connections after first meeting on Internet discussion boards and having text discussions about literature, movies, music, and many other topics. Moving that experience out into the real world is a tantalizing prospect, but not as straightforward as it first might seem—and in some cases, a little push from an agent can probably help!

The idea of local media sharing has continued to be developed by several companies after Push!Music. For instance, in late 2006 Microsoft released its first portable music player, called *Zune*. This product had the feature of sending (or as the company called it, "squirting") songs to other users through a local wireless network, much like the active sharing method in Push!Music. However, as with Push!Music, there were no back channels or other means for additional communication. The product flopped, never reaching enough critical mass for people to take advantage of serendipitous sharing, and the Zune hardware was eventually discontinued in early 2011, although the trademark lives on as a music and movie service for Microsoft's Xbox. Similarly, the Bump software mentioned earlier now allows users to transfer music files as well as photos and other content by bumping their phones together, which allows for direct sharing, but not the surreptitious variant afforded by Zune and Push!Music. (To avoid copyright issues, commercial systems like Zune and Bump usually impose limitations on how many times a song can be listened to after it has been shared, or they only allow the sharing of links to streaming versions.)

The idea of media agents is not limited to music. In a follow-up project presented in 2006, *Push!Photo*, we transferred the concept to photo files. We also introduced new parameters to the sharing structure. The intention was to use factors such as when a photo was taken, at which location, and with what other people to inform what files would be transferred. For instance, if a group of friends all attended the same party, they would be taking a lot of pictures individually. However, nobody would have access to all the pictures from the event. But as they encounter each other later during the week, the photos—being media agents—would spread on different devices and would find that they had all been taken in the same time frame, at the same location, and with the same group of people. Thus, they could start spreading over the other devices, so that in time, everybody would have access to the photos. You could even imagine that if there were a person who was normally part of this social circle but didn't attend this particular event, he or she would also get access to the photos. Of course, because photos are much more personal than music files, this raises privacy issues that must be dealt with—or you might have photos appear in places where you definitely would not want them! The system was built and demonstrated to work technically, but because the availability of the technology (expensive handheld computers) was limited, we were never able to see it in full use.

Today, things are different—Push!Music, Push!Photo, and other media sharing applications could be implemented as apps on a variety of smartphone platforms and distributed easily, and a number of companies have launched similar media sharing apps for mobiles. For instance, in 2011 the Silicon Valley startup *Color* launched a system for media sharing in local, personal networks, which works much like the Push!Photo prototype but uses location sensing and the Internet instead of direct connections between the devices (as was the case with our applications and Microsoft's Zune). In its basic form, Color allows you to see and collect all the photos taken around you at the same time. The company claims the distance is 100 feet, about 30 meters, although the real distance will depend on the accuracy of the location sensing. (The company is complementing the regular location data with sensors fusion, including the microphone and ambient light, to determine if users are at the same place.) These photos can be collected and browsed, creating a sort of virtual history of images from places where you and others have used the application. Color also introduces what the company calls an "Elastic Network," people who you are socially connected with but who might not be at the same location, which is established on the fly through your interactions. You can browse the photos that they are creating, thus achieving an effect that is similar to Push!Photo, where you might be able to see party photos taken by your friends even if you did not attend the party yourself. The company has also built in some back channel capability, so that you can actually introduce yourself to other people in the network. Ultimately, the company hopes to provide value by further developing the algorithms that facilitate local sharing and networking, possibly to serve ultra-targeted advertisements.

But even though proactivity in digital products can be useful in certain situations, there is a fine line to walk, especially when it comes to personal data. In the previous chapter, we saw how sensors can pinpoint the location and context of everything from cups and shelves to people. In fact, location tracking is one of the most complicated issues affecting digital products, although it is sometimes naively treated. Even as far back as the experiments with the Active Badges by Olivetti and Xerox PARC, attempts at producing location tracking technology have been treated with suspicion. In one presentation, Roy Want, one of the developers of the Active Badge, explained how Xerox originally called the press to demonstrate the new technology. The researchers had been anticipating how the media would extol the virtues of knowing the position of every employee of the lab and sharing the useful functionality built on top of it. However, the press reaction was quite different. They saw a *1984*-esque instrument for surveillance and control. The 1992 New York Times headline was typical, "Orwellian Dream Come True: A Badge That Pinpoints You," as was Business Week's "Big Brother,

Pinned to Your Chest." Clearly, something had gone awry in communicating the bold new vision of location awareness—or perhaps the concept is just plain creepy.

The fact is that location tracking happens to most of us all the time, whether we like it or not. The location of every cell phone is constantly tracked through the carrier's network, and if your contract is tied to your name, it is easy to find out where you are—or have been. Authorities of many countries often use this capability to, for instance, put together evidence against suspected criminals. But in this case, the information is highly safe-guarded and only given out based on a court order or other legal decisions. Other tracking information is not necessarily so well guarded. As we already mentioned, when you use Google Maps or some other mobile map applica-tions, the company will typically take your global positioning system (GPS) position, if available, and combine that with data of nearby cell towers and Wi-Fi stations in order to improve their location database. Google also uses information from Google Maps usage to calculate congestion on highways. By collecting data from many users, they can derive the speed and location of cars on the road, thus creating a real-time map of congestion. At present, all of these data are sent anonymously, but there is, in principle, nothing to stop Google from getting your identity along with the data, something that would, of course, greatly help the company to refine its targeted advertising system.

A large part of the problem with location tracking lies in the fact that it is often done without the user being aware of it, or being able to control it. It does not necessarily have to be so, and different technologies afford differ-ent types of tracking. For instance, the Hummingbird (discussed in the previ-ous chapter), which detected the radio signals of other Hummingbirds nearby, did not leave any persistent traces of the user's location. It was also fully symmetrical; only if I know your location will you know mine. Unlike most location-based systems including the Active Badge, GPS, cell tower triangula-tion, and so on, it never provided an absolute position—only one relative to other nearby users. However, this technology also has many drawbacks, includ-ing battery life, imprecise accuracy, and lack of critical mass. Today it makes much more sense to solve the problem of finding out who is nearby by using the absolute location provided by smartphones, but this might also mean giv-ing up a certain amount of privacy.

Although many services now use so-called check-ins to let users share their current position, the most natural and easy way of approaching location seems to be to have your location constantly updated in the background, as you move. Then it would be easy to share it with your friends and family, provide on-the-fly information and alerts, and, of course, that ultimate location-based thrill (at least for the commercial actors), provide place-based advertisement and deals. Technically, there are many different ways of achieving this. The

Active Badge solved it by having a custom-built local infrastructure that picked up the signal from the badges and communicated this to a central server. (This is somewhat analogous to using the phone network for location, as detailed later.) The Hummingbird, on the other hand, did not provide a real location but instead relied on constant radio contact between individual devices to determine if two users were near each other. Some current smartphone services, such as Germany's Aki-Aki, use the same principles by connecting to other devices through Bluetooth radio. Nintendo's portable game system, DS, has similar provisions for finding other users through radio contact. However, constantly scanning for other users with radio is an energy-consuming approach and has currently not gained wider traction, although new hardware and communication standards may well make it more feasible in the future.

For modern smartphones, there are two obvious ways to gather continuously updated location information: through the phone network or the device itself. In the first case, used, for instance, by U.S.-based service Loopt, the system finds your location based on the network operator's knowledge of which wireless base station the phone is connected to (similar to when your phone finds its position by triangulating the signal from nearby base stations). However, because location is sensitive, this requires an agreement to access the location information from the operator; in Loopt's case, major U.S. phone companies such as AT&T provide this information (based on the end user's consent). The advantage with this approach is that the user's location is constantly tracked without actually using the phone's resources, such as the GPS and network connections, thus not draining the battery. The main problem is that because all operators have different ways of providing location information, and often charge for the privilege to boot, it is not certain that your particular location is even accessible, meaning that it requires a complex set of deals with national and international carriers to provide true critical mass.

The other approach is to use the phone's own location sensors, including GPS, GSM triangulation, and Wi-Fi, as we discussed in the previous chapter. Here, a piece of software runs in the background of the phone at all times. This has the advantage that no deal with operators is required—every phone can look up its own location and send it to a central server for further processing. The location provided by a modern smartphone is also typically more accurate than what the operators can find out. The disadvantage is that it requires the device to run software constantly in the background (software that also uses the phone's location sensors) and send updated information through the network, both of which can be a serious drain on battery life. However, with new optimization techniques, this is not so much of an issue; for instance, it is possible to use less power-consuming sensors on the phone, such as the accelerometer, to determine if the user has actually moved, which makes it possible to only update the location when it is actually needed.

Google Latitude is one example of a service that uses this on-device method to provide constantly updated location information.

In other words, technically, there is nothing stopping a system from keeping track of you and sharing this information with other parties, be they your friends, employers, or advertisers. But location is a much more sensitive issue than taste in music or the other examples we discussed before! In fact, if we start looking at the issue of location sharing in digital products, it really cuts to the core of how much proactivity is acceptable in a digital product.

In the research world, continuous tracking has been the norm in virtually all location-sharing systems ever since the Active Badge and the Hummingbird. One reason is because this allows applications to be more proactive. Compared to the check-in model, where the user only declares her position when she chooses, continuous tracking provides both much more accurate and more timely location information. This in turn makes it possible to constantly monitor the user's relationship to other points of interest and provide useful information on the go. It also allows for people to monitor the location of others, whether for peace of mind, social awareness, or practical considerations. But managing the privacy in such systems has turned out to be very complicated.

Case Study: To Share or Not to Share

A study presented in 2011 by Clara Mancini and a group of researchers at the Open University offers a typical example of the concerns many have about location tracking and privacy. They studied two family groups who used a location tracking system for three weeks. The system tracked each user continuously and showed the whereabouts of the other members in the extended family on a map. Although some of the users got a sense of security from knowing the whereabouts of their children, for instance, even this short test seems to often have been an uncomfortable experience. Like with many similar systems, participants felt conflicted on how much it was acceptable to look up the position of others and felt an uneasiness about how their own position was interpreted. The researchers found that the tracking technology reduces an important *margin of tacit misunderstanding*—that is, how much leeway we give others in acting out their own action. It also created a sense of over-accountability and made the participants feel it necessary to explain even innocuous actions for fear of misunderstandings. But the most interesting result was that even though the system had tried to prevent this reluctance by introducing a set of privacy controls, the controls provided even more conflict! After all, if your children were suddenly to turn off the automatic tracking, wouldn't that make you *even more* worried and suspicious, and wouldn't you then expect even more of an explanation from them when they did turn up? Thus, the practical use of controls that limited the effects of the tracking turned out to cause conflict, because it opened up the opportunity for even more misunderstandings.

Compare this with the check-in model, which is used in Foursquare, Gowalla, Facebook Places, and many other location-based systems. Here, the user actively declares when he is at a certain place, or "venue." This is done by first letting the system find the most likely venues in the vicinity of the user's physical location. Then he chooses the best match from a list (although as we saw in the previous chapter, it is also possible to photograph a barcode or even the place itself) and "checks in." This approach, of course, has a distinct disadvantage: If I don't check, the system does not know where I am! Thus, systems based on the check-in model cannot automatically alert users of points of interest, tips, deals, other users, and so on. In fact, compared to the continuous location tracking model, check-in based systems seem inadequate in providing relevant information. Yet, from the current usage trends, they are vastly more popular than continuous tracking systems.

One reason is because, as we already noted, current location technology is simply not good enough to disambiguate between different nearby places—in fact, most of these systems do not even have a sense of vertical direction! Thus, it is often technically impossible to automatically determine whether you are in a coffee shop or in the hairdressing salon next door. This problem led to the practice of letting users choose the place they are at manually from a set of likely candidates.

But a more complex issue has to do with what actually constitutes a "place." As Steve Harrison and Paul Dourish, then researchers at Xerox PARC and EuroPARC, noted, a "place" is much more than a "space"—it is not just a set of geographical coordinates, but has semantic meaning. A space turns into a place depending on how it is used. This meaning is very difficult for an automatic system to determine. Here, the fact that users can create their own names for venues in the popular check-in systems has lead to instances of use that no automatic system would allow. For example, during a heat wave in New York in 2010, a user created the Foursquare venue *Heatpocalypse NY*. This "virtual venue" received 9,426 check-ins! This is obviously not a real place in the physical world, but rather an expression of the user's feeling or state of mind, and something that struck a note with many other users during this particular period. Foursquare users have also created many other "non-places," such as a freeway traffic jam, or "In your pants"! This kind of openness to new definitions of places gives users of these systems the opportunity to define their own world, rather than have it mechanically tracked by a computer.

So why do people check in in the first place? In a study performed in 2010, Henriette Cramer in my group interviewed 20 users of check-in services and complemented this with surveys of another 47. She found that there were many reasons to check in, and some of them did not have anything to do with sharing location at all! When it came to "virtual" venues such as those discussed earlier, one interviewee said, "Because it is an imaginary place, as opposed to a 'venue,' I want to express myself in terms of place, not just create a history of my consumer behavior." There were also other reasons, such as game aspects (Foursquare lets users collect points for various types of check-ins and become "mayors" at places where they check in the most), getting access to deals and coupons, creating a personal history of where the user had been, and so on.

Most interestingly, the study showed how the check-in model changes location from being a property—something you *have*—to a performance—something you *do*. This is significant, not least because it elegantly solves many of the privacy issues associated with automatic tracking. You can choose to check in whenever you feel like it, but you can also ignore it without anybody taking much notice, thus declaring your position only when you feel it is validated by the situation. Much like Facebook, Twitter, and other social media services let us express ourselves in a manner we choose, the check-in model lets us declare our location for an audience—real or imagined. (Josh Williams, the CEO of the popular location service Gowalla, even said that "Check-ins are the status updates of location.") Thus, the purpose of a location-sharing system becomes not to slavishly tell other people where we are but to create a public identity through our actions.

Ultimately, proactive digital products must walk a fine line between doing too little and doing too much. The experiences from Push!Music showed how getting recommendations from an automatic system let users feel less uncomfortable about sharing music with people around them. On the other hand, automatic location tracking puts users in a complex position where they worry about infringing on others' privacy and feel the need to be accountable for their actions and at the same time have little recourse in the privacy mechanisms provided, because these create even more anxiety! The solution may lie somewhere in between, where the check-in models of Foursquare et al. allow the user to be creative and create her or his own identity yet provide both social and commercial opportunities for service providers to capitalize on. One thing is clear, however: the proactive digital product that is as annoying and inappropriate as Microsoft's Office Assistant will not have a long shelf life!

At this point, we have looked at the various properties that make up a potential digital product, as well as methods that can be used to create new product concepts. In the next and final chapter, we will put it all together by looking at past and current technology trends as well as taking a glimpse at the future of digital products.

CHAPTER 10

CREATING DIGITAL PRODUCTS: MASHING IT UP AND GETTING IT OUT THERE

At this point, we have made a journey through both the innovation processes and the technical properties of digital products. We have seen how there are systematic ways to ground innovation in both technology and human needs, how we can generate ideas that go outside the box, and how we can use the power of prototyping and trying out potential concepts in order to get essential feedback from real users. In the examples, we have also seen several ways that digital products have gone beyond being merely information processing machines and have become integrated in the real world in various ways, through metaphors as well as direct integration with everyday artifacts. We have seen how computation can augment real-world objects (such as coffee cups!) as well as the human senses. We have also seen various ways of interacting, both directly (such as scanning a barcode) and indirectly (for instance, by having sensors read and react based on the context). Digital products can both transform existing activities (such as photography) and create shared spaces that afford entirely new ones (such as the collaborative games). Ultimately, we can see how the focus in developing innovative digital products has gone from a search for new interfaces to information processing, and from being the creation of new digital artifacts to being the creation of new activities, in which the digital technology is a facilitator rather than the end goal.

But let's get back to the properties of digital products: information processing, interaction, networking, sensing, and proactivity. In various examples, we have seen how they have served as the jump-off point for a number of novel ideas, some of which are already found in products used by millions, others which may never leave the research lab. Going through the properties in turn, information processing continues to be fundamental for all digital products. However, this does not mean that every digital product has to be doing the computation by itself! As we saw, technologies like barcodes and radio frequency identification (RFID) tags can enable even "dumb" objects to be part of a computational system, and with advanced image recognition techniques, even tags are becoming unnecessary. Thus, to equate digital products with a computer in every device—the paradigm of ubiquitous computing—is starting to look like a fallacy. Instead, a few devices, including smartphones and pads, are capable of recognizing and working with data from the environment. But even these devices will not be doing most of the work; more and more, computation is offloaded to the "cloud," which means that it is performed by centralized servers rather than on any particular device. Most web services, from Facebook to Google Docs, already function in this way. With faster and more pervasive networks, it makes sense to store most data in a central and secure location rather than on a particular memory chip. This also means that services will be accessible through a multitude of devices and not tied to any particular hardware instance.

Interaction is by now almost as fundamental as information processing. However, in human-computer interaction, the field that has spent the most effort in understanding interaction with digital products, there is a necessary and ongoing move from focusing on traditional screen-based systems to focusing on interaction that is situated in the "real" world. With more computing services being done on mobile devices, such as phones and pads, this development is accelerating. However, again it is a fallacy to believe that "interaction in the world" is the same as interaction without a screen. At present, a screen is still the most expressive and flexible output mechanism available, and it can be integrated in the physical environment in many different ways. Furthermore, touch technologies are making screens increasingly available for direct input, and technologies such as electronic ink are making the screen more affordable and suitable for embedding in new types of objects. As we saw with many of the examples in the chapter on interaction, simply situating a screen in new physical circumstances can radically change how we interact with it and create entirely new usage patterns.

At the same time, although screens are currently probably the most well-developed and understood interaction technology, we may soon start to see new input and output paradigms making it into the mainstream. Research in tangible and embedded interaction have already produced many inventions that may be where we see the true innovation in interaction happening in the future, especially as new prototyping and manufacturing methods become available. However, although the screen is a sort of Swiss army knife that can accommodate many different digital products, tangible interfaces so far have had a hard time presenting general-purpose interaction techniques. Perhaps the future for tangible interaction lies in specialized, low-cost devices, along the lines of the various health monitoring sensors that have been recently introduced (e.g., Fitbit and Nike+). As we have seen, a low-cost tag can transform an object into a digital product, and this can open up new interaction paradigms.

With literally every computer and smartphone connected to the Internet, networking is also often taken for granted in digital products. However, as we saw in this chapter, sometimes objects can be part of a network without actually communicating directly among themselves. The "Internet of Things" is as much or more about making the real world available for information processing as it is to put a networking chip in every device. In fact, because of the cost issues, it may be a long time before digital products have true, always-on networking. There are many innovations that use workarounds to provide more powerful networking than a product itself can muster. For instance, the Nike+ step counter is only connected to the Internet after each run to calculate results; by not including full-blown networking capability, the cost and battery life has been kept down to a reasonable level, thus making the product practical for the average runner. Similarly, Fitbit is also a technically simple step counter that gets most of its value from the aggregation and processing that is done after the data are collected. In the future, as new technologies such as printed electronics make networking hardware cheaper and less energy consuming, we may see more real-time networking between objects.

Sensing is already a major factor in many digital products, but again it may not be necessary to distribute a sensor in every device. Currently, the most powerful consumer sensing device is the smartphone, which typically comes with a location awareness function, an accelerometer, a microphone, and a camera. However, with its roots as a personal communication device, current phones are not yet fully equipped to be sensing constantly. There are already successful experiments with background sensing on phones—for instance, for location awareness. By cleverly using hardware such as the accelerometer to "wake up" a phone as the user moves (and presumably changes location), rather than having it report its location constantly, it is possible to give updated location and other context information without unnecessarily draining the batteries. As more compelling applications come along, and more application programming interfaces (APIs) become available, this area will continue to grow. Direct sensing, such as with the camera, is already on the verge of becoming a major source of innovation, with image-recognition systems such as Google Goggles giving a tantalizing glimpse of where these technologies will take us very soon. When it comes to sensors distributed in the environment, the technology is not yet small or cost effective enough to do this on the grand scale envisioned by, for instance, the furniture assembly system. But as the cost and energy consumption of simple components like accelerometers and light sensors continues to go down, we may see them embedded in everyday objects soon.

Finally, proactivity is in some way the newest, and also the least understood, of the properties of digital products. Although recommendation systems and intelligent agents have proven themselves more than useful for pure information processing tasks such as finding a good movie or sorting out spam e-mails, the impact on applications connected to the real world is still limited. Partly this has to do with the capabilities of existing sensors and the associated algorithms used to process the data. Most sensors are still too unreliable to correctly recognize human activities, and the algorithms need much more development to be able to correctly identify complex situations. Another issue is that even in cases where sensing is fairly reliable, such as location detection, the effects of acting proactively (for instance, with a system revealing a user's position) can be both hard to understand and "creepy," in the sense that they are an unwanted invasion of privacy. But we also saw that proactivity can be a way of giving an "alibi" in awkward situations, such as music sharing. Balancing the effects of proactivity with user control is an important challenge that must be addressed before such systems can become truly mass market.

When it comes to generating new ideas, a lot of the power of digital products comes from the combination of these properties. As we saw, beyond pure information processing, it is almost impossible to separate out any single property and build a meaningful digital product. Sensors need to network to share interesting data; proactive systems need to be able to interact with users; and so on. We can imagine the properties as capabilities that can be combined and associated at will. What happens if you add a new type of sensor to an interactive display? If you network the data from several users? And then if you let the system in the background do information processing on the results and proactively suggest new courses of action? Thinking like this, new digital product concepts can emerge out of mix-and-match combinations much like with the bootlegging technique described in Chapter 4.

That said, another way of seeing digital products is from the perspective of *infrastructure*. By this I mean that given today's networks, hardware, and software capabilities, it is possible to do things with a much higher efficiency and on a completely different scale than before. Twenty or even ten years ago, achieving many of the things described in this book was very difficult. To sense somebody's position, you would have had to build a specialized device, at a high cost and with little chance of distributing it beyond a lab setting. Today, complex location-based services can be included in the software on any smartphone. Similarly, to use networking between devices used to require extensive implementation, and even then it usually did not function properly. Now, it is possible for any smartphone or tablet device to open up an Internet connection just about anywhere in the world and share data, not just locally but with any service. Sensors that were previously expensive and rare, such as accelerometers, can now be found in cheap accessories like Nintendo's *Wiimote* game controller. Even more impressively, Microsoft's *Kinect* game controller includes hardware for visual gesture recognition that would have cost tens or hundreds of thousands of dollars a few years ago. Algorithms for image recognition, collaborative filtering, and other complex information processing tasks are now readily available for licensing, free, or at a small charge. Completely new forms of infrastructures are also springing into place, like the social graphs provided by social networks like Facebook and Twitter. Building on all of this, it is becoming possible for small teams and startups to do the same things as was previously the domain of multimillion-dollar funded government and industry research labs. Ultimately this means there has been a democratization of the invention and capitalization of digital products, the long-ranging effects of which we have barely seen yet.

Another aspect that is changing rapidly is the ability to prototype digital products in hardware. Perhaps the best-known example is the Arduino system, which is widely used in education to create interactive installations. A similar but in some ways even more capable system is Microsoft's *Gadgeteer*, which started as a research project at Microsoft Research Cambridge by Nicolas Villar, Steve Hodges, and James Scott, and was released commercially in 2011. Much like Arduino, Gadgeteer allows the developer to easily snap together different components, like sensors and actuators, and write software that uses the many supplied libraries and APIs to get a prototype up and running quickly. However, Gadgeteer adds tight integration with 3D printing, the technology that allows the literal printing of real-world objects. There are a number of systems for 3D printing, and some can produce sturdy end results, more than enough to use in a prototype. Gadgeteer takes advantage of this by integrating the assembly of electronic components with software that also lets users design the physical shape of their prototypes.

For instance, if you want to make an actuated birdhouse, where a light sensor is set to trigger a camera to take a photo every time a bird enters, you can first put together the components and write the required software in Gadgeteer. This will give you the digital function of your birdhouse, but not the actual house. For this, you can then go into the compatible computer-aided design (CAD) software and design the building blocks of a birdhouse, complete with predetermined holes to fit the camera, sensor, and central processor. The components can then be printed out using 3D technology, assembled together with the electronic parts, and result in a finished prototype ready for some birds to move in. Impressively, with Gadgeteer this whole construction process can be completed in days rather than weeks or months, even taking into account the hours needed for the slow process of producing the actual printouts.

Although this technology is still out of reach for most consumers, there may be a time when 3D printer technology has gone down in price in the same way that ordinary laser printing already has. When this happens, it may become possible to construct or download plans for just about any digital product, print out the physical parts, and assemble it together with the required hardware and software—a "desktop publishing" revolution for the physical world, so to speak. An exciting example is the *RepRap* project, which has the goal to produce a low-cost, do-it-yourself, 3D printer that has the capacity to print many of the parts required for constructing another instance of itself! In this spirit, all the designs produced in the project are released as open source and available for others to use. Based on the success of the RepRap, a commercial company has also been formed, MakerBot, which produces open source hardware and sells an affordable 3D printer, the *Thing-O-Matic.*

The access to inexpensive physical prototyping and electronics is leading to a revolution in do-it-yourself (DIY) hardware, much like the availability of home computers created a boom in amateur software hacking in the 1980s. Although electronics used to be the domain of experts and serious hobbyists, the availability of platforms such as the Arduino is democratizing hardware hacking and exposing it to entirely new demographic groups. For instance, Leah Buechley at Massachusetts Institute of Technology (MIT) created the *Lilypad Arduino,* which is a microcontroller board specifically designed to be sewn into textiles—for instance, to create digitally augmented clothes. This kind of platform could make it easier to interest groups who are not normally exposed to electronics, such as young girls. In another example of unorthodox hardware hacking, Sweden's *Syntjuntan* is a female artist collective that performs music on instruments that they have sewn themselves using textile-based components. They are also inviting interested amateur hackers (both male and female) to synthesizer sewing parties—"syntjuntor"—thus bringing a traditional women's activity, the sewing club (or "syjunta" in Swedish) into the world of digital products.

There is also an ongoing revolution in software-based digital products, thanks to emerging technologies for the mobile web. With HTML 5, the new HyperText Markup Language standard for creating web pages that is currently being formulated, the links between web content and hardware are becoming much stronger. Together with server-side software, HTML 5 will let web services tie in directly to resources that were previously only accessible to native apps. For instance, it is already possible for a web service to determine the location of a user by tapping into the built-in positioning capabilities of a phone or even a laptop. This means that when you open a web page on your device, the page can adapt to where you are—for instance, by showing the search results that are near you first. Other sensors are also being integrated in the standard, such as the accelerometer (making it possible to interact with web pages by moving the device) and even the camera (making visual input available). Furthermore, new standards also make it possible to use web services when you are not actually connected to the Internet, or even run them in the background while other processes take precedent. The significance of this capability is not so much the function itself—all this can already be done with the use of dedicated apps for the Android, iPhone, or other platforms—but that it is being folded into the web standard. Thus, rather than having to write

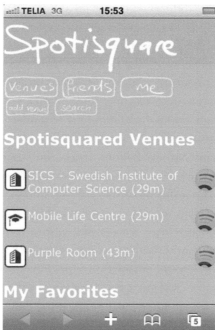

Figures 10-1–10-2

NearMe *and* SpotiSquare *are examples of* mobile mash-ups—*mobile web services that combine various online resources (e.g., Facebook social graphs, Foursquare venues, and Spotify music streaming) with the capabilities of mobile phones such as location awareness. They are not apps but instead run completely in the mobile web browser, taking advantage of the emerging HTML 5 standard. (Images courtesy of Mobile Life Centre)*

a location-aware app for each operating system, we can tap into the generalizability of the web and write web apps that take into account all the properties of digital products, yet are as easy to distribute as a single web address or URL. Rather than download and install an app, you simply visit the required web page.

Intrigued by this possibility, Ph.D. student Mattias Rost and I recently constructed a few examples of mobile web services that take location into account. For instance, with *NearMe*, it is possible to see the physical distance between you and your Facebook friends. All you do is visit the web page through your mobile browser and sign in with your Facebook identity; the page then takes your location from the phone, correlates it with other people who have visited the page, and returns a list of names ordered by the distance to you in meters. In essence, this service performs almost the same function as early location experiments such as the Hummingbird or the Active Badge, but with some crucial differences. First, whereas the earlier projects required specialized hardware that took the experts months to build and install, NearMe was programmed by a single programmer in a matter of days. Furthermore, there were a limited number of Hummingbird devices, produced at a high cost, which restricted the potential critical mass and uptake of the system to a handful of users. NearMe, on the other hand, is simply a web page—it can be shared as easily as sending a URL in an e-mail or posting it on a social network, and it works instantly on compatible browsers. It does not even make any difference if it is an iPhone, Android, or other type of phone, because HTML 5 is becoming standardized across all mobile browsers.

With these new web capabilities, it is easy to mix and match existing web services with the new sensors that are becoming available. This lead me to formulate the concept of *mobile mash-ups*—services that are created quickly and easily from existing components, yet perform functions that only a few years ago would have required extensive software and hardware development. A good example was created in my group by Henriette Cramer, Mattias Rost, and Nicolas Belloni. They combined the location-based service Foursquare (which we talked about previously) with the music streaming service *Spotify*. The result was *SpotiSquare*—a web service that does exactly what it sounds like: it gives you the capability to bind music to places. Remarkably, it was literally created over a weekend, with a fully functioning version ready on Monday morning. With SpotiSquare, you can create a Spotify music playlist and then tie it to a Foursquare venue. For instance, a café can create a playlist that everyone will get access to when checking in to the venue at Foursquare. You can have another for the office, for the local bar, for the supermarket, and so on. This creates a virtual location-based soundtrack. This kind of service has been tried many times in research, but always with specialized hardware and long development times—and virtually no critical mass. SpotiSquare, on the other hand, immediately gained several thousand users after the address was simply put on Twitter. This shows how mobile mash-ups are radically shortening the time between idea and usable product.

Of course, we cannot just look at the technology—innovation also has to be grounded in real-world use. Looking at the examples from this book, we can identify a number of ways to approach the design of digital products, which are sometimes orthogonal to the technical qualities. For starters, in the interface to the original desktop computer, and in most of the screen-based designs that followed for a number of years, it was common to *bring the real world to the digital*. Think of the trashcan icon and other metaphors in the original Xerox STAR interface, still used in computers today, or my Flip Zooming visualization that mimicked a stack of papers. However, the increased availability of input and output screens made it possible to *bring the digital to the real world*. For instance, the Mondrian bus display in the informative art project took information that was until then situated in the digital domain and placed it in the physical world. There are many other ways in which digital information can be brought into the real world, such as through augmented reality overlays.

Informative art is also an example of *augmenting real-world objects*, in this case a painting. Other examples of augmented real-world objects included the MediaCup, an ordinary coffee cup with added sensors, or the flat-pack furniture with built-in instructions. As sensor and display technology gets cheaper, we might continue to see more objects with added functions, such as the umbrella that tells you if it is likely to rain or the key that remembers if you locked your door (incidentally, both of these concepts have been launched as products, but so far they have not become successful). It has also become possible to *augment human senses* to detect actions and activities that are not normally available to our senses. The Active Badge was a first example of such "superpowers," letting users keep track of people in a building. Similarly, the Hummingbird would tell you when your friends were nearby, even if you could not see or hear them. With mobile phones we are now able to keep track of our friends on Foursquare, Facebook, and other location-based social media, and we can be informed about actions we normally would not know about.

When it comes to interacting with real-world objects, the Smart-Its Friends technique and the similar Bump application, as well as touching an RFID card to a reader or scanning a barcode, are examples of *direct actions on objects*. As more products become digitally enhanced, we will have to find interaction techniques that let us perform actions on them that are clear and obvious, even if the artifact does not have any buttons to press or a screen to give output. But we can also build in *implicit interactions*—for instance, when the furniture is being assembled and the progress is detected by sensors, or when the MediaCup (which does not require any conscious action on the user's part) divulges a great deal of information. Commercial examples include fitness sensors, like the Nike+, which record data simply by being placed in a suitable position on the body. Automatically updated location services offer another example, but as we noted earlier, these services also indicate the complexity of this approach; if everyday actions have consequences that users are unaware of, the users may become uneasy and find that their privacy has been invaded.

Another interesting opportunity is to *transform existing activities* with digital technology. For instance, the context camera took the normal activity of taking a photograph and added sensors and visual filters, thereby changing the way users approached the activity. Rather than just looking through the viewfinder, users also started to be more conscious about the sound, movement, and other factors in their environment. Similarly, the distributed Pac-Man game changed the way players thought about their computing devices. In addition to looking at the screen, they had to take into account the environment around them, as well as the very physical reality of other players. Finally, digital technologies can be used to create *shared spaces for interaction*, as shown in the Ubiquitous Graphics system, where the same image was available over multiple devices and displays. In a similar way, the Push!Music system connected a user's music collection with that of other users, so that songs literally started to move between the boundaries of the devices.

The preceding is, by necessity, a nonexhaustive list of potential design approaches, but each of them could be applied to digital products in many different domains. However, from these examples we can also see a more systematic trend in human-computer interaction (HCI) emerging. The original aim of HCI was to create *interfaces* to digital products, such as the windows-icons-mouse-pointer paradigms of the desktop computer. Here, the idea was literally that the "interface" was the mediator between the human and the machine, sitting in the middle with the "computer" on one side and the "user" on the other. By designing a better interface, the interaction with the data residing on the computer would become more efficient. However, as digital products become more diverse, this division has become increasingly meaningless. What is the "interface" to a product such as a smart shoe or coffee cup? Instead, there has been a trend toward creating *artifacts*, which are complete user experiences in themselves and where there is no clear division between computer and interface. For instance, the Hummingbird and the Informative Art display are self-contained devices where the "interface" (the hum of the Hummingbird, the changing hue and size of the abstract color fields) is inseparable from the artifact itself.

But as digital products become more integrated with everyday life, we go from designing artifacts to facilitating *activities* that are supported by digital products. This goes for many of the systems used as examples, from the context camera (photography) and Pac-Man Must Die! (gaming) to Push!Music (music sharing) and so on. In each of these cases, we envisioned an activity that users would engage in, and then we created the appropriate technology to make it happen. This does not mean that the process was in any case straightforward—it was still a case of using many different types of inspiration and grounding, combining and collecting ideas, and testing and evaluating prototypes. But rather than producing a particular physical or digital object, the end result would be an activity that engaged users without setting itself as the center of attention. This way of thinking—creating activities rather than interfaces or artifacts—also corresponds well to recent user study and design methods in HCI, which strive to put the context and the activities of users in the center of attention.

However, the nature of innovation is such that even the most novel inventions or well-grounded designs are only the seed of a true innovation as Denning defined it—that is, something that gets taken up and used by a community. This means that the concepts and methods of this book can only take you so far; as we saw in Chapter 2, to turn any invention into a lasting innovation involves much more than "just" coming up with a great product that people want! In fact, as we have learned from Peter Drucker's studies of entrepreneurs, the new knowledge and great interactive technologies produced by researchers, engineers, product designers, and inventors all over the world are, in the bigger picture, only one of many components in what creates lasting innovations. Yet at the same time, new technological inventions seem to have been an important driving force in just about every successful digital product to date, from the personal computer to the smartphone.

So what acutally is the role of new technologies in innovation, and is there a better way to predict the impact of it in the long run? Bill Buxton at Microsoft Research put his finger on this dilemma by pointing out that by the time most digital technologies make it big, they will already have been around for a long time, often 20 years or more. Buxton called his observation "the long nose," inspired by the "long tail" theory introduced by Chris Anderson that postulated that Internet companies can be sustained on a wide range of specialized products rather than a few blockbusters. A typical example of a new technology that took a long time to become a successful product is the computer mouse. It was invented at Douglas Engelbart's lab at Stanford in the 1960s; its use was refined at Xerox PARC during the 1970s; but the first commercially successful version did not come until the launch of the Apple Macintosh in 1984; even then, it took another decade and Microsoft's Windows 95 to make it a truly mass-market product. Another example would be the multitouch screen technology that is now a major feature of many smartphones and tablets, including those based on Apple's iPhone and iPad as well as similar products based on Google's Android operating systems. Touch screens have been around since the 1970s, and the first known multitouch versions were produced in the early 1980s. Many important multitouch interactions, like "pinching," were introduced as early as early as 1983 by video artist Myron Krueger in his seminal Video Place pieces. Building on this concept, it took another two decades before the first large multitouch displays made it to the mainstream—for instance, those based on Jeff Han's work in the early 2000s. When the iPhone finally came along in 2007, the repertoire of multitouch interaction gestures and technologies had been developed to the point where Apple's new product seemed like the next logical step. Thus, even though the pinching and other gestures demonstrated on the iPhone seemed new and novel, they were at the same time intuitive and logical—the result of over two decades of refinement.

Of course, given the basic concepts of innovation we gave in the first chapters of the book, this lag from technology to product is not really surprising: we know that an invention in itself is not nearly enough to lead to a successful digital product. But if we accept the timeline of approximately 20 years from the first demonstration to the first successful digital product, Buxton derives a helpful corollary: Any technology that is going to have an impact over the next decade has always already been around for 10 years. This means that the technological key to the next multibillion-dollar business—the next Google, Apple, Amazon, you name it—is not only already here, but it has been here for a long time! For those working in high-tech fields of research and development and academia, this is particularly important to remember. It means that among those concepts that were published so long ago that we have grown bored with them, and probably just about forgotten about them, could be the ones that will demand attention if we aim to develop innovations with lasting impact for the next decade. Of course, the timeline from technical invention to product might get more compressed, sometimes to 10 or even 5 years, but the basic insight still holds: the most important technologies of the future are already here, and have been for some time.

A lot of this is visible in the examples given in this book, even going beyond the obvious ones of the personal computer. For instance, as we saw in Chapter 8, location awareness has been around for a long time, building on a variety of technological platforms. Personal location technology arguably started with the Active Badge in the early 1990s, which was designed for an office environment and required a fixed infrastructure to work. This concept was designed to give the location of people in a professional setting, supporting distributed and collaborative work. Inspired by this concept, the Hummingbird in 1996 also provided support for locating other users, but with two key differences. First, it worked without any infrastructure and could thus be used anywhere. Second, it was used to support not just work tasks but also social connections, thus breaking out of the professional environment. But neither of these technologies had any chance of becoming commercial products, because of their cost and other factors. It took another decade of work in improving and bringing down the cost of positioning technologies—designing inexpensive consumer global positioning system (GPS) chips, building databases of GSM cells and Wi-Fi nodes, and so on—before it was feasible to put positioning technology in consumer products, like phones. Today, numerous companies are trying to provide consumer services based on location awareness, and it is easily one of the hottest areas for new innovation. If we go through the examples given in the previous four chapters, we will see that some technical breakthroughs in digital products are already producing innovations right now, whereas others are still limited in their reach but are poised to become important in the future.

What has happened in the case of location-based services is not that they have suddenly become useful—they already were—but that a number of factors have converged to make them practical and accessible for a larger audience. There was first of all the required technology and technical infrastructure to make them feasible at a reasonable cost while covering a large area rather than being limited to certain spaces. But furthermore, there was the gradual introduction of the idea of using location as a data point in digital products. There were early location-based games for mobile phones, such as BotFighter, a game launched in the early 1990s that used the standard SMS (Short Message Service) capability for interaction. There were dedicated GPS units for car navigation. There were early stabs at social location-based services, such as *Dodgeball*, a precursor to Foursquare, which was also SMS based. There was also the gradual acclimatization to performing social actions over digital networks, started by the general public's adoption of e-mail and continuing over social services such as Friendster, MySpace, and Facebook. Finally, as GPS receivers were small and cheap enough to put into mass-market consumer phones like the iPhone, the idea of using your location to get information on the go and connect with friends seemed natural. At this point, nobody has quite cracked the location-based services space yet (even the most popular dedicated services have far from universal reach, and just about none are making any money), but we can be sure that somebody will do it soon.

What we are seeing with location-based services, as well as many other digital products, is the emergence of a *paradigm*. Remember Verplank's spiral in Chapter 2; what eventually comes out after a series of hunches, hacks, prototypes, and products is something bigger, something that is more than just another isolated product to put in shops. To emerge, a paradigm requires the convergence of not just technology, but a number of factors. No matter how good the technology is and how well it has been engineered, there has to be a clear use story that can be understood and easily explained to potential customers. The best way to create it seems to be to iterate over and over again until everything falls into place. This is not easy, and usually the first try is not right—nor the second, third, and fourth. An excellent recent example is the development of tablet computers or "pads." Although there were visions of similar devices as early as the 1960s, the first working example was produced by Xerox PARC around 1992 as part of Mark Weiser's ubiquitous computing experiment and was called the PARCPad (an original PARCPad device can still be found exhibited at PARC to this day, among other examples of ubicomp devices). However, the PARCPad could never make it as a product; it was too expensive, too underpowered, and required a wireless networking infrastructure that simply did not exist at the time. But even from this primitive example, it was clear that the pad or tablet form had the potential for a lot of usage situations. During the years, researchers and R&D departments at many major companies continued to try to produce successful versions of the tablet device. There were experimental electronic book readers, and there were handheld devices with touch-sensitive screens such as Apple's Newton and the Palm Pilot. Technology progressed continuously, and Microsoft introduced its so-called Tablet PC devices in 2002, a decade after the PARCPad. But even though it had the power of the world's (at the time) largest computer company behind it, the product was a flop. The operating system—a version of Microsoft Windows—was somewhat clumsily adapted to the touch screen, and the screen itself required a specialized pen for input. But to borrow Buxton's terminology, the pad concept was now peeking its nose out into the world. PC manufacturers continued to attempt to produce successful tablet computers, including laptop-like hybrids with regular keyboards that could be folded away to create a tablet.

When Apple introduced its iPhone in 2007, a lot of the technologies and interaction techniques were starting to converge. The phone, which actually started its life as a padlike computer, consolidated several important factors, including a robust touch screen that did not require a pen, a graphical interface that was a clear break with the mouse-driven desktop metaphor, and a number of interaction techniques developed specifically for multitouch. There was also an ecosystem around the device, including a media store (iTunes) and soon a dedicated channel to buy software (the App Store). There was also the global infrastructure that had gradually been built over the 20 years since the PARCPad: a pervasive wireless network of both high-speed local Internet nodes and wide-area GSM and 3G data networks. Overall, it meant that in addition to creating the actual hardware, Apple could fall back on a strong background of established services (making it clear that the emerging discipline of service design is one of the company's key strengths—even more so than hardware and interaction design).

Finally, as the Apple iPad appeared in 2010, it slotted right into all of these preconditions, built up over two decades. One would think that at this time it would seem to be the most natural device in the world. But even up to the announcement, many commentators were dubious that a tablet computer of any kind would have commercial potential. After all, there had been so many attempts already that there was a strong precedent for this one to also fail. I am sure that despite their belief in the product, even the Apple executives were nervous about its reception. But as we know, they need not have worried. Although the iPad in itself, as we saw, was in no way a completely new product, it was the first of its kind to be commercially successful. It therefore created a completely new market for tablet-like computers, and was followed by a slew of devices by Samsung, HP, Motorola, Amazon, and others. Although the iPad is still by far the leader in this segment, there is no doubt that other manufacturers will in due time also have success in this space. Thus, what the iPad did was to solidify a paradigm—the tablet or pad computer—that had been percolating for 20 years or more. But unlike singular technologies like multitouch or the mouse, the pad paradigm is a collection of many different elements: interaction techniques, infrastructure, ecosystem, use cases, and so on. It is tempting to say—and many have done so—that Apple single-handedly created the pad product segment. Instead, as we saw, it was the opposite: it was the convergence of a great deal of work in many diverse areas, from 3G networks to software architectures, that happened to find its inflection point in this particular device.

The paradigm way of thinking helps us understand how to innovate successful digital products that are not just singular instances but part of a larger movement. We can assume that most of the time, every truly cutting-edge product developer will always be too early—any really new product will need a few iterations before it is right. However, if it is really part of an emerging paradigm, it will add to the creation of a new product category—even if this particular instance is not successful. Many of the examples in this book are exactly that—instances of emerging paradigms that have not gelled yet but might possibly make total sense in the future, as the paradigm they belong to is better defined. For instance, the ambient information display like Informative Art is such an emerging paradigm; the technology, infrastructure, and use cases are not quite in place so these displays are not yet viable as products, but it is a fair bet to assume that it will happen sooner or later. Even if they are not ready to be put on shop shelves yet, instances of potential digital products such as the bus timetable Mondrian can teach us a lot about how to eventually create a truly successful product in this space. Thus, if we can anticipate emerging paradigms, we can also identify and learn from the instances that are already here. These will become like little sneak peeks into the future, a way to understand what the world will look like when the paradigm is truly formed.

If I were to make a bet on the next paradigm, or at least one that will dominate our lives in the future, it would have to do with the first quality of digital products: information processing. For the bulk of this book, we have been taking information processing for granted—it is simply the fundamental part of any digital product. This still holds true for products where the computation is harnessed inside of dedicated devices—like our personal computers, mobile phones, and pads. But increasingly, information processing is seeping out into the world. By applying interaction, networking, sensing, and proactivity, information processing is coming to grips with the real world, beyond the computers and screens where it is already well understood. By applying information processing to the real world around us, everything becomes a potential digital product. Imagine a day when information processing reaches so far that every object is part of a digital database, even the most mundane of everyday things. Then, to run a digital search for a pair of lost socks in your apartment becomes as easy as looking up the word "socks" on Google. Sometimes this vision is called "the Internet of Things" or "ambient intelligence," terms with roots in logistics and home automation. I prefer to think of it as "applying information processing on the world." Then every place, every action, every physical artifact, and every human relationship becomes part of a database and immediately available for processing. This is not nearly as radical as it might sound right now—remember that we are already running information processing on social interactions. Services like Facebook routinely scour your list of friends for the news items and updates that it thinks you will be most interested in; it even goes so far as to suggest new friends for you based on your existing social relationships.

Although terms like "ubiquitous computing" and "the Internet of Things" lead to thoughts of devices with electronics embedded and radio transceivers chattering between each other, for the most part this will probably not be the case. Instead, a lot of information gathering can be made through sensors in devices such as phones, and using passive technologies such as image recognition. Furthermore, the trend toward Internet-connected devices and web-based services means that fewer information processing tasks are running on the actual devices around us. Instead, processing takes place in "the cloud," the vast collection of servers where popular services such as Google, Twitter, and Spotify store their data. In the actual world of ubiquitous computing, rather than having many computers for every user, we are in many ways going back to the mainframe world where many users were connected to the same central processor using terminals—except the terminals are phones and pads with wireless connections. This also means that even in the cases where a digital product has embedded interaction, sensing, or other active components, the processing may very well be happening somewhere else. This makes more sense, as it becomes more important to aggregate information over many devices and actions—rather than, say, every household utensil in a smart kitchen having its own memory and processing unit, it is better to store all data and do all processing in the cloud. Not only does this minimize the cost of each object, it also makes it easier to potentially combine the readings from the cooking in my kitchen with that happening in other kitchens around the world.

These future digital products will thus not necessarily be doing much processing themselves, but they will become *windows into services.* Just like we today use different terminals—one minute a smartphone app, the next a web page—to look into the popular services on today's web, such as Facebook, tomorrow's digital product will in similar ways provide means of accessing services running somewhere in the cloud. If they are physical artifacts, they will always need to be connected to the network, which becomes the gateway to other products and services. In this way they become distributed input and output nodes to the cloud. But they may also be completely digital, residing on devices such as phones and pads, using the devices' sensors to connect to the world around us and taking into account factors such as location, the weather, who else is nearby, what configuration of objects is available, and so on. In many cases, they will be *personal*—physical artifacts that we own and can literally put in our pockets or in our homes. But they will also be *social*—tied in to our extended social network of likes and dislikes, recommendations and reviews, contributed by close friends as well as strangers and dedicated professionals. This multiplies the information processing power we can apply to the world manifold, because it allows products to go way beyond the immediate surroundings and any particular user, drawing on the same kind of mass dynamics that powers everything from Google to Wikipedia on the Internet today.

The technological development and user-oriented groundwork for this new paradigm has already largely been done. In fact, this is exactly what much of this book is about. We have seen that by using grounded innovation methods and starting from the qualities of digital products, we can construct examples of how information processing can engage directly with the world, far beyond the digital products that exist today. As the technologies become refined and cheaper, and as the use cases build, we will see them gel into paradigms for new product categories—ones that for the average consumer will seem at the same time entirely new yet oddly familiar, because of the decades of percolating refinement that has happened under the surface.

In this emerging space, there is room for a lot of innovations. Of course, we will need to see the novel and compelling services and products that will make people interested in using this new technology. This is what we have seen in the examples in the book. But there will also need to be innovations on an ecosystem level. How can we charge money for these new services, some of which may be running in the background, making use of implicit interaction, and latching onto everyday objects and activities without us even knowing? What are the demands on the new infrastructures—both the purely technical (networks, routers, sensors, actuators) and the virtual (data, algorithms, social graphs)—that will power these products? How do we build stories and use cases that make the products compelling, and how do we avoid the potential privacy and trust nightmares that will by necessity come from having virtually every aspect of the world available for search and processing?

The barriers for constructing and testing instances of these products are much, much lower than even five years ago. New technologies—such as the mobile mash-ups for phones, the rapid prototyping construction kits, 3D printers, cheap and easily embedded electronics, low-powered and inexpensive displays, interactive textiles, and all the other technologies that have been emerging during the past decade—are getting to a tipping point. There is a pervasive infrastructure of networking and smart terminals in the hands of most of the people in developed countries (and the rest of the world is catching up fast). On the consumer side, this means we may be entering an age of *hyper-customization*. Just like the early adopters of the World Wide Web and HTML took to looking at existing code and modifying it slightly to make their own web pages, soon it may be possible to take an existing digital product—an app, a web service, even a physical device—alter a few parameters, and create your own customized version.

For creating tomorrow's digital product paradigms, those ideas that lead to real and viable innovations, this new world is both a challenge and an opportunity. Today, users are already used to having all the information in the digital world readily available at their fingertips, and having their social life and connections organized by online services. They expect their technologies to be able to process information more and more intelligently, to make informed decisions about not just which book to buy on Amazon but which street corner to turn at in order to meet a friend or have a new, interesting experience. And technological developments happen more and more on "Internet time," even for physical products—by pushing out a product as soon as it is ready and correcting errors afterward by updating the software. Tomorrow's researchers, engineers, inventors, and designers who will have to navigate this supercharged world must have a strong foothold in what really works and what humans are fundamentally interested in. To gain this foothold, the concept of grounded innovation, the methods and processes presented in this book, the many technologies and examples we have gone through, and the future trends we have hinted at can all help. But ultimately, there is no surefire way to create innovations, and there is no guarantee that these methods will be successful. The only way to find out what works is to try. The way to do this is quite literally to take all the resources that are available, all the methods and materials you have learned about in this book and elsewhere, and *mash it up and get it out there!*

BIBLIOGRAPHY

The following are suggested books, articles, and other sources that can help broaden the reader's understanding of the topics addressed in this book. This list is not exhaustive, but the titles listed here should serve as a good starting point for further searches. Many of the research fields touched on in the book are young, and definitive books have not yet been published on these topics, which is why a large part of the list is composed of academic papers. Even if most of these articles come from specialized journals and conferences, they have been chosen because they are accessible for the reader who does not have prior knowledge about the subject beyond what is given in this book, and most of these publications should be only an Internet search away.

Chapter 1

Early computer history and the development of the personal computer:
   Freiberger, P., Swaine, M., 2000. Fire in the Valley: The Making of the Personal Computer, second ed. McGraw-Hill.
   Swedin, E.G., Ferro, D.L., 2007. Computers: The Life Story of a Technology. The Johns Hopkins University Press.

On the history of interaction technology:
   Moggridge, B., 2007. Designing Interactions. The MIT Press.
   Rheingold, H., 2000. Tools for Thought: The History and Future of Mind-Expanding Technology. Second revised sub ed. The MIT Press.

On the origins of the graphical user interface and the innovations of Xerox PARC:
   Hiltzik, M.A., 2000. Dealers of Lightning: Xerox PARC and the Dawn of the Computer Age. Harper Paperbacks.

On ubiquitous computing and other paradigms for digital products beyond the desktop computer:
   Begole, B, 2011. Ubiquitous Computing for Business: Find New Markets, Create Better Businesses and Reach Customers around the World 24-7-365. FT Press.
   Dourish, P., Bell, G., 2011. Divining a Digital Future: Mess and Mythology in Ubiquitous Computing. The MIT Press.
   Kuniavsky, M., 2010. Smart Things: Ubiquitous Computing User Experience Design. Morgan Kaufmann.
   Weiser, M., 1991. The computer for the 21st century. February. Scientific American.
   Weiser, M., 1993. Some computer science issues in ubiquitous computing. Communications of the ACM. July.

On other interaction paradigms, including virtual, augmented, and mixed reality, tangible interfaces, and so on:

Benford, S., Giannachi, G., 2011. Performing Mixed Reality. The MIT Press.

Ishii, H., Ullmer, B., 1997. Tangible bits: towards seamless interfaces between people, bits and atoms. In: Pemberton, S. (Ed.), Proceedings of the SIGCHI Conference on Human Factors in Computing Systems. March 22–27, 1997, Atlanta, GA. ACM, New York, pp. 234–241.

Rheingold, R., 1992. Virtual Reality: The Revolutionary Technology of Computer-Generated Artificial Worlds—and How It Promises to Transform Society. Simon & Schuster.

Wellner, P., Mackay, M., Gold, R., 1993. Back to the real world. Communications of the ACM—special issue on computer augmented environments 36 (7).

Chapter 2

On some popular views on design and software development:

Kolko, J., 2011. Thoughts on Interaction Design, second ed. Morgan Kaufmann.

Löwgren, J., Stolterman, E., 2007. Thoughtful Interaction Design: A Design Perspective on Information Technology. The MIT Press.

Norman, D., 2002. The Design of Everyday Things. Basic Books. (Originally published as The Psychology of Everyday Things, 1988.)

Schön, D.A., 1983. The Reflective Practitioner: How Professionals Think in Action. Basic Books.

Simon, H.A., 1969. The Sciences of the Artificial. The MIT Press.

William Verplank himself has not published on his model, but an original "napkin sketch" and an account of the spiral model can be found in the author's Ph.D. thesis:

Holmquist, L.E., 2000. Breaking the Screen Barrier. Gothenburg Studies in Informatics, no. 16, ISSN 1400-741X.

Also see www.billverplank.com

On innovation and entrepreneurship:

Denning, P.J., 2004. The social life of innovation. Communications of the ACM 47 (4).

Denning, P.J., Dunham, R., 2010. The Innovator's Way: Essential Practices for Successful Innovation. The MIT Press.

Drucker, P.F., 2007. Innovation and Entrepreneurship, second ed. Butterworth-Heinemann.

Johnson, S., 2010. Where Good Ideas Come From: The Natural History of Innovation. Riverhead Hardcover.

On the failure of Xerox to capitalize on PARC's invention of the graphical user interface:

Smith, D.K., Alexander, R.C., 1988. Fumbling the Future: How Xerox Invented, Then Ignored, the First Personal Computer. W. Morrow, Reissued by iUniverse, 1999.

On participatory design and the Scandinavian school:

Bødker, S., Ehn, P., Kammersgaard, J., Kyng, M., Sundblad, Y., 1987. Autopian experience. In: Bjerknes, G., Ehn, P., Kyng, M. (Eds.), Computers and Democracy: a Scandinavian Challenge. Avebury.

Ehn, P., Kyng, M., 1991. Cardboard computers: Mocking-it-up or hands-on the future. In: Greenbaum, J., Kyng, M. (Eds.), Design at Work, Laurence Erlbaum Associates.

Greenbaum, J., Kyng, M., 1992. Design at Work: Cooperative Design of Computer Systems. Lawrence Erlbaum Associates.

On lead users and user-driven innovation:

Spinosa, C., Flores, F., Dreyfus, H.L., 1999. Disclosing New Worlds: Entrepreneurship, Democratic Action, and the Cultivation of Solidarity. The MIT Press.

von Hippel, E., 2006. Democratizing Innovation. The MIT Press.

von Hippel, E., 1986. Lead users: A source of novel product concepts. Management Science 32 (7).

von Hippel, E., Thomke, S., Sonnack, M., 1999. Creating breakthroughs at 3M. Harvard Business Review 77 (5).

On the Persona design method:

Cooper, A., 2004. The Inmates Are Running the Asylum: Why High Tech Products Drive Us Crazy and How to Restore the Sanity. Sams–Pearson Education.

Pruitt, J., Grudin, J., 2003. Personas: practice and theory. In: DUX '03, Proceedings of the 2003 Conference on Designing for User Experiences, ACM Press.

On transfer scenarios:

Ljungblad, S., 2000. Beyond Users: Grounding Technology in Experience. Ph.D thesis. Department of Computer and Systems Sciences, Stockholm University, No. 08-004.

Ljungblad, S., Holmquist, L. E., 2007. Transfer scenarios: grounding innovation with marginal practices. In: CHI 07, Proceedings of the SIGCHI Conference on Human Factors in Computing Systems, ACM Press.

Ljungblad, S., Walter, K., Jacobsson, M., Holmquist, L. E., 2006. Designing personal embodied agents with personas. In: Proceedings of RO-MAN 06, Hatfield, United Kingdom.

On the GlowBots robots:

Jacobsson, M., Bodin, J., Holmquist, L.E., 2008. The see-Puck: a platform for exploring human-robot relationships. In: CHI '08, Proceeding of the Twenty-Sixth Annual SIGCHI Conference on Human Factors in Computing Systems, ACM Press.

Jacobsson, M., Fernaeus, Y., Holmquist, L.E., 2008. GlowBots: designing and implementing engaging human robot interaction. Journal of Physical Agents 2 (2).

On the Flower Wall:

Petersen, M.G., Ljungblad, S., Håkansson, M., 2009. Designing for playful photography. New Review of Hypermedia and Multimedia 15 (2).

Chapter 3

User-centered design and inquiry methods:

Bødker, S., Buur, J., 2002. The design collaboratorium: a place for usability design. ACM Transactions on Computer Human Interaction 9 (2), 152–169.

Kuniavsky, M., 2003. Observing the User Experience: A Practitioner's Guide to User Research. Morgan Kaufmann.

Mackay, W. E., Ratzer, A. V., Janecek, P., 2000. Video artifacts for design: bridging the gap between abstraction and detail. In: Proceedings of ACM DIS 2000 Conference on Designing Interactive Systems, ACM Press.

Sharp, H., Rogers, Y., Preece, J., 2007. Interaction Design: Beyond Human-Computer Interaction, second ed. Wiley.

A parallel view to my account of the history of the HCI field can be found in the notion of three "waves" of HCI:

Bødker, S., 2006. When second wave HCI meets third wave challenges. In: NordiCHI '06, Proceedings of the Fourth Nordic Conference on Human-Computer Interaction: Changing Roles, ACM Press.

Discussions on the role of user inquiry and evaluations in HCI:

Crabtree, A., Rodden, T., Tolmie, P., Button, B., 2009. Ethnography considered harmful. In: CHI '09, Proceedings of the Twenty-Seventh International Conference on Human Factors in Computing Systems, ACM Press.

Dourish, P., 2006. Implications for Design. In: CHI '06, Proceedings of the SIGCHI Conference on Human Factors in Computing Systems, ACM Press.

Greenberg, S., Buxton, B., 2008. Usability evaluation considered harmful (some of the time). In: CHI '08, Proceedings of the Twenty-Sixth Annual SIGCHI Conference on Human Factors in Computing Systems, ACM Press.

On studies of the Pleo robot toy and the ActDresses system:

Fernaeus, Y., Håkansson, M., Jacobsson, M., Ljungblad, S., 2010. How do you play with a robotic toy animal? A long-term study of Pleo. In: IDC '10, Proceedings of the Ninth International Conference on Interaction Design and Children. ACM Press.

Fernaeus, Y., Jacobsson, M., 2009. Comics, robots, fashion and programming: outlining the concept of ActDresses. In: TEI '09, Proceedings of Tangible and Embedded Interaction, February 16–18, 2009, Cambridge, UK.

Jacobsson, M., Fernaeus, Y., Tieben, R.K, 2010. The look, the feel and the action: making sets of ActDresses for robotic movement. In: DIS '10, Proceedings of ACM Designing for Interactive Systems 2010, ACM Press.

On Smart-Its Friends and other similar interaction techniques:

Holmquist, L., Mattern, F., Schiele, B., Alahuhta, P., Beigl, M., Gellersen, H., 2001. Smart-Its Friends: a technique for users to easily establish connections between smart artefacts. In: Proceedings of UbiComp 2001, International Conference on Ubiquitous Computing, Springer.

Hinckley, K., 2003. Synchronous gestures for multiple persons and computers. In: Proceedings of UIST '03, Sixteenth Annual ACM Symposium on User Interface Software and Technology, ACM Press.

Details on the Bump sharing app, by Bump, Inc., can be found at the company's website, bu.mp.

Chapter 4

On inquiry and blue-sky innovation (source of the Apple Research Labs quote):

Rogers, Y., Belotti, V., 1997. Grounding blue-sky research: how can ethnography help? Interactions 4 (3).

On the Cultural Probes method, including discussions of its—sometimes contested—use in HCI:

Boehner, K.,Vertesi, J., Sengers, P., Dourish, P., 2007. How HCI interprets the probes. In: CHI '07, Proceedings of the SIGCHI Conference on Human Factors in Computing Systems, ACM Press.

Gaver, W., Dunne, T., Pacenti, E., 1999. Cultural probes. Interactions 6 (1).

Gaver, W., Boucher, A., Pennington, S., Walker, B., 2004. Cultural probes and the value of uncertainty. Interactions 11 (5).

On brainstorming:

Osborn, A.F., 1953. Applied Imagination: Principles and Procedures of Creative Thinking. Scribner.

The preceding book contains the original description of the technique; today there are literally hundreds of texts on the subject, offering various practical guides to successful brainstorming. Websites such as www.brainstorming.co.uk also offer free brainstorming tools and tutorials.

Other idea-generation techniques:

Djajadiningrat, J.P., Gaver, W., Fres, J.W., 2000. Interaction relabelling and extreme characters: methods for exploring aesthetic interactions. In: DIS 2000, Proceedings of the Third Conference on Designing Interactive Systems: Processes, Practices, Methods, and Techniques, ACM Press.

Oulasvirta, A., Kurvinen, E., Kankainen, T., 2003. Understanding contexts by being there: case studies in bodystorming. Personal and Ubiquitous Computing 7 (2).

On cut-ups, bootleg mixes, and musical mash-ups:

Burroughs, W.S., 1982. The cut-up method of Brion Gysin. In: Vale, V., Juno, A. (Eds.), Re/Search, Issue 4/5. Re/Search Publications.

Mashup (music), from Wikipedia, the free encyclopedia. <http://en.wikipedia.org/wiki/Mashup_(music)>.

For the reader curious to hear actual bootlegs and mash-up remixes, examples are readily available from websites such as mashstix.com and remix.vg/category/mashups.

On the bootlegging brainstorm method:

Holmquist, L.E., 2008. Bootlegging: multidisciplinary brainstorming with cut-ups. In: PDC '08, Proceedings of the Tenth Anniversary Conference on Participatory Design, ACM Press.

Chapter 5

On what prototypes represent:

Holmquist, L.E., 2005. Prototyping: generating ideas or cargo cult designs? Interactions 12 (2).

Houde, S., Hill, C., 1997. What do prototypes prototype? In: Handbook of Human-Computer Interaction, second ed. Elsevier Science B.V., Amsterdam.

On sketching:

Buxton, B., 2007. Sketching User Experiences: Getting the Design Right and the Right Design. Morgan Kaufmann.

Speculative prototyping and design methods:

Buchenau, M., Fulton Suri, J., 2000. Experience prototyping. In: DIS '00, Proceedings of the Conference on Designing Interactive Systems: Processes, Practices, Methods, and Techniques, ACM Press.

Gaver, B., Martin, H., 2000. Alternatives: exploring information appliances through conceptual design proposals. In: CHI 2000, Proceedings of the SIGCHI Conference on Human Factors in Computing Systems, ACM Press.

Iacucci, G, Kuutti, K., Ranta, M., 2000. On the move with a magic thing: role playing in concept design of mobile services and devices. In: DIS 2000, Proceedings of the Conference on Designing Interactive Systems: Processes, Practices, Methods, and Techniques, ACM Press.

Practical prototyping guides:

Banzi, M., 2008. Getting Started with Arduino. Make.

Igoe, T., 2007. Making Things Talk: Practical Methods for Connecting Physical Objects. Make.

O'Sullivan, D., Igoe, T., 2004. Physical Computing: Sensing and Controlling the Physical World with Computers. Thomson.

Reas, C., Fry, B., 2010. Getting Started with Processing. Make.

About the Melanesian cargo cults:

Jacopetti, G., Prosperi, F., Cavara, P. (Dirs.), 1962. Mondo Cane, Italy. Available as Blue Underground DVD, BU1011DVD.

Lindstrom, L., 1993. Cargo Cult: Strange Stories of Desire from Melanesia and Beyond. University of Hawaii Press.

On the cargo cult as metaphor:

Fernaeus, Y., Jacobsson, M., Ljungblad, S., Holmquist, L.E., 2009. Are we living in a robot cargo cult? In: HRI '09, Proceedings of the Fourth ACM/IEEE International Conference on Human Robot Interaction, ACM Press.

Feynman, R., 1997. Cargo cult science. In: Surely You're Joking, Mr. Feynman!, reprint ed. W.W. Norton.

McConnell, S., 2000. Cargo cult software engineering. IEEE Software 17 (2).

On the design of the context camera:

Håkansson M., Gaye L., Ljungblad S., Holmquist L.E., 2006. More than meets the eye: an exploratory study of context photography. In: Proceedings of NordiCHI 2006, Oslo, Norway, October 14-18.

Håkansson, M., Ljungblad, S., Holmquist, L.E., 2003. Capturing the invisible: designing context-aware photography. In: DUX '03, Proceedings of the 2003 Conference on Designing for User Experiences, ACM Press.

Ljungblad, S., 2007. Designing for new photographic experiences: how the lomographic practice informed context photography. In: DPPI '07, Proceedings of the Conference on Designing Pleasurable Products and Interfaces, ACM Press.

Chapter 6

On focus+context visualization:

Holmquist, L.E., 2011. Commentary on "Bifocal Display" by Robert Spence and Mark Apperley. Retrieved October 3, 2011, from Interaction-Design.org: www.interaction-design.org/encyclopedia/bifocal_display. html#lars + erik + holmquist.

Spence, R., Apperley, M., 2011. Bifocal display. In: Soegaard, M., Dam, R.F. (Eds.), Encyclopedia of Human-Computer Interaction. Available online at www. interaction-design.org/encyclopedia/bifocal_display.html.

On calm technology and ambient information displays:

Holmquist, L.E., 2004. Evaluating the comprehension of ambient displays. In: CHI '04, extended abstracts on human factors in computing systems, ACM Press.

Mynatt, E.D., Rowan, J., Craighill, S., Jacobs, A., 2001. Digital family portraits: supporting peace of mind for extended family members. In: CHI '01, Proceedings of the SIGCHI Conference on Human Factors in Computing Systems, ACM Press.

Stasko, J., Miller, T., Pousman, Z., Plaue, C. Ullah, O., 2004. Personalized peripheral information awareness through information art. In: Proceedings of UbiComp 2004, Springer.

Weiser, M., Brown, J.S., 1997. Designing calm technology. In: Denning, P.J., Metcalfe, R.M. (Eds.), Beyond Calculation: The Next Fifty Years of Computing. Copernicus/An Imprint of Springer-Verlag.

Wisneski, C., Ishii, H., Dahley, A.G. Gorbet, M.G., Brave, S., Ullmer B., et al., 1998. Ambient displays: turning architectural space into an interface between people and digital information. In: CoBuild '98, Proceedings of the First International Workshop on Cooperative Buildings, Integrating Information, Organization, and Architecture. Springer.

On Informative Art:

Holmquist, L.E., Skog, T., 2003. Informative art: information visualization in everyday environments. In: GRAPHITE '03, Proceedings of the First

International Conference on Computer Graphics and Interactive Techniques in Australasia and South East Asia, ACM Press.

Redström, J., Skog, T., Hallnäs, L., 2000. Informative art: using amplified artworks as information displays. In: DARE '00, Proceedings of DARE 2000 on Designing Augmented Reality Environments, ACM Press.

Skog, T., Ljungblad, S., Holmquist, L.E., 2003. Between aesthetics and utility: designing ambient information visualizations. In: INFOVIS'03, Proceedings of the Ninth Annual IEEE Conference on Information Visualization, IEEE Computer Society.

On the Ubiquitous Graphics system:

Sanneblad, J., Holmquist, L.E., 2006. Ubiquitous graphics: combining hand-held and wall-size displays to interact with large images. In: AVI '06, Proceedings of the Working Conference on Advanced Visual Interfaces, ACM Press.

On multidisplay games:

Sanneblad, J., Holmquist, L.E., 2003. OpenTrek: a platform for developing interactive networked games on mobile devices. In: Mobile HCI '03, Human-Computer Interaction with Mobile Devices and Services, Fifth International Symposium, Springer.

Sanneblad, J., Holmquist, L.E., 2004. The GapiDraw platform: high-performance cross-platform graphics on mobile devices. In: MUM '04, Proceedings of the Third International Conference on Mobile and Ubiquitous Multimedia, ACM Press.

Sanneblad, J., Holmquist, L.E., 2004. "Why is everyone inside me?" Using shared displays in mobile computer games. In: ICEC 2004, Proceedings of Entertainment Computing, Third International Conference, Springer.

Chapter 7

On one-dimensional barcode systems:

Brody, A.B., Gottsman, E.J., 1999. Pocket Bargain Finder: a handheld device for augmented commerce. In: HUC '99 Proceedings of the First International Symposium on Handheld and Ubiquitous Computing, Springer.

Ljungstrand, P., Redström, J., Holmquist, L.E., 2000. WebStickers: using physical tokens to access, manage and share bookmarks to the Web. In: DARE '00, Proceedings of DARE 2000 on Designing Augmented Reality Environments, ACM Press.

More information on one- and two-dimensional barcodes, QR codes, the CueCat, and the like can be found on Wikipedia and other online resources.

On RFID tags:

Holmquist, L.E., 2009. Automated journeys: automated connections. Interactions 16 (1).

Want, R., 2006. An introduction to RFID technology. IEEE Pervasive Computing 5 (1).

Want, R., Fishkin, K.P., Gujar, A., Harrison, B.L., 1999. Bridging physical and virtual worlds with electronic tags. In: CHI '99 Proceedings of the SIGCHI Conference on Human Factors in Computing Systems, ACM Press.

On crowdsourced image recognition:

Bigham, J.P., Jayant, C., Ji, H., Little, G., et al., 2010. VizWiz: nearly real-time answers to visual questions. In: UIST '10, Proceedings of the Twenty-Third Annual ACM Symposium on User Interface Software and Technology, ACM Press.

On visual tag-based augmented reality:

Billinghurst, M., Kato, H., Poupyrev, I., 2010, November. The MagicBook: A Transitional AR Interface. Computers and Graphics.

Rekimoto, J., Ayatsuka, Y., 2000. CyberCode: designing augmented reality environments with visual tags. In: DARE '00 Proceedings of DARE 2000 on Designing Augmented Reality Environments, ACM Press.

On markerless augmented reality:

Azuma, R., Baillot, Y., Behringer, R., Feiner, S., Julier, S., MacIntyre, B., 2001. Recent advances in augmented reality. IEEE Computer Graphics and Applications 21 (6), 34–47.

Feiner, S., Macintyre, B., Seligmann, D., 1993. Knowledge-based augmented reality. Communications of the ACM 36 (7).

Several augmented reality applications are available for download to mobile phones running Android or iOS, including Layar and Sekai Camera, as well as for many specialized tasks. The following article provides a rundown of some interesting iPhone apps:

Hamburger, E., 2011. 10 iPhone apps that will make you feel like you're in the future through augmented reality. Business Insider, www.businessinsider.com, March 16.

Chapter 8

On how context was used in the context camera:

Håkansson, M., Gaye, L., 2008. Bringing context to the foreground: creative engagement in a novel still camera application. In: DIS '08, Proceedings of ACM Designing Interactive Systems 2008, ACM Press.

On context-aware applications

Dey, A.K., 2001. Understanding and using context. Personal and Ubiquitous Computing 5 (1), 4–7.

Dey, A.K., Abowd, G., Salber, D., 2001. A conceptual framework and a toolkit for supporting the rapid prototyping of context-aware applications. Human-Computer Interaction 16 (2).

Dourish, P., 2004. What we talk about when we talk about context. Personal and Ubiquitous Computing 8 (1), 19–30.

Schilit, B., Adams, N., Want, R., 1994. Context-aware computing applications. In: Proceedings of the First International Workshop on Mobile Computing Systems and Applications, IEEE Computer Society.

Schmidt, A., Beigl, M., Gellersen, H-W., 1999. There is more to context than location. Computers & Graphics 23 (6), 893–901.

On the Active Badge:

Want, R., Hopper, A., Falcão, V., Gibbons, J., 1992. The active badge location system. ACM Transactions on Information Systems 10 (1), 91–102.

The use of the Active Badge at Xerox PARC is detailed in Weiser's Scientific American article on ubiquitous computing (see Chapter 1).

On the Hummingbird:

Holmquist, L.E., Falk, J., Wigström, J., 1999. Supporting group collaboration with interpersonal awareness devices. Personal and Ubiquitous Computing 3 (1–2).

Weilenmann, A., 2001. Negotiating use: making sense of mobile technology. Personal and Ubiquitous Computing 5 (2).

Videos of the systems mentioned in the chapter (ϕ^2, Pic-In, and Subway Art Information System) are available on Vimeo at vimeo.com/user1308867 (or by a search for the user "Mobile Life").

On the MediaCup:

Beigl, M., Gellersen, H-W., Schmidt, A., 2001. MediaCups: experience with design and use of computer-augmented everyday artefacts. Computer Networks 35 (4).

On the load-sensing table:

Schmidt. A., Strohbach, M., van Laerhoven, K., Friday, A., Gellersen, H-W., 2002. Context acquisition based on load sensing. In: UbiComp 2002, Proceedings of the Fourth International Conference on Ubiquitous Computing, Springer.

On the Smart-Its system:

Gellersen, H-W., Kortuem, G., Schmidt, A., Beigl, M., 2004. Physical prototyping with Smart-Its. IEEE Pervasive Computing 3 (3).

Holmquist, L.E., Gellersen, H-W., Kortuem, G., Schmidt, A., Strohbach, M., Antifakos, S., et al. 2004. Building intelligent environments with Smart-Its. IEEE Computer Graphics and Applications 24 (1).

On the Smart-Its–based furniture assembly system:

Antifakos, S., Michahelles, F., Schiele, B., 2002. Proactive instructions for furniture assembly. In: UbiComp 2002, Proceedings of the Fourth International Conference on Ubiquitous Computing, Springer.

Chapter 9

On intelligent agents:

Maes, P., 1994. Agents that reduce work and information overload. Communications of the ACM 37 (7).

Wooldridge, M., Jennings, N.R., 1995. Intelligent agents: theory and practice. Knowledge Engineering Review—KER 10 (2).

On recommendation systems and collaborative filtering:

Sarwar, B.M., Karypis, G., Konstan, J.A., Reidl, J., 2001. Item-based collaborative filtering recommendation algorithms. In: WWW '01, Proceedings of the Tenth International Conference on World Wide Web, ACM Press.

Shardanand, U., Maes, P., 1995. Social information filtering: algorithms for automating "word of mouth." In: CHI '95, Proceedings of the SIGCHI Conference on Human Factors in Computing Systems, ACM Press.

On Push!Music and mobile media recommendations:

Håkansson, M., Rost, M., Jacobsson, M., and Holmquist, L.E., 2007. Facilitating mobile music sharing and social interaction with Push!Music. In: HICSS '07, Proceedings of the Fortieth Annual Hawaii International Conference on System Sciences, IEEE Computer Society.

Håkansson, M., Rost, M., Holmquist, L.E., 2007. Gifts from friends and strangers: a study of mobile music sharing. In: ECSCW 2007, Proceedings of the Tenth European Conference on Computer-Supported Collaborative Work, Springer.

Jacobsson, M., Rost, M., Holmquist, L.E., 2006. When media gets wise: collaborative filtering with mobile media agents. In: IUI '06, Proceedings of the Eleventh International Conference on Intelligent User Interfaces, ACM Press.

On problems with location-aware systems:

Mancini, C., Rogers, Y., Thomas, K., Joinson, A.N., Price, B.A., Bandara, A.K., et al., 2011. In the best families: tracking and relationships. In: CHI '11, Proceedings of the 2011 Annual Conference on Human Factors in Computing Systems, ACM Press.

On space and place:

Harrison, S., Dourish, P., 1996. Replacing space: the roles of place and space in collaborative systems. In: CSCW '96, Proceedings of the 1996 ACM Conference on Computer Supported Cooperative Work, ACM Press.

On the use of check-in systems:

Cramer, H., Rost, M., Holmquist, L.E., 2011. Performing a check-in: emerging practices, norms and "conflicts" in location-sharing using Foursquare. In: MobileHCI '11, Proceedings of the Twelfth International Conference on Human Computer Interaction with Mobile Devices and Services, ACM Press.

Chapter 10

Some examples of novel hardware prototyping and DIY systems:

Buechley, L., Eisenberg, M., Catchen, J., Crockett, A., 2008. The LilyPad Arduino: using computational textiles to investigate engagement, aesthetics, and diversity in computer science education. In: CHI '08 Proceedings of the Twenty-Sixth Annual SIGCHI Conference on Human Factors in Computing Systems, ACM Press.

Villar, N., Scott, J., Hodges, S., 2011. Prototyping with Microsoft.NET Gadgeteer. In: TEI '11, Proceedings of the Fifth International Conference on Tangible, Embedded, and Embodied Interaction, ACM Press.

On mobile mash-ups:

Holmquist. L.E., 2010. The age of the mobile mash-up. TechCrunch guest article, May 29, 2010. Available at www.techcrunch.com.

On the "long nose" of technology:

Buxton, B. The Long Nose of Innovation. Bloomberg Businessweek, January 2, 2008.

INDEX